# Help for Today's Troubled Marriages

# Help
# for Today's
# Troubled Marriages

## by Esther Oshiver Fisher, LL.B., Ed.D.

Hawthorn Books, Inc.
Publishers
New York

1455

To Mitchell Salem Fisher, my husband
these thirty-four years

# Preface

People have many emotional needs and a major one is for a satisfying and rewarding marriage. Faltering, troubled, or untenable marriages are a frequent and urgent reason for seeking professional guidance and help. Bewildered and confused, people may turn to the minister, the psychiatrist, the physician, the lawyer, or the social worker. Given the opportunity—and this is ever increasing—troubled husbands and wives are calling more and more upon the clinically trained marriage counselor.

*Help for Today's Troubled Marriages* is based on the possible adult life experience of men and women today and attempts to convey the many problems marriage presents within the broad sweep of modern-day life. Consideration is given to the socio-economic, psychiatric, religious, and legal aspects of marital distress, especially in relation to marriage counseling.

Marriage counseling is an old art and a modern technique—a specialty that is on its way to becoming a profession. The aim of this book is to help clarify and crystallize the philosophy, goals, and techniques of marriage counseling so as to further an understanding of its scope and potential for helping today's troubled marriages. Marriage counseling as practiced today includes premarital counseling which seeks to prevent marriages from becoming too troubled. In my view and experience, marriage counseling includes and should include the predivorce and divorce periods in order to aid those who divorce in their recovery from troubled marriages, and includes and should include aid to the widowed, together with pre-remarital and remarital counseling. Such a scope should serve to dispel the popular misconception that marriage counselors are always and inflexibly for marriage, whatever the human cost.

To develop a sound technique of marriage counseling, clinical marriage counselors must be keenly aware of marital interaction and family living from a diversity of points of view—religious, psychiatric, legal, sociological, and cultural—and must have psychological insight into personality development as well.

My experience as a clinical marriage counselor and as a teacher of marriage-counseling process and techniques leads to a conclusion that the clinical marriage counselor's educational and clinical preparation is and must be far more extensive than is generally appreciated.

*Help for Today's Troubled Marriages* deals with the development of the marriage counselor's philosophy, theories, and techniques as a member of a clinical team or in private practice. Marriage counselors come from varied disciplines, and furthermore, marriage counseling is practiced at various levels by different professionals within the framework of their professions. Consequently, to help resolve some of the confusion about marriage counseling, it becomes important to describe for professional and lay interest the philosophy and practice of marriage counseling today in various professional settings.

Those in the helping professions—medicine, psychiatry, counseling, psychology, the law, the ministry, and social work—recognizing their respective capacities, skills, and limitations, can cooperatively perform a useful and welcome task for the troubled matrimonial client. For this reason, considerable attention and time will be devoted to the relationships between the various helping professions and the clinical marriage counselor.

# Acknowledgments

During the academic year 1964-1965, a lecture course in marriage counseling was offered under my guidance to students of pastoral counseling at the American Foundation of Religion and Psychiatry. The lectures were given by myself and other professional members of the staff. The views expressed in the lectures and discussions were interdisciplinary in character—those of psychiatry, the ministry, medicine, the law, psychology, education, and social work. I tried, as a teacher of marriage counseling, to orient the material presented by these various professionals to the perspective of marriage counseling.

At the conclusion of the course, both groups—the students as well as the members of the clinical staff who attended or participated—suggested that a book reflecting and synthesizing the material would advance the teaching of marriage counseling, its philosophy and technique, and would be a potential contribution to mental health and to marital and family stability.

All the views expressed and the positions taken in this book are mine or, in various instances, those of individual lecturers. They do not represent any view or position of the American Foundation of Religion and Psychiatry itself. If any errors appear, they are mine.

I am especially indebted to the following persons for their contributions and thoughtful cooperation in the initial lecture course: Dr. Smiley Blanton, Dr. Fred U. Tate, Dr. Nathaniel S. Lehrman, Dr. Hector J. Ritey, Dr. Yves J. Kron, and Dr. Alan M. Levy, all psychiatrists; Dr. Lawrence Winkelstein, obstetrician and gynecologist; Mitchell Salem Fisher, a specialist in matrimonial law; the Rev. Arthur M. Tingue, marriage counselor; the Rev. C. Clifford McLaughlan, the Rev. Frederick C. Kuether, and Thelma F. Dixon, pastoral counselors; Renée Fodor, clinical psychologist; and Helga Aschaffenburg, social worker.

Words of thanks must be offered also to the students who gave life to the bare bones of academic presentations—among them a number of ministers and rabbis—and to the many clients who gave me the impetus to crystallize and present my views and feelings about marriage counseling.

All the case studies presented involve the experiences of people who have sought my help for the trouble they were having with their marriages. Marriage-counseling cases are notably complex and at no time is the entire story presented. Only those parts have been selected in each case that are pertinent to the point I am trying to make. I have disguised identities, and if there are those who think they recognize themselves, let them hold their peace in the interest of helping others who find themselves trapped in troubled marriages.

Unfortunately, Dr. Smiley Blanton, director and co-founder with Dr. Norman Vincent Peale of the American Foundation of Religion and Psychiatry, died while this book was being written. Dr. Blanton gave the project and the entire marriage-counseling program his continuing support, advice, and supervision. He encouraged me whenever I became uncertain or anxious about not being able to carry out various projects in this comparatively uncharted field. He taught me how fear and anxiety are enemies that block our way to accomplishment and how we must have the courage of our convictions. In all the years I knew him, he rarely taught me technique; he taught me instead how to *be*. I am deeply grateful for having known him. I can only hope that this present effort will prove worthy of this kindly healer of men.

Despite all the difficulties that people have with marriages today, there are marriages that give sustenance to husband and wife and help them to grow and to realize much of their potential. As a result, husband and wife develop a feeling of oneness that in turn respects the uniqueness of each. This book and all the experience that led to its writing could never have been achieved without such understanding, consideration, and cooperation on the part of my husband, Dr. Mitchell Salem Fisher, who is a matrimonial lawyer.

ESTHER OSHIVER FISHER, LL.B., Ed.D.

*New York*

# Contents

# Introduction

## *Changing Marriage in a Changing Society*

As I write, I sit in the warm, intimate library of my apartment overlooking the Hudson River, where I counsel people whose marriages are troubled. On one wall is a brightly colored pastel drawing showing a loving exchange of greetings between a husband and wife; in their enthusiasm, the man did not even take time to remove his coat. Their small daughter is tugging at her father's leg, and one gets the feeling that she will soon get her share of her parents' affection. Clients are frequently made tearful by the drawing; they say it depicts something they themselves have never experienced. On another wall is a painting of a rowboat that has gone adrift and lies stranded on a barren shore. In the distance, beyond tumultuous waves, is the busy city. Some who see that picture weep in self-pity for their own isolation and loneliness; others propose ingenious ways to reach the far shore.

I sit at my desk trying to think of one startling and dramatic case in my experience that will give those concerned with troubled marriages the incentive to read this book. I cannot. Instead, the hundreds of distressed husbands and wives I have known and counseled seem to be clamoring for such recognition. Perhaps this is as it should be, for the work of the clinical marriage counselor is many-faceted, and he must be able to help many kinds of marriages for him to be fully equipped to deal with the problems of one. I think of all the troubled husbands and wives I have seen and remember the variety of relationships we established, and I am pleased that so many felt they could work their problems through with me. I am sorry about those

who could not, for the establishment of a good working relationship between a marriage counselor and his clients is imperative
if anything is to be achieved.

I recall the things that were said—in passion, in disdain, in indifference, in despair—the confidences and the confessions that
people had been unable to give vent to elsewhere, and I medi-
tate on the variety and intricacy of their problems. So many came
because of dissatisfaction with their sexual relationship—either
there was too much sexual activity or too little, or the sexual relationship had failed to live up to their expectations, or they were
upset by what one partner or the other considered "not normal"
behavior in their marital bed, or they were upset because of
adultery. Others worried over their children's difficulties, but had
been unable to resolve their own sufficiently to cope with those
of their offspring. Still others were enmeshed in money problems,
real or fancied. Some had in-laws with whom they had been unable to cope. Alcoholism or compulsive gambling devastated
many more. There were those who were overwhelmed by the
difficulties and the hazards of intermarriage or mixed marriage.
Finally, there were the divorced, widowed, and remarried with
their peculiarly difficult and complex life situations.

The urgency with which they came for help—their distress,
their anger, their fright, their anxiety, and their tension—haunts
me still. I have come to feel deep humility and compassion for
their struggle for life itself and a keen admiration for the many
whose courage and fortitude motivated them to strive for a
sounder existence, to understand and finally make a decision on
the future course of their lives and marriages, and to take responsibility for their decisions. With the aid of counseling, they were
gradually able to reject despair and self-pity, and accept a commitment to life that minimized their self-involvement and emphasized concern for others. Some, I hope, recognized how everyday loving was far more rewarding, if more difficult, than "falling
in love" or "being in love."

Why do so many people today have this pressing need for
professional help with their marriages? Why does the trend to
divorce remain at its high rate?* Certainly it is not because mar-

---

* The chance of divorce in the United States at present is generally said
to be one for every four new marriages made per year. This is not true for
every segment of society.

riage is disliked; else why the boom in marriages and the numerous remarriages?

Is the reason our quick-changing, ambivalent society—a society in which we often say one thing and do another? A society increasingly beset by confusion about human values and goals, and by frustration as to the means to achieve them despite a scale of affluence never before attained by man? Society's confusions frequently compound the confusions that inevitably confront the individual. If a society does not succeed in defining what it expects of its members in their various roles, if it does not substantiate those expectations with intellectual, legal, and moral sanctions necessary to impart structure and content to role expectations, what is the individual to do?

Why the confusion? For one, the mid-twentieth-century world is moving and changing too quickly for the social institutions that were developed in a less restless age. Today's events seem to give inadequate preparation for what may happen tomorrow. A theme of the times is that all problems are solved quickly and all "stories" end happily. Unfortunately, the reality is that in life there are no quick solutions and no pat endings, but only constant struggle and ever-present potential for growth.

Another contributing characteristic of contemporary society is its growing horizontal mobility (a result of cheap and easy transportation) as well as its improved vertical mobility on social and economic ladders. As people are swept along in cars, planes, and boats, as they move from city to suburb and from region to region, they pay a price for their freedom in rootlessness and loneliness and the feeling that there is no need to answer to anyone since no one really cares. However, there is always the gnawing need to answer to oneself, but just who is that?

As a result, young people, not quite aware of who they are themselves, often do not get to know one another in varied situations prior to marriage. Small wonder they make tragic mistakes in their judgment of potential mates. Relationships are formed on the basis of superficial likenesses, with little awareness of the differences in culture and tradition that, in their deeper intangibles, tend to become crystallized in the intimate relationship of marriage. Many are so eager for love and affection that they are likely to marry in haste and without adequate preparation. Underlying all this is a wide discrepancy between the realities and responsibilities of marriage and the unreal expectations concerning it that are created by what appears in the mass media of communication and entertainment.

Moreover, there has been an actual change in marriage expectations from those of fifty years ago that only further compounds young people's problems in the selection of their mates. It used to be that one generation passed on to the next within the family the values, the traditions, and the expertise that kept marriages going despite the many disappointments and difficulties. Today the barriers between the generations have grown more resistant, and the family has ceased to be the integrated economic unit with a place for everyone from Junior to Father's maiden aunt. Instead there is a small family group of Mama, Papa, and children, all of whom seek "happiness"—whatever that may be. Years ago, a man expected the woman he married to be strong and healthy, a good cook and a good housekeeper, and a woman expected her husband to be a good provider and manager. Today men and women look for mates who will be good companions and for whom they will feel affection and love.

Our society places particular value and emphasis on individualism. Individuals are expected to be free to make their own choice of a mate, but this puts a tremendous responsibility on the young, especially if they are immature and naïve. It is no longer fashionable to seek parental approval. This is a far cry from the practice of yesteryear, when choice was based on economic and social position, family background, and parental approval.

Mass culture and mass education are other sources of confusion because of the havoc they have wrought with concepts of class and status. It does not help that superficially we all look more alike. We may look alike, but we are not alike in fact; our society, made up of many cultural, religious, ethnic, and racial groups, is notably pluralistic. Inherent differences frequently have peculiar effects on communication between two people. We live in a world of vast and wondrous communication, but few of us are able to speak to others and be certain that they will really comprehend us. There is, then, the recurrent danger that men and women, marrying as they do, will have only external layers of understanding of each other and of the deepest values in life. Inevitably, disappointment and anger will follow.

The emphasis on the romantic ideal places on romantic love alone the whole weight of the marital relationship. We mate now for love, but the meaning of this is not clear. Distortions will arise: only one person in the world will do; love alone is enough for a decision to marry and, therefore, happiness will be forever.

This emphasis on happiness and romance has been accompanied by a radical revision in sexual attitudes and behavior. We have swung away from Victorianism and the double standard, toward a trend in the direction of a single standard for both sexes, patterned after that of the male. This takes little cognizance of the inevitable concern for home and children that many women have when they are involved in sexual behavior. The pendulum has yet to come to a stabilized position where values and behavior meet. In the meantime, some good has come of it. Shame and prudishness have waned, at least in the upper and middle classes, and there is more understanding of the meaning of sex and affection between men and women.

Whatever liberation has been achieved in sexual matters has also had its price, however, for it has increased confusion about sexual and social roles and has accelerated the deterioration of underlying values. On the one hand, people enter marriage with a clearer understanding of what sexuality involves; on the other hand, they are all too frequently beset by doubt and uncertainty about what they want and what will be expected of them.

Women are equal partners in marriage; yet they are treated as overwhelming and potentially omnipotent beings and at the same time as members of a somewhat despised minority group. With this dual orientation, confusion in many marriages is inevitable. What is more, in a world where more and more women are working, the character of marriage must change. If the wife works, the husband is likely to share more of the home responsibilities and care of the children. There is an increasing similarity in the roles of men and women and a tendency for the two sexes to become more alike in their behavior and, accordingly, in personality. Women are becoming more aggressive, as well as more educated; with more education, women seem to become more masculinized in attitudes and behavior, while many more educated men seem to become more feminized in their approach to life. The gap between the sexes appears to be narrowing.

We live in a world where education has suddenly taken on a new importance. In my experience, the high school graduate or the woman who attended college for only one or two years tends to view her limited education as another symptom of her inadequacy. Such a woman needs to be motivated to further educational pursuit and goals that would help take some of the emotional burdens off her marriage and contribute something to it instead. Husband and wife may or may not find something more in common, but the wife's energies are directed away from making demands on the marriage toward satisfying her own needs. Other women need to be motivated toward part-time jobs, even to working with their husbands where it is feasible, or to outside volunteer interests that bring them into contact with other people. This is not the total answer to a troubled marriage (no one thing ever is), but the joy of personal achievement is real and obtainable, whereas the "happiness" that so many people seek in marriage is not.

We have the peculiar phenomenon today that is labeled the nuclear family. This family group is made up only of father, mother, and children. No one else is allowed to be involved. This kind of family is frequently mobile, rootless, and makes a demand for privacy which tends to result in isolation, especially in the suburbs and particularly for women who stay at home. The loneliness and confusion that result need to be assuaged by furthering interest in the community and its needs and activating a concern for others.

I remember leading a group of young women in discussions about marriage for some ten or twelve sessions in a development on Long Island where they lived. I never got over the feeling, each time I went, that I was in some kind of glorified camp where the parents were the counselors, for better or worse, of their young children. No one in the group had children over sixteen, which was generally true of the development at large, and no one who lived there was more than forty-five. The first question they asked was: What is a woman and what makes a man?

Life is lived, especially today, by many generations, and each has much to offer the others. I am not suggesting going back to the old way of life of the extended family, but there is a middle ground between the extremes. Grandma and Grandpa have much to offer their grandchildren. (I am not including in this discussion the neurotic, the extremely aged, and the chronically sick older person, but rather the many independent, healthy grandparents who have lives of their own.) Too often they are pushed off for special visits that have to be tolerated, or they live too far away for the casual visiting that should take place.

Mobility brings more tensions as tradition and heritage become less important. Whom you come from no longer matters—just what you are—so there is no past and no future, only today. Men and women set up homes, determined to forget Mama and Papa as much as possible. This seems like a step toward independence. Whether it is or not, the individual is left with little to go on, for to have a future there must be recognition of the past.

It is not very surprising then that many people, disturbed by the troubles they may have in marriage, seek professional help —consciously and ostensibly for the distress they feel because of their marriage, but unconsciously and less obviously for the distress they feel because of themselves. They want help to explore and understand many things: the meaning of being a person; a redefinition of their sexual roles; the differences between freedom and license; the significance of adult responsibility; the need for commitment to life; and the difference between falling in love or being in love and loving in the day-to-day relationship of marriage.

How can I help my marriage? Shall I keep my marriage? These are the conscious questions each person asks when he seeks help. The marriage counselor does not make the ultimate decision whether to keep the marriage unless there is a danger of serious physical or psychic harm. Instead, he helps the marital partners, individually and together, to explore their life situation and their feelings about themselves and their marriage as the basis for making the decision on their own. This can be properly accomplished only if the marriage counselor has little or no need to act out his feelings and can be objective, has perception and knowledge, stands for the positive and constructive factors in life, and despite his awareness of all the negatives, is able to find some of those constructive factors in all those who seek his help.

# I

# *Problems Troubled Marriages Present*

# 1

# *Sex Is Not Always*
# *What It Should Be*

Attitudes toward sex have been constantly changing in modern times, particularly since World War II, when a whole new outlook on sexual relationships began to evolve. The first part of the sexual revolution took place in the twenties and was much more easily understood than the one we are going through now because that sexual revolution was openly directed against Victorian standards, which still pervaded many areas of life. The current transformation is more difficult to comprehend because it is not so much a reaction against old standards as it is a search for entirely new ones. The effort to formulate the new standards makes inevitable and understandable the current open and free discussion about sex. The talk ranges from Victorian values, remnants of which still pervade the feelings of many people, to those values associated with new-found freedoms of sexual expression and activity.

There is some question whether the changes in sexual behavior have in fact kept pace with the changes in attitudes, despite the fact that there would seem to be much less inhibition in discussion and a good deal of flagrant behavior. The difficulty lies in establishing a standard for comparison, namely, the extent and kind of sexual behavior that generally existed in fact when people did not find it easy to talk openly about sex.

Of far more importance to note is that whatever the changes in attitudes and behavior may be, feelings have a way of lagging behind, so that there remains a painful gap for many between what they may say or do and what they really feel.

3

Changes of this kind have a way of bringing confusion, particularly since a single standard for men and women is sought by the many groups that make up our pluralistic society. For example, we speak of women's right to equality with men. What do we mean? Many think it means that women have the right to the same sexual standards as men. We talk of a single standard, meaning the male standard, and say that women should have the same rights as men, without any regard for their difference in need. A man and a woman have basic physical and psychic differences that cannot be denied.

The difficulty lies in what we mean by equality. "Equal" need not mean intrinsically "the same." What it means is, rather, that men and women have the inalienable right to equality of opportunity, each to live to his own best potential. This does not necessarily even mean the same opportunities. The view that equality in sex is sameness fails to take into account fundamental differences and different levels of meaning in regard to sex.

We talk of physical sex. Most men can deal with this kind of sex and move on. However, despite the single standard and the talk, many women are in fact unable to cope with physical sex devoid of emotional involvement. For these women, sexual intercourse is usually accompanied by a conscious or subconscious desire for home and children. Such women inevitably become emotionally involved with their sexual partners.

There is much stress, too, on the need for mental and spiritual understanding; both men and women express this need, especially in better-educated groups. To satisfy such a need, companionship and mutual acceptance must be established before intercourse takes place. To have physical sex first and to hope that companionship and mutual acceptance will follow involves taking a long chance on achieving the intimate relationship for which most of us strive.

Also to be considered are the differences in needs between men and women. Women generally are somewhat slower to arousal than men. Men who love their wives know this and are interested in foreplay. Those who are overconcerned with themselves, for whatever reason, are impatient and leave their wives wanting. Indeed, there should be what I have termed "foreplay before the foreplay"—the prior mood cannot be one of hostility and anger if a woman or, for that matter, a man is to respond easily and freely in bed.

Men, especially young men, tend to seek sex as such, with affection being a secondary gain. Most women seem to seek affection first. Women ask for romance, they react to a mood, a touch, to their feelings; they are slower to react to what they see. Men respond quickly to touch, and to what they see and smell but lose their capacity easily. It has been my experience that many women are unaware of how quickly an erect penis can deflate. Women who unconsciously emasculate their husbands need to be educated in how not to destroy what they want—basically, a man who will give them affection and love.

TODAY'S IDEAL

In no other relationship does there exist the intimate psychosexual tie that we find between husband and wife. For the purposes of this discussion, the focus is on marital intercourse and the frequent deviations from the marital ideal. The current ideal for a satisfactory marriage stresses the necessity of sexual satisfaction for women as well as men, the measure of happiness being often expressed according to the degree to which husbands and wives have been able to achieve this mutual satisfaction.

Clearly, when primary emphasis is placed on the ideal of mutual sexual satisfaction, there is much room for disappointment and dissatisfaction, with the possibility of termination of the couple's sexual activity and even of their marriage. On the other hand, if the emphasis is on companionship, love, and understanding, with sexual activity another important and wonderful way of communicating feelings, the ideal of mutual sexual satisfaction can be abandoned in large measure for a loving and affectionate sexual relationship that poses much less threat to the marriage. It would seem that the elusive one-to-one relationship within the framework of love, sex, and marriage that is presented in our culture as the optimum is a possibility— not always a realized ideal.

The result of all this is that the marriage counselor is frequently faced with the question, What is "average" or "normal" sexuality? Time and again clients want to be told that there is a standard for performance, frequency, and gratification in marital sexual relations. The fact is that there is no standard because individuals vary. Dr. Lena Levine, a gynecologist and marriage counselor, noted that nearly every couple needs to make several adjustments in order to achieve a good sexual relationship.* These adjustments depend upon the needs and capacities of each partner, the emotional and physical stimuli that arouse them, the frequency of their desire, and the very techniques they use.

Too many husbands and wives feel that their sexual relationship is a failure if bells do not ring out every time. They try to conform to some romantic ideal and believe themselves deficient when they cannot consistently achieve it. What they must do is take a closer look at the reality of themselves and their marriage and accept the ebb and flow of life. In this way, they will understand that an ongoing, loving marital relationship means that sex may sometimes be delightful, sometimes so-so, sometimes nonexistent, sometimes not very successful, and sometimes even a failure, only to return to being exciting and active again. While the act of intercourse may be a one-time thing and may or may not be successful, the sexual relationship in marriage has the advantages of time and of loving care. If the emphasis is on the love husband and wife feel for each other, a single act of intercourse will not take on undue importance but will become part of the whole relationship. That is why sex becomes most meaningful within the framework of love and marriage.

A question is often asked about the frequency of marital intercourse. Sex is an important part of our lives—certainly it is not the whole of life. There are clients who overemphasize the frequency of their sexual activity as though the quantum of their activity indicates "success." I sometimes say to them, "Let us assume that you are indeed a very active man sexually and have sex twice a day, seven days a week. Such activity, I assume, must take you an hour or two each day. There are twenty-four hours in the day. What do you do with the remaining twenty-two hours besides sleeping?" The implication is caught, and we go on to talk of other aspects of their lives and let sex, at least for the moment, fall into place.

---

* Lena Levine, *The Frigid Wife*, Julian Messner, 1962, p. 99.

Almost everyone wants to be "normal" and to be recognized as such. Here again we have confusion. So many people think normality means conformity to a rigid standard. But variety is normal. There is a variety of sexual stimuli and of response. Both partners need to understand their own needs for arousal and for stimulation. Frequency is based on what both spouses like and not on what one wants or demands. Variations in sexual techniques are often considered departures from the norm by the unknowledgeable, resulting in disgust or distress. Counseling that helps both spouses to a mutual understanding of needs and preferences will aid sexual harmony.

Marriage counselors constantly battle ignorance, fear, and guilt. When a counselor destroys the concept of normality in sex and suggests a process of sexual adjustment, he inevitably challenges the illusion of romantic love and perhaps destroys the client's belief in its spontaneous, untutored, unthinking, and absolute perfection. Sooner or later, every couple has to learn that there is rarely such a thing as immediate, casually achieved sexual happiness and that love and sex are not to be equated but are to be used in each other's service, if a good sexual adjustment is to be made.

UNSATISFACTORY SEXUAL ADJUSTMENTS

If husband and wife do not consciously adjust, they will inevitably make an unconscious adjustment that can cause any number of problems. More frequently than not, an unsatisfactory sexual adjustment is a symptom rather than a cause of marital unhappiness. In other words, what is happening in the marriage sexually is an excellent barometer of what is going on in the relationship as a whole. Symptoms must be treated, however, and sexual maladjustment is a major marital problem.

Disorders such as impotence or frigidity may be either physical or psychogenic in origin, or may reflect elements of both. A marriage counselor must know his professional limitations and make appropriate referral to medical men whenever there is any indication of a physiological problem. We have a tendency these days to brush off everything as just emotional; the counselor must be careful not to ignore any physical symptoms.

### FRIGID WIVES AND IMPOTENT HUSBANDS

Mr. and Mrs. A had married after a year of courtship in which there was much heavy petting. Mr. A had no reason to suppose they would have difficulty. He was young and somewhat inexperienced but eager to achieve a successful marriage. This was also true of his wife. However, when she found herself in bed with Mr. A, she was unable to participate. Mr. A did not have successful intercourse with Mrs. A until six months had gone by.

Twelve years and two children later, they were in real trouble and sought marriage counseling. Mr. A had a girl friend and Mrs. A had guessed it. He refused to give up his girl—he had waited long enough for Mrs. A to warm up and he was going to continue to punish her. After a few weeks, he refused to continue with marriage counseling since he knew counseling would mean the end of his affair. I saw Mrs. A more frequently in this interim because of her depression. A soft-spoken young woman, well-dressed and well-mannered, she had tried for the "perfect"—or what she thought was perfect—marriage, with just the right furniture and everything in its place. Actually, she had lived like a little girl in a doll house of her own creation. Her doll house was certainly physically different from the small apartment where, for most of her life, she had shared her bedroom with an older brother. Emotionally she had simply exchanged partners. She could not understand her frigidity, her disinterest in sex, and was not motivated to help herself. When her husband refused to continue counseling, she felt to continue counseling by herself would be perilous because she might then discover that her marriage was not really very "perfect." This would have led to divorce, and she preferred the status quo.

The marital situation of Mr. and Mrs. A reflects a problem that is frequently presented to the marriage counselor—frigidity. There are various definitions of frigidity: one says that if a woman does not have an orgasm in intercourse, she is frigid; another says that frigidity exists only where a woman has an abhorrence for intercourse.

The first viewpoint has colored the thinking of many women (and men, too) who feel that a woman is frigid if she does not experience more or less simultaneously a counterpart of what men experience. Such women have much to learn about the various gradations of orgasm before they can call themselves frigid.

The second viewpoint gives much more scope to the definition of frigidity. The fact is that many times a woman's frigidity may never be discovered by her husband because she can assume a passive role in which she is perfectly capable of participating in the sex act without erotic arousal. She can feign a response—something a man cannot do. A woman who consistently does this may not be able to be a loving, warm, giving wife to her husband, but she may earnestly desire to keep her marriage for other reasons—money, status, children, or whatever—and be successful at her pretense. To accomplish this, she consciously makes an effort to please her husband and gain his approval. Such a woman is not likely to seek counseling.

The woman who asks for help is one whose frigidity is causing marital discord because of her husband's dissatisfaction or her own, or both. She may be one who is capable of becoming sexually aroused but who never or infrequently experiences an orgasm. She has read or heard that unless she is having this experience, she is frigid. She may feel that her husband is to blame for his inability to arouse her fully and may become angry with him, thereby setting off feelings of guilt and inadequacy in her husband that can only create more difficulty. This kind of woman is usually dependent and immature, waiting for her husband to give her something. She has little or no awareness of what and how much she must give to him to achieve anything for herself. Another woman may blame herself inordinately and not take into account her husband's lack of participation and interest in foreplay. Instead, her initial feelings of inadequacy lead to growing anxiety, and she becomes more and more unable to perform.

In recent years too much emphasis has been placed on orgasm and not enough on the loving relationship between husband and wife in sexual intercourse. This emphasis on orgasm, the demand by women that they be satisfied by their husbands in marriage, parallels other demands by women for equality. Women are confused and uninformed about the extent of the satisfaction that they can expect and about the manner in which a successful relationship should be achieved. For example, unknowledgeable women who demand that their husbands make certain that they both have an orgasm at the same time place an unreasonable burden on them. For most couples, this rarely if ever occurs, and does not really make much difference. The woman who expects the "perfect explosion" as a sign of her adequacy as a woman and of her husband's interest, love, and abilities is doomed for disappointment. Men who measure their virility in terms of such an expectation are often reflecting their own feelings of inadequacy and their tendency to disparage their wives.

A more realistic expectation is for a woman to recognize that her orgasm may occur at any random time in relation to that of her husband. What should be of far more concern is that women are sometimes unaware that the basic requirement for having any sexual fulfillment lies in their ability to have a day-by-day loving relationship with their husbands. A man can only activate what a woman feels; he cannot make her feel. She must come to marriage feeling that she is a woman and not depending on her husband to make her one. Her feelings of sexual inadequacy are her responsibility, and blaming her husband is not the answer any more than developing psychosomatic equivalents, such as dysmenorrhea or back and pelvic pains.

There are three principal neurotic sources of frigidity—fear, hostility, and a conflict in loves. A woman may fear that if she reacts too freely she will be ridiculed by her husband or will arouse his suspicion that she has had more sexual experience than she acknowledges. Fear of pregnancy inhibits some women and fear of rejection others. Not only hostility against the husband, but deep, long-sustained hostility against men generally may be a crippling factor. When a woman loves someone else, consciously or subconsciously, she may find it impossible to participate fully in sex with her husband. Such a love may range from an affair to an unresolved relationship with her father or a brother with whom her husband just cannot compete.

Mr. and Mrs. B had met when they were finishing college. They were attracted to each other, and before long they were having sexual intercourse on a fairly regular basis. She pressed for marriage but he felt that he was not really ready and, besides, he still had to complete professional school. He was persuaded. They married and she went to work while he continued in school. This arrangement was satisfactory until Mr. B began to resent being cared for by his wife. Somehow, her concern made him feel like a little boy. Their sex life deteriorated, and even though he continued to make some sexual attempts, he somehow could not go through with the act. Unable to tolerate this, Mrs. B sought help. She wanted to know whether her husband was impotent.

Impotence, as used here, can mean that a man is cold and has little or no sex drive, or that he has some desire but not enough to render him adequate in sexual performance, or that he has a functional problem such as an inability to have or maintain an erection, premature ejaculation, or an inability to ejaculate.

Fear may make it impossible for some men to function with any woman. Unconscious feelings of guilt or shame may prevent others from having successful intercourse with their wives; the sexual success of such men lies only with prostitutes or with women they consider inferior. Guilt feelings about masturbation, fetishism, or homosexual activities, or unconscious incestuous feelings or fantasies involving a mother or sister can be strong enough to paralyze a man's sexual performance in marriage. Anger and resentment toward women generally for their competitive strivings with men may make still other men refuse to have sex with their wives. The desire not to take responsibility in an exacting world may influence others. The passive husband of a domineering wife may in fact be so hostile as to withhold sex from her as his only way of getting even with her.

Coldness tends to feed upon coldness, with each spouse complaining that the other does nothing to stimulate. Some men use sex as a reward or punishment, and frequently this use of sex is part of a power struggle that precludes deriving mutual pleasure from intercourse. There are cold men whose need to denigrate their wives is so great that they enjoy masturbating in their presence to show how contemptuous they are of their wives as sexual partners.

The impotent man can well breed frigidity in his wife. Anger, contempt, frustration, and disgust are some of the results. In an era that proclaims the right of every woman to sexual satisfaction in marriage, such wives are demanding that their frigid or impotent husbands seek therapeutic help lest there be adultery or divorce. Men are finding that they can no longer hide behind their marriage to avoid taking responsibility for their sexual roles.

The marriage counselor has the advantage of being able to see and hear both husband and wife and thereby come a little closer to the truth. A man may complain of his wife's frigidity and may himself be its cause, for example, by not bothering about foreplay to arouse his wife. A wife who complains of her husband's passivity and lack of interest may be the precipitating cause by her domineering, castrating maneuvers. No amount of loving attention will, however, make a man potent and sexually interested in his wife if he has an abhorrence of her because she reminds him of his mother or has not met his romantic expectations. Such a man needs intensive help. The marriage counselor uses the individual sessions to get at intimate feelings that cannot be too easily verbalized by one spouse in the presence of the other. Then, in joint sessions, the counselor can, if it is feasible, help both spouses to communicate their desires and hopes, to open up a whole new level of communication, with awareness of themselves and each other. Then, hopefully, they will be able to do something about their sexual relationship.

ADULTERY

Mrs. C, who had been married eighteen years, came in depressed. She did not know how to deal with what had recently happened and asked whether she should seek a divorce. She had discovered that her husband had been having an affair with a married woman who lived in their town. After several months, her husband had told her about it because the woman's husband threatened to tell her himself. Mr. C had been frightened and had recently stopped seeing the other woman. His wife felt that she did not know how to handle what had happened. She was ashamed when she went out socially. Her anger and hurt seemed to be making whatever was left of the marital relationship worse, and she did not believe that her husband would continue to stay away from the other woman.

I called Mr. C and told him that his wife had sought my help and asked if he would like to come in and tell me what it was all about. When he did come in, he said he had come to see me against his wishes. He asked, "Is it a man's job to always maintain harmony? Every man in his forties goes through what I have in recent months." He thought his wife was great sexually and he was dependent on her, but he felt capable of loving two women at the same time. Anyway, his wife did not flatter him as his paramour did, and he needed this flattery. His wife was a great girl, a hard worker who did many things well. He did not hate his wife as the other woman hated her husband.

Mr. C saw his paramour twice more after this session, then broke off the relationship. He was a man with feelings of inadequacy who needed his wife's strength and hated her for it. He asked to continue counseling to help him with his feelings about himself as a man.

In counseling, Mrs. C learned not to permit any talk about the other woman and explored the role she had played in her husband's adultery. She began to understand how she had prevented him from growing as a man. They had married at a very early age and she had mothered her husband, being so over-concerned for him that she had then done a turnabout and treated her children as though they were adults while treating him as a child. She had a naïve approach to life and required much guidance, education, and support. At first she resented making a conscious effort to change what she had been doing. Her resentment decreased as she realized how much she set herself up to suffer in her marriage. The marriage had a good foundation and the adultery posed much less of a threat as time went by. She began to help her husband on the road to achievement in his business, of which she owned a part, rather than edging him out, as she had been doing prior to the adultery.

Nowhere is the effect of the ambivalence of society more poignant than in the adultery situation in New York. Adultery has been, until recently, the only ground for divorce in this state. A new divorce law, fully effective in September, 1967, changes this at long last. The retention of adultery as the sole ground for divorce was largely due to the strong influence of the Roman Catholic Church, despite efforts by legal, social, and religious groups to change the law. Adultery itself continues to be a crime in New York, but the criminal law of adultery is not enforced despite the many divorces obtained on this ground.

For the person who is basically confused about right and wrong and whose ego is weak and burdened with conflict, society's anomalous position on adultery compounds his confusion and hurt. To add to the confusion, adultery is many-faceted. When we speak of adultery, we can mean anything from a fleeting liaison, to bed-hopping, to a prolonged affair.

To counteract the confusion and the hurt of those who seek help, the counselor must develop something of a realistic approach to marriage that will help husband and wife deal with the "emergency" elements that an adulterous situation frequently presents. Perhaps the premise should be that if the client is for the marriage, then anything that undermines that marriage is wrong. This is true whether the "innocent" spouse knows what is going on or not. The fact that this approach coincides with what is popularly known as "morals" is important but, at best, it is only a secondary gain. In substance, this approach relies on the modern single standard for husbands and wives.

The marriage counselor has to help the client determine his own standards in the light of the client's goals in life. If one goal of the "guilty" spouse is to keep the marriage, then no further adultery can be permitted since such activity would be a drain on that marriage. Attention must be paid to the marriage if the marriage is to survive on a healthy basis. This makes it imperative for the counselor to confront the guilty spouse eventually with the necessity of making a choice between the marriage and the affair if the adultery continues despite counseling. His spouse's unawareness of the continued adultery is of no consequence. The important factor is that the adultery is draining the marriage.

The counselor does not put pressure on the errant spouse to terminate his extramarital activity; rather he confronts him with the necessity for choice. When the decision continues to be delayed and the counselor is helping both husband and wife, the necessity may arise for the "guilty" spouse to be sent to another therapist, particularly if the "innocent" spouse does not know about the adultery. I find that there is usually a need to refer the indecisive spouse to a psychiatrist at this juncture while I continue to help the other spouse and support the marriage. The roots of adultery may be quite deep, and may require long-term help to cope with them. If the adultery is continuing, the counselor cannot permit himself to be manipulated by the errant spouse and thus fortify what he is doing. Then, too, the "guilty" spouse may be able to explore his feelings more freely alone with another therapist than with the marriage counselor who is also seeing the other spouse.

When the "innocent" spouse comes for help alone and has knowledge of the infidelity, the counselor develops enough of a relationship and rapport to be able to help him see what must be done if the marriage is to be saved. After anger and hurt are vented, an effort is made to have the errant partner attend a counseling session if at all possible. If no other way is feasible, I will call the other spouse in myself with the permission of my client. The errant spouse is frequently eager for the opportunity to tell his story.

The next step, one of the more difficult aspects of adultery cases, is to confront the "innocent" spouse with his contributing acts and feelings. Short of the misguided Don Juan who tries to find his satisfaction in bed-hopping, comparatively few adulteries occur without at least some unconscious help from the "innocent" spouse. Even the person who is married to a Don Juan or his female counterpart must ask himself how, to begin with, he came to marry as he did.

The marriage counselor must be able to help the "innocent" spouse to see his role in the adultery. Inevitably, this takes some of the onus off the offender and transfers it to the innocent bystander. The latter has much to do if he wishes to keep the marriage. Despite hostile and hurt feelings, he must no longer indulge in accusations or bring up the adulterous relationship. The innocent partner's role is to forgive his errant spouse for his misdeeds and himself for somehow playing into the other's weaknesses and neurotic needs. This is not easy when one's ego has been shattered and one needs consolation and warm understand-

ing for himself and punishment of the spouse whose behavior
has been intolerable. Yet the "innocent" spouse must recognize
that everyone must save face, the "guilty" spouse most of all,
if the marriage is to be saved.

The next step is for the innocent spouse to develop faith in
himself and in the offender. I have had several cases in which
I have been called upon to give what I call an injection of faith.
Often this injection has been given to clients who came across
the country searching for help they refused to find or were
unable to find where they lived. They and others have asked
for quick, concentrated doses of faith when, heartbroken, they
asked me how to continue their marriages in view of their feelings about their spouse's activities. I am no minister or rabbi,
but a marriage counselor frequently deals with faith, hope, and
trust. Eventually, each partner must recognize the other's need
to save face and must have renewed trust and faith, despite the
record of mistakes, if there is to be any hope of continuing the
marriage.

Adultery, like any other unsatisfactory sexual adjustment, may
be a symptom rather than a real cause of marital unhappiness—
yet this does not lessen the importance of what happens when
adultery occurs. The marriage counselor must be able to distinguish causes from symptoms and must be prepared to determine treatment for husband and wife and the marriage, and to
refer clients where necessary.

### HOMOSEXUALITY AND LATENT HOMOSEXUALITY

Mr. and Mrs. D came into the lawyer's office. Mrs. D wanted
a divorce because her husband had been having an intense and,
to her, peculiar relationship with his friend Sam. Mrs. D could
not understand what was happening. They had been married
ten years and had two daughters, but she just could not compete
with his friend Sam any more. A later investigation indicated
that Mr. D and Sam had been having a homosexual relationship
for several years. After the inevitable divorce, Sam and Mr. D
bought a house and set up housekeeping.

This case is easy enough to comprehend. When this sort of
thing occurs, it usually destroys the marriage because the devia-

tion from the norm is so clear-cut that the injured spouse is left with little alternative to breaking the marriage.

Mr. and Mrs. E had married and had three children quickly. Mr. E struggled to make a living. Everything had happened too fast, and he resented the responsibilities life had imposed upon him. He felt his wife was to blame. Women were all the same. Everybody talked about how much women gave to marriage, but all his wife did was to take care of the house and the children. She had little if anything to do with him except to insist on a weekly supply of money; no matter how much he gave her, it was never enough. In his experience, all women were takers and not givers and his wife fitted the pattern—she was a taker who would absorb him if he let her. Also, she was not to be trusted—no woman was. Mr. E consoled himself regularly with too many beers. Doing so made him feel more relaxed and even affectionate toward his wife. With no preamble, he would insist upon having sex. His wife would submit despite her feelings of revulsion. Time and again Mr. E would find that he could not successfully complete the sexual act.

Cases involving overt homosexuality rarely come to the marriage counselor, but many cases needing counseling involve men and women who are not consciously so much interested in members of their own sex as they are unable to become involved in a permanent, ongoing, constructive relationship with the opposite sex despite marital vows and good intentions. This inability to relate constructively to a member of the opposite sex has been called, for want of a better term, latent homosexuality. I dislike the term because it is negative, vague, and accusatory and ignores the positive attributes of human beings and their marriages. This label, like many in the psychological field, fails to reflect the vast range of any human trait. Life does not always present clear-cut patterns, and deviations from the norm often take on a blurred, shadowlike quality.

In these cases, and there are many, there is usually no peculiar or asocial behavior pattern. Rather, men and women so afflicted come to marriage generally hating and not trusting the opposite sex and eventually direct their hate and mistrust toward their spouses. Sex, if and when it occurs, is superficial and intensifies resentment. Frigidity, impotency, and adultery are frequently the presenting problems, but the deeper psychological problem is usually apparent to the marriage counselor.

Rarely does the term "latent homosexuality" appear in the diagnosis of one spouse without appearing in that of the other. Husband and wife may display the trait in their relationship differently, but they both find difficulty in communicating in bed and out—they find difficulty in becoming involved with each other. When there is a good marriage, husband and wife gradually mesh, if not all their life together, at least for a good part of the time. They develop a oneness that is highly rewarding. In marriages involving those with latent homosexual traits, the partners have little capacity for meshing, nor do they really want to; indeed, any closeness can be frightening. However, if the marriage counselor can reduce the distance between them, they can often be helped to achieve a certain amount of communication, understanding, and acceptance of each other and themselves so that they can exist within sight of each other. In fact, with help, and depending on their ability to respond to counseling, they might even be able to make some occasional, albeit momentary, emotional contact. This might not be enough sustenance for other couples, but would be highly satisfactory for these people and others like them.

ABORTION

After Mr. F and Mary had lived together unmarried for six months, Mary became pregnant. Mr. F insisted that she get an abortion although he liked her enough to marry her. She agreed. They married, and there followed a search for an abortionist that ended in the back quarters of a city in Europe. Mrs. F never got over the trauma of the abortion, and her hatred of Mr. F became intense. They came for help when he threatened divorce because of her hostility. Mr. F was immature, confused, unable to assume responsibility—he was a taker and not a giver. Mrs. F was dependent, frightened, and immature. She had tried, but the abortion had left her bitter, with feelings of guilt and of hatred toward her husband from which she was unable to recover.

After exploration in counseling, Mrs. F made the decision not to continue in a marriage in which she felt so much hatred and anger. She acted quickly on the decision and left the city. Mr. F continued in counseling for a while and developed some insight into his immaturity, confusion, and hatred of women and then was referred to a male psychiatrist for further help.

Mr. and Mrs. G were married for twenty years and had two teen-age daughters when Mr. G began asking for a divorce. A rigid man with deep feelings of inadequacy, he saw everything as either black or white, right or wrong. Mrs. G felt inadequate, confused, frustrated, for she had put all her efforts into her home and family, with little success and less personal satisfaction. Eight years before, she had gone for therapeutic help so that she could deal with the problems her children had begun to present. She had become more relaxed in her relationship with her husband and suddenly she found herself pregnant. She had been totally dismayed by the prospect of another child when she was about beginning to hold her own with her present family. Her husband overtly went along with the professional advice they were getting at the time, which indicated that an abortion was in order to avoid a breakdown. He never forgave his wife, however, for having the abortion and eliminating the possibility of his ever having a son—a "good" married woman just did not do this. Abortion was illegal for a reason—everyone knew it was criminal. He felt that his wife's obtaining the abortion was another act of castration on her part and he became angrier than ever.

After a year of counseling, Mrs. G resolved her guilt feelings about the abortion and recognized how her husband had used it to punish her for not behaving exactly as he wished. She gathered enough strength to seek a divorce rather than continue in a marriage in which there would only be frustration and little satisfaction.

Legal abortion must inevitably come, and this is good for many reasons, but legal abortion will never of itself resolve the feelings of a man and a woman toward themselves and each other. The movement toward legal abortion is becoming stronger and more vocal, and the unnecessary pain and suffering caused by illegal abortions are no longer being passively accepted. At the same time, marriage counselors are aware that couples who have a good marriage tolerate an abortion with little effect on their relationship. When an abortion becomes necessary because there is no marriage, it, too, will have little effect if the later marital relationship is a really loving one.

CONTRACEPTION

How people use contraceptives is often a clue to their feelings about sex and about each other.

Mr. and Mrs. H had two young children. Mrs. H complained of Mr. H's isolation, withdrawal and, above all, his passivity in bed. Mr. H felt that his wife was angry and aggressive, and he had difficulty making love to her.

After six months of counseling, Mr. H began to understand that his passivity was not a reaction to his wife's anger, since she was no longer very angry, at least not at him. He became anxious at this point and, one night, he impulsively determined to show her what a man he really could be. Mrs. H was at once delighted with and angry at his aggressiveness. She thought of her diaphragm but felt her husband should take responsibility. Mr. H thought of using one of the condoms he had close by, but was afraid to stop his love-making. Mrs. H became pregnant.

Since pregnancy had conveniently put sexual distance between them before, it was not too surprising that Mrs. H's pregnancy did so again. They continued counseling until the baby was born. They came to admit their feelings of inadequacy and their hostility toward themselves and each other, which had resulted in their failure to use birth control.

Mr. and Mrs. I, married twenty years, bordered on forty and had two teen-age daughters. Mr. I had continued difficulty relating to his wife sexually. His greatest satisfaction came when his wife helped him masturbate. Theirs was a sadomasochistic, immature relationship into which each had fitted well for many years. Mr. I despised women generally, and it suited him to show how little he thought of his wife's abilities as a sexual partner by refusing to complete their sexual activity with intercourse. Mrs. I, who was immature and frightened of men and their potential aggression, went along with his demands but was deeply angry with him and herself.

In counseling, Mrs. I moved quickly in her awareness of how matters stood between herself and her husband. On the counselor's suggestion, she had herself fitted with a diaphragm. Mr. I was unable to accept the freedom this gave him and the closeness that might be achieved as a result. He proceeded to use a condom even though his wife used the diaphragm, on the ground that he did not trust the diaphragm and that they certainly did not want any more children. He then became furious with his wife because he had to use the condom and demanded that she stop using the diaphragm so that he could stop using the condom and they could go back to their old sexual pattern. Mrs. I stopped using the diaphragm but eventually she gathered enough emotional strength to be able at times to leave the marital bed rather than go on helping her husband to masturbate. He was a disturbed man who had little motivation to understand and help himself or his marriage. Mrs. I's ability to get out of bed when her husband refused intercourse in favor of masturbation showed at least the beginnings of personal strength, from which she derived a certain amount of self-respect.

Recently developed contraceptive methods appear to be bringing much greater freedom and spontaneity to sexual relations, and they may also be changing the pattern of female psychology. The principal innovations are the well-known "pill" and the less well known but equally effective and, perhaps, eventually more satisfactory intrauterine loop. The anovulent pill, which is fairly well established medically, does not lift responsibility since if it is to be effective the required schedule must be adhered to. On the other hand, the loop, a spiral of plastic inserted in the uterine tract by a physician, requires no further attention except an occasional checkup.

The pill and the loop free a woman, if she so desires, to act as spontaneously in sex as does a man. Although this freedom has obvious merit, it can also precipitate a woman into situations with which she is not fully prepared to deal. Within marriage, it enables her to become the pursuer, and such pursuit may unsettle her husband if he finds that he cannot always meet her demands.

As new freedoms are gained, there is a pressing need for each person to assume more responsibility. Otherwise there is no true freedom, only license, and perhaps chaos.

The condom is disliked by many men, who feel that it interferes with their sexual satisfaction, but the condom remains popular. A man who has agreed to use this method must make sure that he keeps a supply available; if he persistently neglects to do so, his wife can well question his motivation.

A woman who decides to use the diaphragm must assume her responsibility, too. Sensitive wives are aware of when intercourse might occur and make it their business to be prepared. A difficulty arises for the woman whose husband is not sexually active: each time she inserts the diaphragm she prepares herself for another disappointment. If she feels inadequate as a woman or feels rejected easily, her emotional difficulties are intensified, and her anger and bitterness can be devastating.

STERILIZATION

Mrs. J, a young, attractive woman, was quite upset by her husband's disinterest and his refusal to do something about their having a baby. When they married, she knew that she could not expect to have children with Mr. J, but she had a hope for a miracle that had some foundation in reality. She was Mr. J's second wife; he had a child by his first marriage whom he saw about twice a year. After this child's birth, he had complied with his first wife's request and had himself sterilized. His present wife had been asking him to undergo the somewhat serious operation that might possibly restore his ability to have children, but he had consistently refused.

I called Mr. J and asked if he would come in so I could better understand the problems with which his wife was struggling. He was a tall, good-looking man who was a commercial pilot, and it did not take long to unearth the reasons for his behavior. He had welcomed his first wife's suggestion for sterilization because it had freed him permanently from any responsibility in his many extramarital affairs. Basically, he despised women and could not constructively relate to one in marriage. He felt inadequate as a male, and the sterilization only compounded this feeling. However, he compensated by continuing to use women to prove his masculinity. He was immature and unable to accept adult responsibility in relationships with others on the ground. In the air, he felt manly and was able to function as a responsible pilot.

When Mrs. J gained some insight into her husband, she left him—reality had washed the glamour away.

Sterilization at a wife's request does not always produce this result in a second marriage. Mr. K had subjected himself to the operation in his first marriage, after several children. His wife had been an aggressive, destructive woman who dominated their relationship. He had passively but angrily accepted the marriage. When he could no longer endure her emasculating maneuvers, he got a divorce. After a while, he married an active woman who knew how to assert her rights constructively. She asked that he undergo the operation that might restore his ability to have children, because she loved him. Mr. K loved her in return for her help and understanding. After some deliberation, he underwent the operation. Today they have two children of their own and maintain a relatively happy relationship.

Clinically, the significance of sterilization for the persons involved must always be explored. Men and women have many feelings about themselves and each other that cannot be routinely labeled and let go at that. Feelings have a way of taking another turn depending on the particular life partner and the dynamics of the life situation.

ARTIFICIAL INSEMINATION

Mrs. L came for divorce counseling—she had received her divorce decree two months before. She was depressed and angry because her ex-husband was insisting upon his legal right to visit their children, a boy of five and a girl of four. She could not understand or accept his need—the children were not even his, they were all hers!

Mrs. L had known when she married that her husband could not have children. He had told her that his inability had been the major reason for the breakup of his first marriage, and he had thought that if she was willing, they might adopt a child after their marriage. Later, Mrs. L developed another idea and, with her husband's consent, turned for help to a doctor she knew, who helped her to conceive by artificial insemination, using the sperm of a donor unknown to Mr. and Mrs. L. No one but her husband and her doctor had known about this until she nervously revealed it to me.

When conception is not possible, artificial insemination may be the answer; the sperm of the husband if possible or that of a donor can be used. There are many legal and ethical problems involved, not all of which have been resolved, and the psychological problems are not too well defined clinically. One can speculate on the feelings of a husband and wife who become involved with artificial insemination—what this can mean to him as a man and to her as a woman.

In counseling Mrs. L, it became apparent that her need for a man was that of a mother for a small boy whom she could manipulate and control. When her husband had begun to express his opinions about the way their children were being raised, serious trouble had started between them. Unconsciously, she felt contempt for men—they were of little use beyond their being necessary partners in marriage, and marriage gave women social status. Moreover, she did not really need her husband financially since she was able to earn a good salary in her profession. Having children by artificial insemination had reinforced her feelings—she did not even need a husband to conceive.

With time Mrs. L began to understand that if she had no need for her husband, her children still had a need for a father, and that she could not ever expect to take his place with them. Eventually, she was able to control her feelings in favor of her children, so that their father was able to visit them under the terms of the separation agreement. When Mrs. L saw how much happier the children were, she began to accept men a little more herself.

---

Marriage demands maturity and the ability to take responsibility, to love and to care. Marriage is a give-and-take affair that is weighted toward the giving. Marriage spells mutual giving and caring rather than mutual taking if there is to be success and satisfaction. This giving and caring must be mixed with judgment, sensitivity, and discretion. For example, a husband may be too concerned about satisfying his wife sexually, so that he is unable to achieve satisfaction himself. In another instance, a woman who cares for her husband might well subdue her desire for intercourse on nights when he is overtired or concerned about his work. Loving concern combined with judgment and discretion will ultimately serve better than the frankness in whose name much hostility is so frequently expressed.

Men and women need to understand the sweep of life and its tapestry woven of human strengths and frailties, love and hate, joy and sorrow, hope and despair, and periods of giving and taking and sharing. Too many people make rigid demands of themselves and of those to whom they are married in order to meet some sex manual's requirement. To do this is to seek a mythical perfection. Such a search arises out of immaturity, ignorance, or someone else's requirements; it is unrealistic to expect sexual perfection or even near perfection all the time. A sexual relationship in marriage is not made up of any single act of intercourse; it is an ongoing, continuous, loving exchange in which acts of intercourse take place. That is why love, sex, and marriage can make such an effective trio. Any combination that excludes one of these is self-defeating—only the three together have strength enough to withstand life's demands and vicissitudes.

# 2

# *Children and Unhappy Marriages*

As husband and wife become father and mother, the sharing of parental responsibility adds another level of complexity to their relationship, with conflict in parental roles superimposed upon such conflicts as already exist. Unfortunately, the child frequently becomes the target of their hostilities.

The framework into which a child is born enables him to experience as he grows an identification process through which, we hope, he will learn who he is and how to stand accountable for himself. The child's need is not only for both father and mother as such but for his parents to be integrated, secure, interdependent people who know and accept who and what they are. This knowledge and acceptance must of necessity include their past. Margaret Mead has commented that American homes are oriented toward the future, toward what children may become—not toward the perpetuation of the past or the stabilization of the present.* It is the houses that people hope to live in that count and not the houses where they were born. The nature of this attitude implies dissatisfaction with a man's conception of his own family and childhood, no matter how good it might have been. She further states that, at the same time, none can attain the ideal prototype of the American mother and father as we know it today. No parent can be all that an American parent should be. This is so not because the ideal is so high, but because it represents something of a myth rather than an attempt to reproduce some of the positive aspects of past family life.

Integrated and secure parents are men and women who accept their identification with their past and in addition accept them-

---

* Margaret Mead, *Male and Female*, William Morrow, 1949, p. 190.

26

selves and each other sexually and as parents who are both important to their children. Frequently women tend to be over-whelmed with their own self-importance, so that I have often had to make the point that where the mother is absent, it is generally not difficult in our culture to find a mother substitute, but far more difficult to find a father substitute. Children in broken homes may grow up without learning their potential as men and women because they will have been unable to establish proper identification with their parents—the answer to the question "Who am I?" will never be completely learned.

Because the relationship of husband and wife affects the well-being of their children, discussion of some of the attitudes and feelings of those with unhappy marriages toward their children and toward themselves as parents becomes appropriate.

WHY HAVE CHILDREN?

We know that years ago people had children for economic reasons. Today prospective children might be considered as in-come-tax deductions, but there seems little inducement in that direction. On the other hand, many parents appear to be having large families for the economic status they reflect. Studies on why people have children have found that although many reasons may be given—the expected thing to do, everybody does it, to keep the marriage, etc.—the most infrequent reason listed by parents is that they had children because they liked them. There are a number of unconscious reasons why people have children, and while these are not necessarily an indication that a particular person does not really want a child or is not going to love him, they do indicate factors that may cause trouble as the child grows.

For example, there is the man who wants a child as a way to punish his wife or to keep her out of circulation. He may have this punitive need because of deep feelings of inadequacy and hostility—perhaps he does not trust his wife to be faithful or, more important, he does not believe himself capable of holding her. These feelings will continue long after the child is born.

Then there is the man who feels inadequate and uncertain and who wants his wife to have a child to prove his potency. His counterpart is the woman with similar feelings who has a child to prove she is a woman. For them a child is primarily an open declaration that he is a man and she is a woman. Such feelings of insecurity may dog the parent-child relationship so that the challenge that maturing personalities of children present to their parents inevitably will not be too successfully met.

Some parents, fearful that their child will die, seek reassurance by having more children. For such parents a child is a permanent possession that must never be separated from them lest they feel intolerable abandonment, so they resist helping him toward independence.

There are parents who have children because of masochistic needs. The family may be in financial difficulty, and having more children all the time keeps it in various states of hardship. Such parents may have a great need to keep themselves this way despite their many complaints.

The conscious reasons for having children, like the conscious reasons men and women give for marrying, are to be considered, but the unconscious reasons form the real foundations of marriage and the decision to have children. These unconscious reasons need exploration and treatment when destructive forces arise in marital and parental relationships.

Some couples nearing the termination of counseling may discover that they are going to have a child. This can be perfectly healthy; the fact that the motivation is unconscious does not mean it is bad or that the children will not be loved and wanted. Such patients may unconsciously be having the child as a gift to the counselor. (I have a number of such "professional grandchildren.") Nevertheless, the parents' attitudes have to be explored and their feelings and behavior watched.

PARENTS' EXPECTATIONS AND FEELINGS
AS CHILDREN GROW

The good intentions of parents are frequently limited by their feelings. Parents often project those feelings onto a child, so that what they want for him may well be something they want for themselves or wanted for themselves when they were children. Such parents may sacrifice to achieve their goal. In these circumstances we often hear them say to the child, "Look at all I do for you, and this is what happens." They see the child as ungrateful and neglect to take into account that he is a separate individual with his own personality and needs. When a son (or daughter) does not choose the path his parents have indicated they would like, they ought to see this as the child's right as an independent human being. Parents often direct their children into fields of endeavor only to reflect their own narcissistic needs. The parents get vicarious gratification when their child accomplishes something they could not achieve.

It is difficult indeed for a parent to recognize fully that a child must answer his own needs, that he must eventually be allowed the freedom to walk away toward his own life if there is to be any hope for him to come back an adult. What was once a parent-child relationship can then be resumed on the adult level.

As children grow, many parents are now becoming less guilty over the differences they are aware of in their attitudes and feelings toward their various children. They are gradually taking into account that their children may be born equal but are not the same. However, parents seem to find it more difficult to accept the fact that their attitudes and feelings toward the same child may vary at different stages of his development. Some parents are highly capable when they deal with a baby who needs a great deal of attention and nourishment, but when the baby reaches age three and begins to show independence and a desire to go on its own, the sweet darling child seems difficult or unmanageable and they have little or no tolerance for his new ways.

At five or so, the child is involved in oedipal fantasies, and a parent may find that peculiar reactions are awakened in himself. Mrs. M was an immature, unhappy, frustrated woman who had a gnawing need for attention, warmth, and affection. She had received some of this from her husband in the beginning of their marriage, but it now had dwindled to nothing. Mr. M's anxiety over his job, his hostility toward his boss, and his hostility toward women had gained precedence. They had a pretty little daughter of six to whom Mr. M diverted some of his attention. The little girl would spend time sitting on her father's lap while he read to her. Mrs. M became inordinately jealous of her daughter and felt rejected by and angry with her husband. Mr. M sensed some of his wife's feelings but he was too hostile to assuage them. Besides, he found pleasure in being close to his daughter, who thought he was wonderful, and let it go at that. He was upset, however, that his daughter asked only for her mother on nights when she awoke crying after a bad dream, and he insisted that he was the one to go in to calm her even though her crying increased. He had to learn that he was using his daughter to punish his wife and was hurting his daughter by playing along with her fantasy of having her father all to herself—a fantasy whose realization she could not in fact tolerate, which made his presence alone in her room at night more than she could bear. Mr. M had to recognize that his own unresolved feelings, rather than a true concern for her well-being, had propelled him into his daughter's room.

Another problem in this period is how to deal with the inevitable questions that arise about sex—where did I come from and how are babies made? If a parent has much difficulty with these matters, anxiety may be aroused in both parent and child.

Later, when the child goes to school, a parent may become overly involved in his own need for the child to achieve perfection, so that tensions may arise that can be quite difficult to erase. In New York City today it is both laughable and true that some parents begin worrying when a child is born, because if he does not get into the right nursery school he may never go to Harvard or Vassar. Many parents are in a constant state of tension over the future of their offspring.

Then there is the need that a large number of parents feel to conform to some external standard so that they will be accepted by their peers. Few parents realize that to do the things that they as individuals may want to do is perfectly all right. Their anxiety breeds a compulsive conformity against which their children will inevitably rebel.

Adolescents are difficult. The biological upsurge in adolescence can greatly threaten parents, and most of them struggle to know what to do. Children, particularly at this stage, tend to reflect the insecurities and uncertainties of their parents. In adolescence, more than ever, a child needs parents who know who they are and what they stand for and what their values are. The child may struggle with these standards and values, disagree, and rebel, and the parents may find themselves most unhappy. This is of minor consequence. What is far more important is that they have given their child something to buck up against for his own determination and resolution rather than leaving him stranded in mid-air searching for something he finds is impossible to define.

Further along in the growth of a child, parents frequently find that an impending marriage is a threat to them. Afraid they may lose their child, they may try to block the marriage in what appear to be well-meaning ways, to the chagrin of the children and themselves.

Pervading all this is the fact that parents are growing older as their children grow older. A parent who may have had problems and who was frustrated too easily in the earlier years of child care may, with age, begin to develop a greater capacity to handle his children. In fact, he may handle a later child in a considerably different way from the way he handled an earlier one. There are always a number of things going on in a family—the parents are changing, the children are changing, more children come along—so that no child in the family can be said to have the same set of parents or circumstances in which to grow.

### PARENTS AND ADOPTED CHILDREN

Is the family that adopts children the same as that with natural-born children? What are the feelings of the husband and wife, of the adopted child, of the siblings? These are important questions that affect not only adopted children but those in foster care and the natural children* of those who adopt.

Mr. and Mrs. N had been married twenty-three years and had one adopted child, Sue, sixteen, and a natural child, Alice, fourteen. Mrs. N visited a psychiatrist in regard to the adopted child, who was breaking down and crying in class when she was called upon. After the psychiatrist examined Sue, he recommended that she be seen privately by a therapist near her home.

About six months later, Mr. and Mrs. N sought help for their marriage, each citing the children as a presenting problem.

---

* The term "natural children" is used here to mean those who are born within wedlock to a husband and wife.

Mr. N felt that his wife used the children as a battleground and as a wedge against him; Mrs. N felt that her husband had to become a father to his children, that his many interests had made his family a side issue.

During the course of counseling, I asked to see Alice, the natural child, having concluded from what was being said by both parents that she might well be feeling somewhat neglected. Her parents and her sister had someone special to go to for help with their feelings. She did not. I also felt that with the changes in the household, she might well need support, if nothing more.

Alice came in for one session. She seemed to have survived the emotional upheavals in her family rather well. She said, when she was alone with me, that matters were much better at home than they had ever been before, except for Sue. Alice had been accustomed to having the upper hand and now Sue was asserting herself, being quite selfish and self-involved. Her parents seemed to be going along with this as they had never done before. This seemingly had more significance to Alice than was apparent on the surface because, in the joint session with her mother that followed, she cried as we talked of Sue's adoption. Then Alice related for the first time how badly she had felt when, years ago, her second-grade teacher had remarked that adopted children were special because their parents picked them out, while other children just arrived. Alice, the natural daughter, had grown up believing that she was a second-class citizen!

Alice was reassured when she saw her mother's amazement at her feelings. The mother had shown the expected concern for the adopted daughter's potential insecurities and had not realized that Alice would have any such feelings. Alice needed to know that her parents had not recognized that the adoption of her sister had compounded whatever feelings of insecurity Alice already had. We discussed this at some length, and Alice came to recognize that her parents were as concerned for her as they were for her sister, even if they had not had the wisdom to display it.

At one time, a child was never told he was adopted. Nowadays, he is supposed to be told as early as possible and the word "adopted" is constantly used so as to become a part of his vocabulary. Whether one accepts this as a better way for parents to handle their adopted child is not the issue. What is at stake, and is far more important for us to consider, is the concept of parenthood. We constantly distinguish between "real parents" and "adopted parents." Apparently we consider biological parenthood to be the only real parenthood; mothering and nurturing parenthood is important to us, but we do not feel it to be real parenthood. Conceivably this is a mistake in our thinking. If we stress biological parenthood as our criterion rather than long-term nurture and care, we are bound to confuse the child who knows he is adopted.

One can well ask why we need to preserve this difference with the very young adopted child. To what end? When the child is exposed to the reality of having two sets of parents or two "parents" of the same sex, such exposure can be most confusing, particularly when he reaches four or five. At this age children normally have fantasies that they are adopted, and they do not need adults to give these fantasies some substance. At adolescence the fantasies are revived, with many saying, "Oh, I am only adopted." We know that this reflects the adolescent's way of dealing with the oedipal situation, enabling him to tolerate his guilt over his incestuous feelings toward the parent of the opposite sex.

When parents who adopt a child maintain the attitude that they are not *really* his parents, they may act in unspoken ways to let him know this. This is seen in more exaggerated form among foster parents and foster children, where agencies are involved. The agencies frequently let the child and foster parents know that he belongs to no one. Foster parents may say, or at least feel, "If it doesn't work out, we'll get rid of you," and, indeed, this may happen. Since every child needs to feel that he belongs to someone who cares about him, the threat can leave him desolated.

On another level, there are people who have or adopt children but reject them. This can create havoc for the children, whether adopted or not, for no child flourishes in an atmosphere of even subconscious rejection. The attitude of the parent toward the child has greater impact on the child than the biological facts.

The feelings parents have toward themselves and toward each

other are very important to their offspring. The woman who feels inadequate, for example, tends to raise a daughter with feelings of inadequacy. A woman who is angry and hostile toward her husband may well resent his child. Fathers, of course, display the same mechanisms.

## PARENTS AND HANDICAPPED CHILDREN

Having a handicapped child can be devastating. Attitudes and feelings vary, depending on the handicap. For example, a parent who can tolerate a child whose health is not perfect may find difficulty in accepting a blind child. Add to this the fact that blind children may not be as responsive in some ways, and the parent may feel that the child is stupid as well. Beyond this, parents may be threatened unconsciously by the nature of the disability. Blindness, for example, can evoke feelings of castration. Some parents can tolerate blindness and yet not be able to tolerate the absence of a limb or the involuntary movements associated with congenital neurological disturbances like cerebral palsy. Inevitably these parents convey a certain idea of handicap that makes the child feel different.

The parents' concept of themselves, their bodily integrity, and their feeling of capability are often reflected in the child's attitude toward what is wrong with him. Society has a way of reinforcing the damage, what with medical examinations, differences in schools, etc., so that the emotional life of a handicapped child can become quite tragic. Frequently friends (and we can include ourselves) give "sympathy" to the child or something that goes under the guise of sympathy, and of this the child or the parent may well say, "I can take care of my enemies, but protect me from my friends."

Counselors try to help parents to overcome an exaggerated sense of sympathy and to see the child and his problems realistically. Parents are helped toward treating their children as normally as possible within the limitations of the handicap.

Handicapped children tend to bring out many facets of the parents' unconscious. The guilt feelings inevitably aroused may augment negative forces between husband and wife, sometimes to the point of divorce. Unfortunately, too, unconscious guilt feelings can sidetrack the parents in their dealings with the child. They may take the child's handicap as a reflection of their own inability or their own bodily injuries, almost as if the child's defect was their defect. This is what the counselor ferrets out and tries to alleviate.

## THE DEATH OF A CHILD

What happens to a child who is seriously ill and is going to die is similar to what happens to an adult. Nobody wants to talk about what is going on. The child may be aware that he is going to die or that he might not get better, and if he is given an opportunity to discuss it openly, at least with the doctor, he can be made to feel much better. Parents have to be given such an opportunity too.

Most of us have an enormous need to blot out the terrible prospect of death. There are probably few events that have such emotional impact. The counselor helps those involved to put their psychological affairs in order so that the struggle is reduced as much as possible for both parent and child. Much depends on what the parents have suffered in terms of loss and how they have been able to cope with their reactions to it.

Parents sometimes produce another child who they feel is representative of the lost child, so that, on occasion, they will react to that child as if he were a restitution of the dead one. The new child, unfortunately, is brought up in a rather unsettled atmosphere because expectations are based on the lost rather than the actual child. Some parents may grieve for years after the loss of a child, so that their other children suffer.

Parenthetically, it should be noted that marriage counselors must explore a client's reactions to the death of a sibling in earlier years because impoverished relationships in adult life can frequently be traced to similar experiences in childhood.

## HOW CHILDREN REACT TO DEATH AND DIVORCE

The impact of death and divorce upon children can be devastating. The child's capacity for understanding and dealing with what is going on is, of course, a major factor. We know that if parents die when the child is a year old, he has no direct awareness of his loss and only later, perhaps, he begins to wonder where his Mommy or Daddy is. When the loss occurs at three or four, children are highly sensitive and death of a parent is such a narcissistic wound that they must, at whatever cost, either totally deny what has happened or convert it into a neurotic symptom such as hyperactivity. If death or divorce occurs at about age eight, the child's conceptual ability is sufficiently advanced so that he is able to verbalize his feelings more clearly; there is still denial or magic thinking because the ego is not as yet strong enough to come to terms with devastating events.

When dealing with divorce, marriage counselors must not lose sight of the fact that the child continues to need two parents and that he is not very interested in the divorce proceedings as such. The important thing is to preserve his emotional bond to each parent. Marriage and divorce counselors must not permit themselves to be pulled to one side or the other; they must avoid the risk of abandoning the child, who has to be helped through the emotional crisis of divorce.

The child retains his attachment to each parent though there is a divorce. If one parent is far away, difficulties are intensified. The child may feel threatened because all of his magic thinking about displacing the parent of the same sex seems to be coming true when, basically, he never wanted the displacement. The inevitable arguments between parent and child frequently raise fears of abandonment; when his parents divorce, the child feels, "Look what happens when Mommy and Daddy get angry—everybody gets upset and somebody disappears. I must never make anybody angry and I must not get angry myself; then no one will disappear or get upset." By way of contrast, children who grow up with parents who have a fairly good and loving relationship learn that the expression of anger is permissible and that nothing dire occurs as a result.

When children are confronted with death or separation, they tend to deny what has been happening. The process of denial may produce neurotic symptoms but, of course, little can be done to alleviate the basic situation; the child has to work his loss out for himself. Attempts to help the child are hindered by the fact that he is extremely sensitive to any criticism of his parents, especially when one or the other has actually left. Most children have deep-seated fears of abandonment, and when it occurs in fact, the aroused feelings are not easy to put aside.

## MARRIAGE COUNSELING AND THE FAMILY

The social worker's interest in the family and family counseling is beginning to take hold among other members of the helping professions in their swing away from the individual-oriented therapy of Freud to focusing on the family and interpersonal relationships.

The marriage counselor may want to include families in marriage counseling if the children are old enough and the severe marital problem has affected them; helping the children will help the marriage just as helping the marriage will help the children. However, the marriage counselor must pick up where the marital problem is, crystallize it, and be careful about the goals and structure of the family-counseling session. Difficult techniques are involved in the joint marriage counseling session, and techniques in the family-counseling session are even more intricate. Family counseling has much in its favor if the counselor is discriminating in what he does. Problems between parents may well affect the child. One may question, however, whether the child has to pick up the tab for them by becoming involved with his parents' problems.

Mr. and Mrs. O, both married for the second time, were concerned about their relationship with Mrs. O's daughter by her prior marriage—Mr. O in particular. They had been in counseling for some time in their effort to straighten out the many difficulties between them and were aware that their daughter had been unhappy in their unhappiness.

In an individual session the daughter, fifteen years old, said she was glad her parents had improved in the last few months and were getting along much better, because she always wanted to leave home when they fought. However, their fighting recently, although less, made her feel she did not belong since they now seemed to use her to fight about.

Hostility has to go somewhere and frequently spouses stop venting their hostility on each other only to vent it on their child. Calling the daughter in for one session did not mean I was treating her, but she perceived I was her friend and was trying to help her, if she would take responsibility too. More fundamental was the fact that this session helped me to more dynamically show the parents what they were doing. I probably could have done this without seeing the daughter, but the parents had wanted me to see her to prove to them she was all right.

Bringing the daughter in for an individual session is one thing, but bringing her in for a family session with her parents somehow did not seem appropriate under the circumstances. The likelihood was that the discussion could have been kept to the daughter's problems as such. And yet, I knew that she was a target for a controlling, selfish, and demanding stepfather and a mother who catered to her and stood between her husband and daughter. What is there to be gained in setting up an adolescent girl to judge her parents and their problems? Those problems reflected the difficulties her parents were having in their intimate psychosexual relationship, and nothing was to be gained in the daughter's realizing this fact more than she already had. Moreover, she would be aware of the marriage counselor as an authority over and beyond her parents, and her parents' authority was already in jeopardy. A family-counseling session would tend to set her up as an equal of her parents and she might have lost even more respect for them than she already had. The daughter mirrored her parents' problems and this needed to be used to help her and her parents, but to have the three, together with the marriage counselor, focus on this was too delicate a matter.

Children cannot be handled on completely equal terms with their parents at all times. If the family counselor believes he can avoid discussion of anything that affects or is in relation to the marital psychosexual relationship then, perhaps, family sessions may be warranted. Difficulty lies in the likelihood of this relationship being opened up for observation and discussion, so that the counselor must be most careful of the structure and scope of the session. I do not believe that to resolve difficulties in a marriage everything has to be put on the table and exposed. There seems to be a certain amount of hostility involved in this that could be likened to the case of people who boast of their frankness and honesty and in the name of these two virtues vent much hostility. In counseling, the counselor must know what to expose and what not to.

Marriage precedes and lasts beyond the children—the marital relationship is part of but apart from the family relationship; the husband-wife relationship is not the same as that between father and daughter, mother and son, or brother and sister. This is so despite the fact that in these other familial relationships there are sex differences and sexual connotations that support various psychological interpretations. If a parent acts out hostile feelings to his child of whatever sex because of his anger at his spouse, this must be picked up and helped in counseling. However, this cannot be done so that the parent is disparaged and denigrated in any way in front of his child if they are to have a constructive relationship in the future.

From my experiences in marriage counseling, I would think that family counseling that uses the family session to discuss and clarify behavior and values, aims for the resolution of familial problems, gives support, and is constructive, leaving to the individual session any probing of the individual member's deeper feelings, should have much to offer toward mental health.

Because the focus of marriage counseling is on the parents and their marriage, marriage counseling is one therapeutic framework that permits for compassionate understanding and help that is concerned primarily with the needs of the parents and their relationship. That the children are not the primary focus of marriage-counseling treatment does not mean, however, that they are unimportant or not to be treated.

The marriage counselor's concern for the husband and the wife and their marriage must inevitably spread to the family. Indeed, the marriage counselor can be helpful to everyone in the family unit. Accustomed to working with interpersonal relations as well as with the feelings of the individual spouse where necessary, the clinical marriage counselor can, at least, bring the children in for several sessions and determine the course that treatment should take. Some counselors are professionally competent and ready to take on the whole family; others refer the children to appropriate agencies or therapists. Most of my experience in this area has involved parents who are about to get a divorce or have already done so. I usually call the children in for some sessions of reassurance, observation, and tentative diagnosis and, if necessary, I motivate them toward further therapeutic help and refer them elsewhere.

In marriage counseling, a husband and wife may present the children as the problem that is tearing their relationship apart, but their feelings toward each other and toward themselves have to be treated as the primary source from which all the difficulties flow. At the same time, the problems that the children create for them in the various stages of growth are real and have to be treated lest the difficulties snowball further.

To be able to help, marriage counselors have to develop a philosophy that mixes up in the pot of reality the regimented schedules for raising children that prevailed in the thirties, the "laissez-faire" attitudes of the forties, and the accusatory approach toward parents by therapists and educators in the fifties. As a result, in the sixties, we can come out with some compassionate awareness, if not always understanding, that parents are human and therefore fallible, confused, and uncertain in a confused and uncertain society. We are able to see that parents need direct, compassionate help for themselves individually and for their relationship, so that they can accomplish something for their children and, through them, for the future of society.

# 3

# *Money—*
# *Mine and Yours*

The earning and spending of money are the obvious symbols of success toward which most people in our society aspire. The "average" individual views money with some economic objectivity and sociological perspective, but the subjective value he places on it is of far more significance. Human beings are often materialistic, and in our society a person's worth is frequently measured by his financial success. It is not too surprising, therefore, that so many measure their personal worth only in terms of the amount of money they make.

As a result of social pressure, many couples start their marriage with almost everything they possibly need, either because of the generosity of their parents or because they have borrowed on their future. They may be in debt, but generally they have a feeling of optimism about the years to come. Young couples expect their income to go up; they do not always realize that their expenditures and tensions will too. The test of their relationship will come at a time of family financial crisis, when underlying feelings about money emerge and tell much about what is really going on between them.

## "NORMAL" AND NEUROTIC APPROACHES TO MONEY

Money can be used in a marriage to give vent to feelings of hostility, inadequacy, anxiety, and emotional deprivation. Mrs. P, who was thirty-five and appeared much younger, was anxious and depressed and very angry. She felt put upon. All her life

41

she had wanted to live like a lady, and when she married she had expected to be able to do so. Instead, her husband had gone from job to job in an effort to find himself, and there had been little money or time for her to play the role of a lady. Husband and wife had withdrawn from each other so that there was not much demonstration of affection between them. At the time she appeared for help, Mrs. P was a love-starved, self-involved young woman whose husband was giving her little affection and money and making her account for every penny she spent.

Mr. P came to see me at my request. He was a pleasant-looking, anxious, angry man, much preoccupied with himself. He had a pressing need to make good in a job in which he felt inadequate, despite proof to the contrary. He considered his wife a poor manager, untrustworthy and stupid with money. He felt that she spent money carelessly, buying antiques to decorate their home when more practical things were needed.

In the process of counseling, Mr. P cut through some of his rationalizations to see the little affection and love he gave his wife. He admitted to his feelings of inadequacy as a man and recognized how money was for him a symbol of masculinity and power and how he used it to control his wife, especially when she attacked him and made him feel like a villain, just as his mother and sisters used to do. Mrs. P was able to verbalize her feelings of rejection to her husband, explaining how she had spent money on the unnecessary antiques because she was angry and felt she had nothing else to go on in her life. She had refused him sex for the same reason. For her, money was a symbol of affection and when Mrs. P did not get it, she felt like a rejected child who was not getting a promised lollipop. In her anger, she would attack Mr. P's inadequacy as a man, and he would become more hostile, more withdrawn, and more controlling with money, using all kinds of rationalizations for what he was doing—the need for security, for planning the future, for a value system that did not emphasize the material-istic. The heavy-handed manner in which he disciplined his wife reminded her of her mother, who had demanded much and given little recognition and affection.

Mrs. P had sought acceptance for years by playing the role of being very young and naïve because, in childhood, her mother had always overlooked the mistakes of her younger sister but never hers. Besides, she had long ago decided that adults led unhappy, dreary lives, so she had determined to be like Peter Pan and never grow up at all. Her feelings about money resulted from this—she expected money to be there and never concerned herself with her husband's problems in obtaining it except when she was inconvenienced by his being out of a job. She took this as a personal affront by her husband in his desire to deprive her of "love." She had little interest in the overall budget, was bored by it, and felt that a budget was none of her concern.

Mrs. P needed much support and help to grow away from being a little girl who escaped into fantasy rather than take responsibility for her position as wife and mother. This took a long time because her anger was so intense. Eventually, as she learned about being a woman, a wife, and a mother, she began to perceive how her attitudes toward money needed to be revised. She found difficulty coming around to accepting her husband's limitations and problems, but as she did, her expectations of him and herself became more realistic. She finally determined to become involved with her husband with regard to their income so that she could better judge how to spend their money to the family's best advantage.

As Mr. P began to feel more adequate as a man, he was able to see his wife as a life companion who could have an opinion different from his without its being an attack on him or an effort to make him look like a villain. The money problems of Mr. and Mrs. P, as in most disturbed marriages, were a symptom of many neurotic feelings.

For many of us money symbolizes security both economic and emotional. As a result, one cleavage that develops in marriage is between those with a "normal" approach to money and those who approach it neurotically.

Mrs. Q was most concerned about her husband's intense ambition to become a millionaire before he was forty-five. He used all his energy in the business he had acquired and displayed little interest in his wife and children. He was a big spender when entertaining prospective customers or enlarging his business, but he doled out the minimum amount to his wife for the maintenance of their home and family.

Mr. Q announced that his ambition to achieve a million before he was forty-five was very important to him. Success, he said, would mean high social status and general acceptance as well as acclamation of him as a man. If he did not succeed within the time stated, he would be ready to die.

No amount of counseling could persuade Mr. Q that he had placed the cart before the horse. He refused to see that first he had to accept himself as a person and a man and then set out to achieve—that no amount of achievement and money could, in themselves, make a man of him. He would not believe that financial success could only enhance what he already had. The truth of the matter was that he could not accept the gift of mature manhood, which would have meant accepting the responsibilities such a gift entails, including those of husband and father, as well as continuing to put forth effort toward success in his business. Mr. Q found such an outlook unbearable, deriding it and his wife with the statement that he could not be expected to run two businesses, his own and his marriage. He ignored any suggestions that he might find his future success, if achieved, meaningless and empty after the first excitement. Mr. Q's anxiety and deep-rooted feelings of inadequacy about himself jet-propelled him toward financial success and achievement that overrode everything else. If his wife wanted to accept him this way, fine; otherwise, she could leave.

Mrs. Q came to the realization that it was up to her to determine whether the marriage would continue. She decided to keep her marriage. The question now was how to do so with the minimum of destruction to herself as a person. The marital history had been marked by violent outbursts of anger from her husband when she, furious because of his lack of attention, would punitively find devious ways to avoid entertaining his customers. She would withdraw after his outbursts, so that there was no communication, and several weeks later her husband would threaten divorce. He was motivated to seek counseling when she had finally called his bluff and herself gone to a lawyer to start divorce proceedings. He wanted the marriage as much as she did—on his terms.

Mrs. Q was an immature, dependent, hostile woman who was frightened of growing up and was primarily concerned with the satisfaction of her primitive needs for food, shelter, and clothing. Her husband could more than answer those needs, provided that she made few other demands on him and answered his needs for a quiet, well-run home in which there were no problems for him to be concerned about.

One day Mrs. Q said: "I learned a long time ago that my mother would never extend herself for me. My husband is like my mother. I never felt free to ask my mother or my husband to do anything. They are not givers of themselves, just of material things, but both expect what they don't give—attention." She began the process of learning how to give what is needed without resentment and with judgment and discretion. She learned how to give herself what she needed and began to feel free to use her judgment and assert herself without the fear of being punished.

As she felt better about herself, she began to see her husband, who had long since left counseling, more objectively. She recognized and accepted his limitations, but looked to his good qualities for sustenance. She began to display feelings of loyalty and support toward him, ran her home better and set personal goals about work that involved going back to school. For the most part, she was able to be relaxed even though she felt his continuous tension.

After six months, I invited Mr. Q to come in to see me—my purpose was to check on the way the marriage was going. He was still driven, self-involved, and tense, but was beaming as he talked about the marriage—it was comfortable, his wife was considerably more helpful now than before and they went out often with his customers. He was staying home more because he was tired and home was more comfortable than it had ever been before. When I asked him what he had done to help make the marriage better, he said, "Nothing—you have done a great job. We have not had a fight in a year. I don't even have to talk to myself any more to keep my anger down—it is just down." He said he knew that his wife considered him too busy and that the marriage could be much nicer, but he was running a race to increase their finances.

Dr. Edmund Bergler,* discussing the differences between the
normal and neurotic approaches to money, says that for those
with what he calls a "normal" outlook, money becomes a means
to an end. The normal person tries not to allow himself to be
taken advantage of in money matters. He seeks to make as much
money as best he can, but in the process he will not sacrifice
health, love, recreation, or contentment. When he says he cannot afford something, that is a simple, objective statement.

On the other hand, the neurotic's attitude is that money is
an end in itself. His fear of being taken advantage of in money
matters is always greatly out of proportion to the threat itself.
Money becomes a center of this type of neurotic's life and everything else is subordinated to the desire to possess it. Any demands or requests for money, even when they are reasonable,
engender excitement, indignation or hostility.

Money runs sex a close second as a stated reason for marital
conflict and divorce. In other words, like sex, in-laws, religion,
alcoholism and gambling, money is frequently presented by
troubled husbands and wives as the problem they cannot resolve in their marital distress. Presenting problems in marital
conflict are the problems that husband and wife may feel are
creating the difficulties between them, but they are usually
only symptoms of deeper emotional problems that a husband
and wife may have either as individuals or as a team. Presenting
problems are dealt with by the marriage counselor as soon as
possible, always with an awareness that "curing" the symptoms
may not necessarily do much about the affliction itself. Some
budget problems presented as a cause of marital stress may not
require more than education and guidance; others will require
exploration and deeper therapeutic treatment. Needless to say,
budget problems, whatever their complexity, are not so serious
as the problems presented by gambling. (See Chapter 6.) Between simple budget difficulties and gambling lies a broad range
of problems involving money.

## "MINE AND YOURS"

The danger of the "mine and yours" cleavage becomes a reality

---

* Edmund Bergler, *Money and Emotional Conflicts*, Pageant Books, 1959,
pp. 18, 19.

in the neurotic marriage, where the unity of the "good" marriage is usually nonexistent. If the wife is not working, she is frequently in the position of having whatever money she needs doled out to her. If she asks her husband for extra money, she is likely to be met by indignation and hostility because of the mere fact that she is using *his* money. If she is immature or thinks little of herself and is easily frightened by the exaggerated anger of her husband, by his need to control and wield his power, the money problem frequently becomes unbearable enough so that she seeks marriage counseling or divorce.

The marriage counselor must unearth the facts to determine whether the money given the wife is indeed enough for her household. Often it is not, but she is afraid to assert her needs. To some husbands every demand is an accusation of passivity and weakness and a lack of manhood. Passive, weak men are often married to immature, dependent "little girls" who are unable to assert their needs because of their fright. If they do get up enough courage to speak out, the furious response elicited is just too much for them to tolerate. Passive men who feel inadequate have a strong tendency to act out their hostility when they are threatened by demands that they give of themselves in love, time, money, or attention. On the other hand, left to their own devices, with no demands made upon them, they may prove to be quite liberal, at least on a superficial level.

Husbands who are of the miserly ilk may be even more difficult. They refuse to spend and frantically accumulate, and they somehow can never make enough. They are often injustice collectors as well, collecting every negative aspect of life to avoid taking responsibility. Therefore, they collect the negatives of their marital relationships to give themselves reasons for not going toward their wives with love and affection—and it takes little for their wives to give them the reasons.

### THE WORKING WIFE

If a wife is working, the first question that might be asked is whether her working is financially necessary. The number of working married women continues to rise. However, comparatively few wives work primarily out of dedication to their careers or professions; when such women do work, the monetary gain is secondary and what they earn usually goes into the family coffers. Most wives work today to help provide essentials or added luxuries. Where husband and wife agree that she can keep the money she earns to devote it to special purposes, this is fine, as long as the "mine and yours" cleavage does not become a major force that overwhelms "ours."

"Mine and yours" is more likely to become a problem in the neurotic marriage if the wife is working. By withholding her money, she can show her hostility and satisfy her need to control. On the other hand, if her husband demands that all her money be thrown in with his, while he frugally hands the money out, he retains control while her resentments build. This is a manifestation of the power struggle that frequently marks disturbed marriages.

The problems of the working wife are enlarged if she is earning considerably more money than her husband. His manhood is greatly challenged then, and he may seek to control her in a dozen little ways other than by money. I remember a couple I secretly labeled the Luxury Queen and the Hot-Dog Man. The wife's work for many years had involved her with luxury attire for women, and her earnings were considerable. She was married late in life to a man whose tastes were as removed from hers as they could be and whose earning power was limited. He had no comprehension of her needs, but left his job to sit home and manage her investments and business. She rather liked this until it became evident that control had replaced management and that she was being reduced to eating at hot-dog stands when she was a luxury queen accustomed to dining in the best of restaurants, which in fact she could afford. At this point, she found her husband's control in all the areas of her life intolerable and refused to continue the marriage.

The problems of the working wife become greater if her husband is unemployed for a length of time while she is able to continue working. He needs her and he hates her for doing what he is not doing and for being what he cannot be—the provider. She, in turn, may be disturbed over feelings that she is now playing the man's role despite the fact that, at the outset, she wanted emancipation and the opportunity to work. More than likely, just when her husband is down, with his manhood being deeply challenged, she attacks.

## A WORKABLE IDEAL

Perhaps it might be best to formulate a workable ideal for the use of money in the good marriage. Let us consider the situation in which the wife is not working. The husband is working to support himself, his wife, and children; that he may be fortunate enough to enjoy his work is an important secondary gain, but secondary nevertheless. He may be ambitious and want to earn more money, in the meantime, for various reasons. The money he earns goes into the family pot, with some amount left, if at all possible, for his personal use and for that of his wife— beyond ordinary expenses. Neither questions the other about how this money is spent. These amounts are agreed upon from time to time, depending on income, expenditures, and plans for savings. If the wife is working and there is no special arrangement for the money she earns, she places her earnings in the family pot as he does. Each recognizes that the other is an individual with a right to a reasonable amount of privacy and separateness. The way they use their money is a reflection of their mutual faith and trust.

Years ago it was generally expected that the husband paid all major bills while the wife managed the rest. In many families this is still true. Nowadays, when a marriage is sound, it is of relatively little importance whether the husband or wife undertakes the general management of the checking account. This usually depends on which one is more efficient with figures and management and is willing to assume the responsibility. In such a relationship, all checking accounts and savings accounts are in both names.* Each trusts the other and recognizes that mistakes will be made (not big ones, we hope), that there will be differences in judgment, but that the money earned will be expended as wisely as possible in the best interests of the family.

---

* Whether these or other holdings should be jointly owned today is often a question for tax experts to decide; we are here concerned with primary attitudes and feelings.

In a good marriage, there is a minimum of "mine" and "yours"—almost everything is "ours."

---

The marriage counselor who has a broad perspective will not be overwhelmed by either the poverty or the wealth of his clients. The problem is not so much the actual amount of money involved as the way money is being managed and what it signifies.

Money can mean many things—to one it is power and control, to another security, to another freedom and independence. Money can mean love—wanted so much but either doled out meagerly, or given in grandiose gifts in the hope of being accepted, or as a way of relating when no other way seems available. The marriage counselor who can help with feelings about money does much more than teach budget management.

# 4

# *In-Laws Can Be*
# *Troublemakers*

People in marital stress generally describe sex and money as their major problems; after these come children and then in-laws. What about in-laws—that peculiar group of relatives that one acquires, to love as one's own, the minute one marries? Relatives are supposed to be loved, and that is frequently difficult enough, but how then to love and accept a spouse's family as one's own? As we grew up, most of us learned to expect that in-laws might make trouble when we married. No wonder then that, having married, we feel we must be sure to keep this in mind.

Especially to be watched is mother-in-law, of course, for she is the most difficult of all. She really has horns. Everyone knows she talks too much, has all the answers—the wrong ones—and is a meddlesome troublemaker. Besides, she is a possessive woman and a nagger who constantly criticizes and complains. We have to watch out for sisters-in-law, too, because they run mothers-in-law a close second. After this, the package deal of relatives is not too bad. We can expect little trouble from brothers-in-law or fathers-in-law, although they may occasionally be difficult.

In any case, many of us are certain we won't have trouble because we are determined to follow the best way to get along with our in-laws, which is to keep as far away as possible—everyone knows that.

So we have a stereotype and a myth that have established themselves in a society where the ideal family consists of husband, wife, and children. That family may be devoid of difficult

51

involvements with in-laws, but it pays a price. Where relationships between the generations are broken off, whatever the reason, impoverishment of heritage and cultural malnutritition can result. Once again, our society has deprived people of something they need if they are to live to their fullest potential.

The mature and the immature as well are conditioned against mother-in-law; trouble with her is anticipated and so trouble is found. Prophecy is a source of its own fulfillment. The mature soon learn to see beyond the stereotype and to perceive their mothers-in-law as persons in their own right. Eventually the myth that staying away is the best thing to do wanes and, all things being equal, an interdependence develops in which parents and married children can have a heart-warming, adult relationship. For the immature, society has done a disservice for, typically, they feed their own neurotic needs with the stereotype of difficult in-laws and the myth that it is best to keep as far away from them as possible.

### SHIFTING LOYALTIES

Everyone agrees, at least intellectually, that certain adjustments must be made in the beginning for any marriage to be successful. The basic need of a young husband and wife is to establish autonomy. Anyone who they feel is threatening their independence can pose difficulties for them, and most families know this.

What parents may not understand or appreciate is that, early in the marriage, husband and wife are involved in shifting identifications and realigning loyalties. This means shifting from being a child to being a spouse; from loyalty to parents and their way of life, to the new loyalty and unity necessary to a good marriage. Along with this shift in loyalties there must develop a strong working concept of the roles of husband and wife. All that was learned before marriage from identifications with father, mother, siblings, and others goes into the making of this concept.

To be able to fulfill this concept of their roles, husband and wife must have developed their own autonomy before marriage. If they have not, and unfortunately they too frequently do not, conflicts in identification ensue, with much confusion about what is expected of self and spouse.

## WHAT'S IN A NAME?

Since we do not tend to encourage in-law relationships, it is not surprising that the nomenclature for them should be so limited. Ethnic attitudes and feelings are reflected in family terminology. The term "in-law" attached to mother, father, daughter, son, sister, and brother is hard, matter-of-fact, and has a legal ring, without warmth or sentiment. Compare this, if you will, with the French emphasis on the word "beautiful" to describe affectionately the in-law relationship—*beau-père, belle-mère, belle-fille, beau-frère*. Hebrew describes the relationship with variations of the word meaning "wedding"—*hatunah*—with the result that the son-in-law is called *hatan* (bridegroom), the daughter-in-law called *kallah* (bride), the father-in-law *hoten*, and the mother-in-law *hotenet*. Since marriage means a happy adding of more persons to the family, rather than any decrease or loss, the Hebrew even has nomenclature for the relationship between a couple's two sets of parents, who forever after feel they are related by the marriage of their children —a father is called *mahutan* by the other set of parents, a mother is called *mahatenat*, and the two sets of parents call themselves as a group *mahutanim*. All terms are again variations of the word for "wedding"—a happy, festive, and loving concept of the union of man and woman. German, Italian, and Russian use terms designating the father- and mother-in-law relationship without any further connotation—German: *Schwiegervater* and *Schwiegermutter;* Italian: *suocero* and *suocera;* Russian: *svekor* and *svekrov'*. These are family terms like "Father" and "Mother," without further meaning, and do not convey the feeling of second-class citizenship that the English "in-law" does.

What a husband or wife calls his parents-in-law is always significant to me. Frequently a first name or no name at all is used until the children are born, when the terms "Grandma" and "Grandpa" resolve a difficult situation in a superficial manner that resolves nothing. In contrast are those young couples whose relationships with their own parents have been sufficiently re-

solved so that they are able to accept their in-laws. Although it
may be difficult at first to call strangers Mother and Father, they
eventually get around to calling them some form of parental
name, usually something other than the ones they reserve for
their own parents.

CAUSES OF TROUBLE

Many marry when they are not emotionally ready for marriage.
They frequently use marriage as a way out of parental domination or an unfortunate home situation, and they tend to have
considerable in-law conflict. They repeat their rebellion against
their own parents in their relations with their in-laws. The result
is that they come to marriage with their minds made up to allow
no parental meddling. The slightest display of interest by any
parent may be construed as meddling by either or both spouses.
The other side of the coin of immaturity is displayed when
emotional ties to parents are very strong and one or both spouses
have difficulty feeling married in any real sense. When things
get tough, it is not unlikely for an immature husband or wife of
this sort to run home to mother.

With so many young marriages depending on parental financial
support, there is often a question as to the effect of such support
on in-law relationships. Much depends on the couple's emotional
maturity rather than on chronological age. If husband and wife
are mature and have developed a sense of autonomy and independence, they are able to establish sound relations with their
parents without feeling any threat to their independence in
accepting financial help. They and their parents are able to enjoy mutual acceptance. This assumes, of course, that the parents,
too, stay within limits and do not use the money they give as a
means to control or gain love.

Marriages made by emotionally immature as well as chronolo-
gically young persons may well need the financial support of
parents in order to survive. Unfortunately, much emotional stress
may follow in the trail of the acceptance of such support. An
up-and-coming young man who had been married for two years
once told me that when he and his wife moved, they would no
longer have a dog. Until now, he said, they had been living in an
apartment furnished by his in-laws and he had not cared when

the dog soiled the carpeting since he had not bought it. In the new apartment, he, himself, would be buying the carpeting and that would be different. To need and want help and feel further defeated each time financial help is offered can only make for anxiety and hostility and for ungracious reactions to the financial support that parents frequently make personal sacrifices to supply.

Many in-law difficulties tend to arise out of early family strains and stresses. In other words, there frequently is latent in-law trouble in the family of origin. Where sons paint a glorified picture of Mother and her ways and overlook the very human disagreements they have had with her, they create a phantom ideal with which their wives must compete, only to lose. This phantom ideal may be a reality in some cases, and a daughter-in-law who feels inadequate can become anxious over the implied competition she senses with her competent, gracious, intelligent, more worldly mother-in-law. As a result, she may rebuff the older woman rather rudely.

Frequently a person may be angry with his in-laws because he feels that they never understood or appreciated their child who is now his spouse. On the other hand, people often lay blame for their spouses' shortcomings on their in-laws.

Mother-in-law makes an excellent scapegoat in any case. If a person has been intensely angry at his own mother, felt guilty about the anger, and pushed it out of the way, he will find it easy enough to transfer his unacceptable feelings to his mother-in-law, who is a member of the same generation as his mother and stands in a similar position. After all, it is much more acceptable to be annoyed at one's mother-in-law than at one's mother.

By the same token, there can be unconscious tensions in Mother herself. Grown children represent a tremendous emotional investment, and she cannot always feel too happy about those who take them away. Besides, she finds it hard to believe that this terribly young stranger is qualified for the important tasks involved in living with her child. Beyond this, a mother may be disturbed when she finds herself with a son-in-law or daughter-in-law whose ideas, standards, and values are radically different from hers.

## WHAT A MARRIAGE COUNSELOR CAN DO

The marriage counselor cannot ever close his eyes to reality, and so he must ascertain the facts and determine of what stuff the in-laws are made. Despite the objections to an in-law stereotype, it does frequently appear as reality. There are parents who, unable to lead independent existences, cling to their children and attempt to live their lives through them. Their overprotection stunts the growth of the children, whose desires for independence end in revolt, especially against the mother. "Momism" is the most common complaint in in-law relationships.

The marriage counselor may find it feasible to call in such an overconcerned, possessive mother. The purpose would be to explain the needs of her married children and to win her cooperation. She may find such cooperation to be painful for her to give and she may prove to be difficult; nevertheless, the marriage counselor who has empathy can appeal to the mother's interest in the welfare of her children.

Mrs. R was deeply concerned that she and her husband would never be able to rebuild their marriage. Mr. R had had an affair, which was over, and Mrs. R was ready to accept her role in precipitating what had happened and the many problems it presented. She wanted, above all, to keep her marriage. The stumbling block was her mother, who lived with them. The older woman kept her silence, but it was apparent how deeply she felt the injury done her daughter. Mrs. R felt that her mother's feelings pervaded their home so that she was unable to relax and accept her husband as she would have liked. Mr. R liked his mother-in-law but was aware of her silent accusation. He needed to save face badly in an uncomfortably charged atmosphere.

I asked the mother to come to see me. She was a sweet, quiet woman who wanted her daughter's happiness. When I suggested that she take a trip for a month and visit relatives she had not seen for some time, she grabbed at the opportunity to extricate herself from what was for her, too, a most uncomfortable situation. This gave Mr. and Mrs. R much-needed privacy to restore their marriage and resolve at least the surface tensions caused by what had taken place.

Let me tell you of a mother who was not such a benign, concerned person as I have just described. Mr. and Mrs. S, married one year, came in angry and upset over Mr. S's mother. Theirs was a rather late marriage and each had kept up the pattern of work to which he was accustomed. Mr. S continued to employ his widowed mother as a secretary-manager in his office. This had resulted in her overinvolvement in her only child's business, so that she was accustomed to working sixty hours a week for him. Mr. S felt that he could never get such loyalty and interest from any other employe. After his marriage he continued to turn to his mother for everything involving not only his business but his personal life. Mama had paid the rent and taken care of his apartment and personal needs prior to his marriage, and this arrangement continued.

In the beginning, Mrs. S, who was a competent executive in her own right, accepted the situation as a convenience. She could go on in her job without much disarrangement of her life beyond moving into her husband's apartment. By the end of a year, however, Mrs. S was an exceedingly unhappy and angry woman. She wanted to stop work and have a child, but she felt that the child would never be truly hers because her mother-in-law would inevitably take over. At first Mrs. S was unable to accept the fact that she had not wanted to assume the responsibilities attached to being a wife, preferring to point an angry finger at her husband and his mother.

Mr. S, like so many "good sons," was angry with his wife, but basically he was far more angry with his mother. Her overinvolvement in his life had left him dependent and hostile, and he had hoped that marriage would perform the miracle and relieve him of her. Instead, he had two angry, competitive women on his hands. He needed help in discarding one of them with a minimum amount of guilt, and he preferred to let go of his mother.

I asked his mother to see me. She was a tiny, unprepossessing-looking woman of sixty who dressed and behaved as though she were a seductive thirty and felt like ten. She believed herself to be far superior to her son's wife in handling his affairs. Any suggestion that she remove herself from his everyday life was met with a belligerent negative.

After seeing his mother, I was able to help Mr. S toward conscious recognition of the damaging aspects of his relationship with her. At first he cut her down to part-time work, thirty hours a week, and employed someone else part-time. Not too long after that he fired her and hired a second person to help him. He had many pangs of conscience until his mother found herself another job. His wife stopped working and assumed her responsibilities in the household. Mr. and Mrs. S have a child now and they see Mr. S's mother rarely, and only when Mrs. S feels that she can control her.

---

The marriage counselor attempts to drain off negative feelings and open the way to wholesome attitudes that will make for more mutually satisfying relationships with the most trying kin. He helps couples see that the oneness they must achieve is constructive only if they use it to relate to others—not least of all their in-laws, and not to cut themselves off. Beyond this, he uses the presenting problem of in-laws, as he does other presenting problems, to get at deeper emotional and psychological disturbances.

To a marriage counselor, the problem of in-laws needs to be dealt with, but is inevitably symptomatic of such elements as immaturity, feelings of inadequacy, lack of marital cohesiveness, and the inability of husband and wife to establish faith and trust on the basis of mutual recognition and acceptance and the respect of each for the other's uniqueness.

# 5

# *Intermarriage—*
# *Does It Make a Difference?*

The minister and the priest speak of the holy bonds of matrimony. The rabbi explains that the word for marriage is *kiddushim,* or "sanctification," deriving from the Hebrew word meaning "holy." Generally speaking, the idea of holiness helps to strengthen marriage, for many people consider that the law of God, as well as the law of man, binds husband and wife together. We all get our licenses from the state and then most of us are married by a clergyman; some have both a civil and a religious ceremony. Religion is the basis for a way of life that includes a set of values and a model for behavior. Such values and definitions of roles, absorbed in the home, give husband and wife a philosophy that enables them to look at their life together and toward their future with some serenity and confidence.

## RELIGION IS A WAY OF LIFE

There is a tendency to take for granted that people can marry without considering the differences between the groups from which they come. Different religious institutions teach different values and standards despite the fact that all religions cherish the home and family and emphasize the sacredness of the marriage vows.

We need only look at the turbulent topic of sex to see that religious denominations differ sharply on the principles by which they seek to preserve home and marriage. The evangelistic churches, for example, are concerned primarily with premarital

59

activities but give little or no thought to marital sex and so contribute to making sexual adjustment in marriage difficult. I remember Mr. and Mrs. T and how anxious they were about their feelings about sex. They met when they joined a church young people's group. They liked each other and, at the time, all their anxieties were assuaged by their church's strong dictate against premarital sexual behavior. Only after marriage did Mr. T's neurotic need to isolate himself and his disinterest in intercourse begin to show. Mrs. T, who wanted and needed affection more than she wanted sex, felt that she was dirty and bad to want her husband to make love to her. They had been taught that sex before marriage was wrong, but nothing had ever been said about the importance of sex within the framework of love and marriage.

Some of the more conservative religious groups link sex with sin, which tends to impede marital adjustment severely. Others accept sex in marriage, but are most emphatic about the evil of premarital experimentation. The more liberal churches view sex as a God-given aid to family cohesion and are trying to develop ways of helping young people overcome their ignorance. They accept sex as a normal part of life, the general rule being continence before marriage and fidelity after marriage.

Since religious values and standards tend to become an integrated part of people's philosophies of life, despite much intellectualization to the contrary, individuals coming from different religious groups may run into considerable difficulty should they marry.

An anomaly has developed in the United States in recent years that further complicates the problems of many interfaith marriages. There are those who say that they do not believe in God; there are those who say that they do not believe in the rites and rituals in everyday living; there are those who do not accept the organized church. These people tend to say they are "not religious" and that differences in religion are of no consequence to their happiness in marriage. They feel that they are free to marry whomever fate presents and however romance sways them, without concern about differences in religious background. Sadly enough, the chances are great that such men and women will find that much of what they deemed inconsequential before marriage seems to take on startling significance after marriage. And no wonder, for no matter how close two people may have been, only after marriage are they finally made aware of how the subtle, elusive differences between them can cause much distress.

All that we have known and felt and experienced in life becomes crystallized with marriage. Things that we never realized meant so much to us suddenly assume a strangely dramatic importance. A husband and wife may be able, with courage and strength, to come to terms with some of their differences, but perhaps not with all of them. It is not always easy to recognize how much we are influenced and conditioned by religion at home. People frequently do not come to grips, until too late, with the realization that religion is more than belief in a deity, rites and rituals, and the organized church. Indeed, religion is a philosophy, a way of life. It is not too surprising, therefore, that those who intermarry are frequently confronted with a sense of loss for which they are unprepared. Their marriage suddenly spells moving out of the framework of the way of life—the values and standards—by which they have been raised and which are a part of them.

This feeling becomes particularly vibrant after children are born. We all intellectualize and rationalize about many values that would seem to be in flux. Only when we have to apply to our children what we have said do we know what we truly feel. In the "good" marriage, by way of contrast, husband and wife are not disturbed by basic religious differences, and are able to more easily mesh their individual philosophies and ways of life to develop a new way of life for themselves and their children.

INTERFAITH MARRIAGES AND CONVERSION

Interfaith marriages are substantial in number and are taking place at an increasing rate. Sometimes one spouse converts to the religion of the other in a hope for unity. The attitudes of the various sects and faiths are quite divergent, so that the problems that present themselves to an interfaith couple can be complex. For example, most rabbis, except for a minority in the Reform group, will not marry a couple if the non-Jewish member has not converted. These rabbis—Orthodox, Conservative, and Reform—feel the Jewish wedding ceremony solemnizes what will be a Jewish household. Judaism places tremendous emphasis on rituals in the home, so that the converted partner in an intermarriage must be able to accept and participate in them. Roman Catholics, too, have rites and rituals in the home. They are exhorted to marry those of the same faith, but the Church is gradually yielding to the times in many ways. Today a mixed couple can have a Catholic ceremony if they agree that their children will be brought up as Catholics. The question of how children will be raised can become a substantial cause for friction in such a marriage, especially when the wife is not Catholic, since she must raise the children without knowledge of the Catholic faith and its rites and rituals, let alone having feeling for those rituals. As for the Protestants, the focus in marriage is on the relationship of the two people as the ceremony is solemnized. No written promise is extracted, nor is there great emphasis on religious upbringing of children. While clergymen of all faiths usually oppose interfaith marriages, Protestant ministers seem to be the least opposed.

The significance of religion to the partners in an interfaith marriage is important in its impact on their children. Mothers do most of the rearing and education in the home; if the mother has a feeling for her religion, the children will be influenced to follow that religion. Unfortunately, the father in such an interfaith marriage may feel like an outsider in the family's religious activities. If he converts to his wife's religion, this may enhance the family's unity. Too often, however, men who convert feel they have given up some of their manhood and have lost something of their feeling of identity. Their submissiveness often conceals deep anger, especially if they have some feelings for their original religion. When a woman converts to her husband's religion, there appears to be less danger of upset, since women still accept the idea that they must assume the name, domicile, and status of their husband and can take the step without undermining their feelings as women. Indeed, if religion has had little meaning to a woman prior to marriage, she may convert to the religion of her husband and find many satisfactions. On the other hand, if religion has been of significance prior to marriage, she may well question the desirability of converting and, indeed, marrying outside her faith.

When persons of different religions marry and there is no conversion, the unity that marriage demands is likely to be difficult to achieve. If religion has played little part in their lives, there may be some chance for success, all other factors being equal. Nevertheless, I am hard put to learn how such couples find the inner strength that religious faith implies to help carry them through the vicissitudes of their life together. Clinically, my experience has been that such people intellectualize and rationalize to cover up the void they feel. If they do not provide a religious environment, their children are often at a loss to answer basic questions about who they are. If the children go to Sunday school, they may struggle over the discrepancy between what they learn and what they see and feel at home.

Some couples resolve their problem by joining liberal congregations where they find many others like themselves and so answer their need for being part of a religious group that accepts them and which they themselves can accept. The difficulty seems to be with the fact that these groups retain overtones of either the Christian or Jewish faiths.

Mr. U was Jewish and Mrs. U was Presbyterian. When they planned to be married by a minister who had known Mrs. U and her family for many years, Mr. U did not mind the arrangement, but he was worried that the minister might say something that would offend his parents. Though he asked the minister to be careful, the ceremony was tinged with Christian symbolism and feeling. Mr. U, who was alienated from his parents and was determined to get as far away from them as he could, had not counted on his own inner feelings about his own religion, so he claimed a concern for *their* feelings at the time of the wedding.

As time went on, Mrs. U insisted that the children go to a Christian Sunday school even if she and her husband did not attend church. To compromise their religious differences, and since Mr. U was unable to make the decision, Mrs. U joined a Unitarian church and sent the children to its Sunday school. Mr. U accepted this and even made several attempts to attend church with his wife, but he could not swallow it and asked her to release him from any obligation to attend, which she did.

In a certain sense, I suppose, every marriage is an intermarriage. Even where there are many basic similarities between two families—religious, cultural, educational, financial, ethnic, and racial—each family creates its own way of life over the years. Children have to be able to take what they have learned and incorporate that learning into the new way of life they are building for themselves. When there are no basic similarities, this becomes even more difficult. If religious or racial differences or those that are ethnic are superimposed on a tenuous marital relationship, it takes much courage, faith, and wisdom to achieve the oneness of the good marriage. Comparatively few people have the requisite maturity, dedication, and commitment to life and marriage to produce that courage, faith, and wisdom. The differences that exist in intermarriage tend rather to be used eventually as added ammunition in the marital power struggle.

### INTER-ETHNIC AND INTERRACIAL MARRIAGES

There are many inter-ethnic marriages in the United States. Years ago ethnic differences in marriage were more disturbing since husbands and wives retained memories and associations with the life in the countries from which they or their families came. Today, inter-ethnic marriages seem to fare well. One can only observe that they hold a potential for difficulties.

Interracial marriages are least in number in the United States and they are least accepted by us. I have never forgotten a session I had with the son of some professional people. He was an intelligent young Jewish man who had married a lovely, intelligent Negro girl he met in college. His parents had renounced him and left him to go it alone. Her parents had accepted the marriage, although they did not like it. However, when their daughter converted to Judaism—they were Baptists—the situation was finally too much for them to accept. Both young people struggled financially and socially but were determined to succeed in their education, in their professions, and in their marriage. Then they had a child, and more money was needed than ever. The young man related his experiences in seeking work and a place to live. I was appalled at the hardship and misery he described and impressed by the couple's strength and fortitude. Why, I asked myself, did they need to suffer so much? Certainly, marriage was never intended to be a source of such martyrdom and suffering. This couple struggled to redefine their place in society and finally compromised by moving away from rejecting relatives and friends to another city, where they were able to establish friendships with other couples like themselves and advance themselves professionally.

## INTERMARRIAGE MAY BE A SYMPTOM OF PERSONAL PROBLEMS

Despite the difficulties inherent in intermarriage, its incidence has increased rapidly and will continue to do so. Superficially, everyone looks alike. The fundamental differences that matter in the intimacy of the marital relationship are not easily recognized by the inexperienced and unsophisticated. "Who am I?" is a question with which the young person is involved. He is hard put to find the answer in a society that sets few limits and changes as rapidly as ours does. Not everyone has the ego strength and wisdom to withstand the bombardment of environmental forces that seem to obscure underlying differences. Youth has always rebelled against parents and authority. Furthermore, social controls have notably weakened in influence and importance. The opportunities for social intercourse have become much greater as the barriers of race and religion have been lowered. Parents are often uncertain of their own standards and values or are afraid to state what they stand for, or are simply permissive. Because they do not state their objections, their children see no reason for not dating outside their religious group, and the stage is set for intermarriage. The mood is further developed by peer-group attitudes and the IBM machine, which have taken the place of parents in determining the basis for dating, be it for better or worse.

Unconscious factors, however, take the lead role. The unconscious, unresolved relationships to parents that play a tremendous part in marital difficulties may well be a propelling force toward an intermarriage. If the unresolved relationship to the parent of the opposite sex has become intolerable, the young person may seek a mate as different from that parent as possible. Unfortunately, this can backfire in the marriage, and the person may find that what he tried to avoid was not avoided at all. For example, Jewish men notably marry out of their faith to escape the overwhelming feelings they have for their mothers. I have seen a number of such men who thought I practiced some kind of voodoo when, sight unseen, I described what their wife or mother looked like. What I did was easy; having obtained the description of one, it was not too difficult to describe her opposite. Rebellion against an unaccepting, domineering father can also set some young persons up to intermarry. Deep-rooted feelings of inadequacy may demand that somehow a person compensate by marrying someone who comes from a minority group and to whom he can feel superior and, at the same time, someone whom he can control. Many people who intermarry are unaware of the significance and the consequences of their act. Their intermarriages are too often no more than symptoms of long-standing, deep-rooted emotional disturbances.

THE MARRIAGE COUNSELOR'S ROLE

Who the marriage counselor is as a person and the nature of his values and beliefs are of significance in conflicted intermarriages. Time and again in marriage counseling there is a need to help clients to forgive themselves and each other and, finally, to do the right thing. Since the rate of intermarriage seems to be advancing, the counselor will have to search even more in such marriages for the unity between husband and wife to help them achieve a feeling of hope for their future together, with faith and trust in themselves and each other. To accomplish this requires a marriage counselor with a strong, positive value system.

The marriage counselor must be keenly aware of his own feelings. He must stand for what he genuinely believes in, but this is never to be foisted upon his clients; rather, it is there for his clients to butt against and, thereby, to find their own values. Above all, the marriage counselor must be able to accept his clients no matter how much he may disagree with them. He must be aware of the effects that religious loyalties may have upon husband-wife adjustment, and he must respect the religion of each spouse. Particularly in intermarriage, he must help husband

and wife seek out whatever basis for unity there may be in the morass of their differences and bring into play the affirmative aspects of religion to transmute the love of God into the love between man and woman. I see nothing wrong in advancing the philosophy that marriage, when it is good, partakes of the Divine Spirit and, therefore, is obedient to the law of life.

On the other hand, the counselor should not allow religion to be a cloak for cruelty and unkindness. Nor should religion be a bar to separation or even divorce when marriage counseling is futile and the marital maladjustment is likely to physically or emotionally destroy husband or wife.

A marriage counselor must know his own limitations in this field and must leave the deeper problems of faith to the minister. The marriage counselor whose basic discipline is the ministry may well stand in an advantageous position when he is treating persons of his own faith. Beyond this, he does well to do as other marriage counselors do and turn the client over to a clergyman of the client's faith when matters regarding religion become too involved.

# 6

## *One More Drink—*
## *One Last Bet*

WHEN IS IT ALCOHOLISM?

A few years ago the World Health Organization published figures indicating the drinking problem to be more severe in this country than anywhere else in the world; 6.5 per cent of the adult male population is alcoholic. It was estimated twenty years ago that the ratio between men and women alcoholics was six to one; since then there has been an alarming increase in alcoholism among women.

Separation and divorce are notably the results of alcoholic excesses. Courts deal also with many other problems that are due to excessive drinking and that have undersirable effects on marriage and the family—financial insecurity, unemployment, illness, preventable accidents, desertion, maltreatment of children, juvenile delinquency, prostitution, and crime.

Though American culture generally encourages drinking, there is a certain amount of ambivalence toward alcohol. We do not approve of heavy drinking since it can be an evil, but we do not wholly approve of abstinence either. Superimposed on this basic attitude are the mores of a number of subcultures in which drinking is encouraged as a part of a way of life.

We speak of drunkenness, the drinker, alcoholism, and the alcoholic, but these terms are not too well defined. Even the arbitrary standard for intoxication set by the Uniform Vehicle Code published by the Federal Government in 1952 has little meaning, since tolerance of alcohol varies between individuals and within the same individual. A drinker may be an alcoholic or the little old lady who downs an eggnog once a year. There is no real agreement on what constitutes alcoholism. "Alcoholism" is a wide term that seems to mean various degrees of heavy drinking. The label "alcoholic" is frequently used disparagingly, for there is a widely held view that the alcoholic is perverse or weak-willed rather than truly sick or addicted.

Dr. Ruth Fox,* who has had many experiences treating the alcoholic, uses the following as a working definition: if a patient is unable to stop drinking after two or three drinks, he is most certainly an alcoholic, even if he can abstain totally for various periods of time. If he just cannot drink moderately, he is driven by unconscious forces that he does not understand and against which rational judgment and will power are helpless.

In counseling marriages troubled by drink, I prefer the definition that an alcoholic is someone whose drinking causes a continuing problem in any department of his life and who finds himself unable to cut down or quit. There are variations in the degree and kind of alcoholism that have varying impact on married life. In contrast to the alcoholic who drinks during working hours there are, for example, the episodic alcoholic and the weekend alcoholic, who keep their jobs and perhaps never drink while working but who create much havoc at home.

THE ALCOHOLIC AND HIS WIFE

Mr. and Mrs. V had been married for fifteen years and had three children. When they had met at college, Mrs. V had been impressed with Mr. V's seeming popularity and leadership. She was a plain woman, born of New England parents who had led a simple and restricted existence. Mr. V came from a Polish background where drinking on payday night was an accepted custom. He had left his home as soon as he was able to get away from it and its old-country customs. When he met Mrs. V, she spelled America to him. She noticed that he liked to drink, but this seemed to be part of the fun of college life.

After they married, Mr. V took a position with an advertising agency and things went well for several years. When the first child was born, Mr. V began to stay away from home, saying his

---

* Ruth Fox, "The Alcoholic Spouse," p. 149 in *Neurotic Interaction in Marriage,* ed. Eisenstein, Basic Books, 1956.

work was becoming heavier. Then he lost his job and there began a series of jobs in which he seemed to fare more and more badly.

When the couple sought help, Mr. V was holding a clerical position in an advertising agency and was frightened of losing that. Mrs. V was a disappointed, frustrated, bitter woman who could hardly contain her anger and contempt for her weak, ineffectual, demanding husband. They lived in a house in suburbia for which Mrs. V's inheritance had paid. Her primary complaint was that her husband did not return on the train most men used, but persisted in going to a bar first and, at times, would come home stupefied with drink. Mr. V insisted that this was the only time of the day when he could relax.

Mrs. V's motivation to help her marriage was greater than that of her husband despite statements that she wanted out. She sought other interests for herself and made a deliberate attempt to get off her husband's neck. While Mr. V was exceedingly dependent on his wife he had little interest in doing much about his relationship to her. He made some feeble attempts to go directly home from time to time but found that he could not tolerate the isolation and emptiness he felt there, despite the presence of his children and his wife, so he went back to relaxing at bars. His wife became even more angry, but was able to remove herself from him sufficiently so as not to have to attack him when he did come home. She finally came around to accepting the idea that her husband had a problem he had no desire to resolve, not because of his anger with her but out of his own deep-rooted difficulties. This made her feel less guilty, and she turned to her children and her work for emotional satisfaction.

Men who meet at bars after work are doing a form of social drinking. However, frequent stops at bars may be a man's way of excluding women and associating with other men because he is unable to relate to women, particularly his wife, on an adult, responsible level. At a bar he is glad to have superficial acceptance, no questions asked. If he goes home, he is sure to be attacked with questions he finds difficult to answer. Going home means taking responsibility for a relationship that demands he be a man.

Another type of alcoholic drinks at home—basically he is a child who wants his mother. His beer or his highball is his bottle and makes him feel good. Alcoholism is associated with oral dependency needs; it is seldom that the alcoholic does not smoke, although there are smokers who do not drink. The woman who marries the home drinker may have a need to dominate him. She may not be able to accept her role as a woman completely and may like having a childish husband.

The wives of alcoholics tend to have their own emotional difficulties. Clinical experience indicates that they may well enjoy their husbands' drinking. Sometimes the wife will drink with her husband or have a bottle of liquor available for him despite her protests against his tippling. These people are immature and relate emotionally on an infantile, oral level. Each searches desperately for another to give him love, but since each is incapable of answering the other's needs, they take to the comfort of the bottle, which becomes their strongest emotional bond. Their way to be together is to drink together. Some dissatisfied wives of alcoholics may eventually begin to nag. The nagging wife is not satisfied with her luck and wants to take the lead, be the boss, wear the pants, her protests to the contrary. Frequently she will do everything to help her husband get away from the bottle, but she is unable to maintain the relationship when he does. The result is that she makes life so unpleasant for him that he goes back to drinking, and then she can feel in control again.

### THE ALCOHOLIC WOMAN AND HER HUSBAND

The alcoholic wife, a comparatively new character in our society, tends to do solitary drinking at home, particularly if she lives in suburbia. Initially she drinks out of a feeling of despair that develops among women who cannot accept the limitations of their lives. She is completely dependent on her husband for emotional sustenance. Like the alcoholic man who has never really been weaned and takes to the bottle when he gets no satisfaction from his wife, the alcoholic woman tries to drain her husband of something he is simply unable to provide. Frustrated or rejected, she wallows deeper in the alcohol.

Many women no longer find completion in marriage, home, and children and so, more and more, they will have to learn early in their lives how to satisfy themselves as persons. The problem of how to motivate women to lead fuller lives is indeed a serious one. The active woman whose children are grown can do all the housework in very little time; frequently she does not want to do it that fast because she needs to fill out her day. Women need to structure their lives after the child-bearing period with long-range and short-range goals that will meet their needs within the framework of marriage and family life. Women who do this need not turn to drink out of desperation and frustration. Women who tap the full resources within are not driven to search beyond themselves for others to give them a sense of completion.

### THE CHILDREN

Children of the drinking father have a poor prospect in life. Boys have a poor male figure with whom to identify. Often, in their attempt to identify, they themselves will become drinkers. They may identify maleness with drinking or they may find in it a good excuse to perpetuate the oedipal conflict. A boy who feels that his father is no good, a drunkard, often tries to become a "good" son to his mother, doing for her what the alcoholic father should be doing. However, this is a surface phenomenon because underneath he feels great hostility not only to his father, who has failed him, but to his mother, who accepts what he has to offer although she is unable to gratify his unconscious feelings toward her—he acts like her husband, yet he is not her husband, and the result is that if perchance he marries, he finds himself unable to relate to his wife.

The damage to girls is probably not so serious. However, there are many ambivalent feelings in daughters for their drinking fathers. The desire to remain deeply attached to the father, to protect him, may later be used as a good excuse to avoid establishing close relations with another man.

The child of a drinking mother feels deeply rejected, and if both parents are drinking, he feels isolated as well. A drinking parent, whether father or mother, tends to unwittingly seduce the children regardless of their sex, so that the latent homosexuality that so frequently accompanies alcoholism is perpetuated in the next generation.

## TREATING THE ALCOHOLIC MARRIAGE

The treatment of alcoholism is extremely difficult. The alcoholic needs courage to repress any feelings of hostility or potential homosexuality. He must be prepared to search deeply to find the reason for his drinking, since drinking patterns are usually more or less sanctioned as a way of escape for men and, consequently, may serve as easy concealment for far more subtle motivations. Few alcoholics will undergo treatment if they have not finished the bottle. Many use the bottle for slow suicide. Alcoholism is a comparatively new way of escape for women in our culture, with the result that the therapist may be able to uncover the reasons more easily and give constructive treatment.

A disproportionately large number of alcoholic marriages terminate in divorce or separation. Usually women who terminate their marriages have suffered more economic hardship and more abusive behavior than those who continue them. On the other hand, alcoholic marriages are maintained when husbands are recovering or when they are continuing to drink. The personality of the wife in alcoholic marriages is not always clearly drawn—there is some question whether the personality of a wife of a man who recovers is in fact any different from that of the wife of a man who continues to drink. Suggestion has been made that families in which the husband recovers tend to be more ambitious and more concerned about social relationships, and so have a greater stake in recovery. In any event, clearly it is the man himself who must make the decision to stop drinking.

Experience indicates that men tend to give up a drinking wife much more readily than women do a drinking husband. Men generally seek divorce rather than tolerate a drinking wife, but women will continue in an alcoholic marriage for a variety of reasons—economic status, children, or their own dependency needs or feelings of inadequacy. Women will struggle with what to them, at least consciously, is a pretty intolerable situation.

Mr. W, a tall, well-groomed man in his forties who drank to

excess, was confronted with his wife's adultery with an arrested alcoholic she had met at a meeting of Alcoholics Anonymous. He sought help because he had a strong feeling of need to preserve the marriage. However, it became apparent as he talked that unconsciously he wanted to break it. Consciously, he was frightened of the loss of someone on whom he had depended for so many years; unconsciously he felt emasculated by her comparative strength and angry at himself for having to depend on any woman. The long-standing problem of his relationship to his wife had now been made acute by her admitted adultery. He was depressed, bitter, and tense.

Mrs. W, also in her forties, was a rather attractive, well-mannered woman who gave the impression of cultivated origins. She showed more than usual concern over questions of right and wrong, she did not trust her judgment and was masochistic and deeply hostile. Mrs. W had told her husband about her affair, which came about when she went to Alcoholics Anonymous to learn what she could do about *his* drinking. She felt her husband to be cold, cruel, and unloving. For years she had struggled with his aloofness, his drinking, and his lack of sexual activity, and suddenly she felt time to be running out. Basically, she wanted to keep her marriage despite her husband's continued drinking. Her father had been a heavy drinker and had been rejected by her mother, and Mrs. W did not want to repeat what her mother had done. She felt that she had invested far too much in her marriage to throw it overboard.

Although Mr. W professed his need to keep the marriage and acted the role of the "innocent" victim, he had little desire to probe his drinking problem. Every so often he would go on the wagon for several weeks, then life would appear to be too much and he would return home to sit in his chair and drink highball after highball. Mrs. W recognized that having an affair was no permanent solution for her. She recognized, too, that in fact she had almost gone from the frying pan into the fire when she had considered divorcing her drinking husband to marry an arrested alcoholic who had already gone through several wives. She began to explore how she could invest what money she had in a business that would make her less dependent, both emotionally and financially, on her emotionally and financially inadequate husband. After some time she went into business. Her husband offered his help, which she needed very much. Gradually they developed an interest in common they had never had before. Mr. W continued to drink, but not so much or so often. Mrs. W made fewer demands on him as she began to look to herself for sustenance. As her role became more clearly defined, the tension between them lessened.

Treating the alcoholic marriage is at best a difficult process. It is important to know whether the man was alcoholic prior to the marriage, how much he drank and for how long, or whether he started after the marriage and if so, when. The marriage counselor must be wary of easy generalizations about the alcoholic and his spouse. To say that the wife of an alcoholic needs the continued drinking of her husband so she can feel adequate is easy. What one has to realize is that this does not mean that she cannot be helped to gain in inner strength or, on the other hand, that she really has the need in the first place. Each spouse brings his basic personality to the marriage, but there is a cumulative effect on the wife, as her husband becomes progressively more alcoholic, that creates constant pressure on her to readjust her role.

When a wife seeks help, the marriage counselor has an opportunity to break through the destructive interaction and pave the way toward recovery of the alcoholic husband as well as of the "healthy" wife and their marriage. The least that can be done is to help the disturbed wife accept and adjust to her husband's illness with reduced anxiety and resentment.

## THE GAMBLING SPOUSE

Gambling in the United States has doubled in recent years. The total amount involved each year has been estimated at $50 billion or more. Professional gambling is so lucrative that organized crime syndicates control most of the "action." Although more men than women gamble, there is considerable increase in the number of women. The gambler, like the alcoholic, is lured by the forbidden. Both are extremely immature, but the gambler is involved with magic thinking. Everyone knows he does not get something for nothing. We know we have to work. The gambler wants to get something for nothing—an almost childish attitude that rejects reality in favor of magic and Lady Luck.

As in drinking, the gambler is usually frustrated and unable to enjoy married life. He wants a miracle and an escape. He wants to isolate himself from the normal relationships he is supposed to have. The drinker is usually determined to give sexual satisfaction to his spouse. Unfortunately, he starts drinking so he can feel better, only to find that, after a few drinks, he cannot do anything—just sleep. The spouse of a drinker can participate with him by drinking with him or babying him. The gambler, on the other hand, is usually not terribly interested in sexual activity. Although he may have a flashy, sexy-looking woman with him, his real love is Lady Luck. The gambler's spouse rarely accepts his gambling and does not share in his quest for a miracle. Men are more likely to seach for the miracle because of the constant economic demands on them or the hope for a "killing" that will give them prestige and power.

The addicted gambling wife is comparatively rare. Women do not tend to spend all their household money on gambling in any serious way. Yet the number of women to be seen standing in front of the gambling machines in Las Vegas and Reno is striking. An inexpensive thrill seems to be their motive.

### TREATING THE MARRIAGE BESET BY GAMBLING

Mr. X had promised his wife that he would stop betting on the horses, but within a week he was doing so again. She had an inheritance which he kept tapping to meet his bets. Mrs. X, in despair, finally sought help for a marriage that had displayed this same pattern for ten years. Her husband's earnings were meager and she had paid for the groceries with what little of her inheritance was left. They had three children. Finally she refused her husband any more money unless he went for counseling. He appeared twice. He was full of plans for reversing his bad luck. After the two sessions, he seduced his wife into giving him the money he needed and promised to continue counseling at some later date. He never appeared, and Mrs. X, depressed, returned to the old pattern of life.

A gambling problem in marriage is likely to be very frustrating to treat. The gambling marriage is more difficult even than the alcoholic marriage because of the magic thinking involved and the frequent inability of husband and wife to relate at any level.

---

There are, of course, other problems which troubled marriages present in addition to those discussed in this and the preceding chapters. Drug addiction, criminality, mental illness, or the physical incapacity of a spouse for long periods of time may evoke a complex of problems to the marriage. A precipitated menopause due to a needed hysterectomy, or menopause in due course, may result in psychosexual problems between husband and wife. Age brings its own problems, so that difficulties that were bearable before become enlarged. Again marriages react significantly differently in relation to the economic extremes of poverty or affluence, especially if they fall suddenly. The prolonged absence of a husband due to war or a series of ongoing, prolonged absences due to a man's work may bring too much pressure to bear on some marriages.

The cacophonies of marital discord are many. Each presents a challenge—sometimes a special challenge to the clinical marriage counselor. To an extent, all these problems have components which are combinations or mixtures of those components I have discussed. All require insight, patience, intelligence, compassion, faith, hope, and love on the part of the counselor and on the part of the spouses. Life with its accidents and incidents raises a myriad of problems for marriage, but there is a myriad of marriages that can be helped.

# II

## *The Problems*
## *Behind the Problems*

# 7

## *What Is a Good Marriage?*

When a man and a woman marry, the relationship they form is a new psychological entity. This entity—their marriage—is stocked full of their personal needs, problems, feelings, attitudes, hopes, and expectations, all of which will affect their behavior toward each other. How each one acts and reacts to the other will determine how satisfying their psychosexual relationship will prove to be to each of them. This interaction sets the degree of satisfaction that each will derive from the other for his personal needs, and determines the extent to which each one's hopes and expectations will be met and his individual personality accepted by the other. In marriage the primary emphasis tends to be on what one partner does, how he does it, and how the other reacts, but feelings and attitudes, both conscious and unconscious, have a way of shining through and coloring behavior.

It does not take much for a husband and wife to become aware that one likes their bedroom window closed and the other likes it wide open; the compromise they make and how they make it and react to it is what will eventually count between them. The person who insists on living in marriage as though he were living alone—keeping the window closed or open or whatever—without regard for his partner's needs and desires will, sooner or later, get a hurt or angry reaction that can only make him react with anger in turn. Such interaction, carried over into other areas of living, certainly does not provide for a loving relationship in which both can thrive.

The person who compromises—who opens the window a little —and yet feels that, in some fashion, he is giving in or giving up rather than seeking a common ground satisfactory to both will do the right thing but will undermine it by his feelings and

81

attitudes. When his partner then fails to show appreciation for the sacrifice that has been made, his reaction to this can be expected to be one of anger—after all, he did do the right thing!

The person who professes to feel love—he may speak about it to his spouse or not—but does nothing to indicate it by his behavior is an armchair lover who can only expect to elicit an angry reaction. Marriage demands kindly action based upon understanding of and consideration for one's partner's needs. Only husbands and wives who understand, accept, and trust themselves and each other can interact in that way. They may make mistakes—this is inevitable—yet they are able to forgive themselves and each other quickly and to move forward again in loving kindness toward each other and toward their goals in life.

There is a tendency to hope for magical changes in personality after marriage, but it is more realistic perhaps to believe in the potential of personality growth, that is, the ability to grow away from complete self-involvement toward involvement with others. Such a maturation process may continue throughout a person's life in a series of psychological adjustments that enables him to use what he has to his greatest satisfaction. I believe that it is this ever-present potential for growth that should give hope to troubled husbands and wives just as it imparts to therapists the faith they need for their work.

When those in the helping professions evaluate a troubled human being, they must consider his strengths as well as his weaknesses. To do otherwise would be to permit him to fall victim to those weaknesses and even to intensify them in treatment. The distressed neurotic is frequently functioning fairly well despite his emotional difficulties, and he is doing so because of counterbalancing strengths in his personality. In troubled marriages this may be even more true but is sometimes even less discernible. There is a tendency for those involved to fall into the trap of becoming so preoccupied with the weaknesses that a negative feeling pervades the marital relationship, which seems to consist of nothing but those weaknesses and destructive forces. Just as latent and active strengths can be employed to overcome destructive weaknesses in an individual, so can they be used to help a failing marriage.

The maturation process is most active in the marital relationship because the continuous flow of action and reaction in attitudes, feelings, and behavior is very intense. In marriage the personality of one spouse interacts with the personality of the other until each eventually modifies the other—it is to be hoped, for the better. That is to say that man and wife each has a certain amount of responsibility—although not the total amount—to help the other as well as himself toward full maturity. It is not unusual in marriage counseling for the counselor to draw on this premise and engage the healthier spouse as a sort of co-therapist to further the other spouse's growth.

Mr. and Mrs. A were yellers. They shouted angrily at each other at the slightest provocation—Mrs. A in constant complaint and demand, Mr. A in derision. During counseling Mrs. A developed enough understanding of herself and her husband so that she was gradually able to control her complaining and demanding until one day she stopped yelling. She recognized at last that she could not expect her inadequate-feeling husband to fulfill her need to feel worthwhile and that she would have to turn to other sources. Since she had always wanted to return to the professional interests she had had prior to marriage, she found a part-time job in her field. Eventually she experienced enough success in her intellectual pursuits and in her relationships with co-workers to satisfy some of her need.

This left her husband in a bad spot. He could no longer blame her for his need to denigrate her and the finger he had been pointing at her began to turn toward himself. Mrs. A was supported in counseling so that she was able to help her husband in his struggle with his gradual awareness that his compulsion to belittle her was a reflection of his need to belittle all women because of his own insecurities. It took some time for Mrs. A to help him resolve this, but her grasp of his problem and her growing ability to deal with it objectively helped him and herself to a more constructive relationship.

Since husbands and wives, and many helping professionals as well, tend to see only the negatives in troubled marriages and give little or no weight to the positives, it might be of some value to consider what goes on in a "good" marriage—with the recognition that not all husbands and wives can be expected to achieve all the qualities and strengths of such a relationship. If marriage counselors are aware of and can define for themselves the possibilities that exist in a good marriage, they will be better equipped to indicate to those who seek their help the direction a marriage can be assisted to take. This does not mean that counselors should (or in fact do) expect those they help to achieve perfection; it merely means that they and their clients, aware of what the possibilities are, use this knowledge as a set of guidelines that must be modified in terms of the potentialities and limitations of the couple under consideration. In this way troubled husbands and wives can be led to an awareness and acceptance of their own limitations as well as those of their spouses so as to set reasonable goals for their marital relationships. This is an important step toward their constructive adjustment to each other.

In a good marriage the interaction is constructive, bringing about growth in each partner so that he is able to live more fully. Each is independent and could if necessary walk the road of life alone, but they feel that together they will be able to walk a better road and help each other to live an even better life. Husband and wife feel they are a team—that they are one, and yet they are two. The independence of each continues, but to the good of the marriage; it does not involve isolation, nor is it compulsively achieved because of selfish or angry withdrawal. There is a healthy mutual involvement that signifies giving of self with judgment and discretion together with an acceptance of and respect for each other's uniqueness. Neither withholds, waiting for the other to give; rather, each gives to the other because it is there to be done, and in the giving each derives sustenance and pleasure.

This healthy interdependence from which each benefits can perhaps be likened to two columns that together with others help support the house of marriage. One column is not taller than the other, nor does one column lean on the other lest the house of marriage collapse, nor do they stand rigid and taut. Rather, there is an architectural interplay, a give-and-take between the two columns so that the house of marriage is safely supported against storms and change. So do husband and wife ideally interact to build a relationship in which each can grow and feel even more worthy—to self, to each other, and to society.

## WAYS OF THE GOOD MARRIAGE

The interaction in a good marriage may not always be perfect, but the general trend is toward support of the marriage, with each helping the other to live to the best of his own human potential. Husband and wife are fundamentally committed to themselves, to their relationship, and to life. They may have occasional fantasies about escaping their difficulties, but termination of the marriage is never seriously in view—indeed, divorce is never mentioned. A good marriage demands maturity; maturity demands taking responsibility for situations and problems that arise according to the particular stage of life in which people find themselves. Mature husbands and wives develop increasing awareness as they proceed through the stages of the marital cycle—awareness of each other's needs as well as the needs of the marriage. They try their best to answer those needs despite any disappointment they may feel. If the romantic notions held prior to marriage are not realized, the disappointments are hurdled and dispensed with, and more realistic expectations supplant them. This is not always easy to accomplish, for reality is sometimes difficult to accept, but there is much compensation to be found in the relief from inner tensions and anger that follows when reality *is* accepted.

Certain needs, like those for acceptance, recognition, respect, and affection, continue throughout life. If one is married, he expects the marriage to satisfy them. Just as new needs develop for the individual in the various stages of life, so do new needs develop in the marriage itself in its several stages. In early marriage, prior to the birth of children, husbands and wives need to develop a special loyalty for each other that will take the place of the loyalty they felt for their parents; the loyalty to their parents may continue but it must become secondary. Newly married couples also need to develop feelings of assurance that each will give the other first consideration and that each will continue so to care for the other. There is an exciting need to discover and enhance common interests. There is much to learn about their roles as husband and wife and, at the same time, to recognize their individual needs and differences. When the wife is working, this may take some doing with regard to the division of labor and support. A young couple's strong need for a harmonious and complete sexual relationship requires maximum mutual understanding and acceptance of each other's wants.

The busy years that begin with the bearing and rearing of children bring many individual and mutual adjustment problems. Each must now let the other find satisfaction in the new relationships with the children and, beyond this, support the other in the parent-child situation, fraught as it is with psychological difficulties, and help the other to avoid using the children to satisfy hidden emotional needs. Each needs to give consideration and affectionate, loving care to the other, for the demands of growing children can be exhausting. This sharing of concern can be exceedingly rewarding and open up new roads toward mutual gratification.

In these years men must seize the opportunity to advance themselves in their work. Women who understand this do not readily feel rejected when they find that their husbands are becoming busier than before. They themselves are more occupied now with the children and the home. Mature husbands and wives who love will find security and strength in the more limited, and therefore more precious, hours they have to spend together alone. Sexually, as well as in other areas of life, there is greater harmony between them despite trying schedules and difficult problems.

The busy years have a way of passing quickly. Suddenly, almost without warning, the children are young adults. They leave home early today—for college, the draft, or marriage—and the period of the "empty nest" begins to have its impact just as parents discover, perhaps with some surprise, that their own youth has passed. All the busyness has ceased, the furniture remains clean and in place, and the noise that used to pervade the house has subsided. This period has much potential, depending on the relationship husband and wife have built. It can be a time of renewed acceptance and closeness, of increased sharing of interests and, indeed, there can be an overtone of satisfaction at just being married and having each other. Both husband and wife feel the departure of the children, but they are equipped to accept the movement of life and inevitable change. The early years and the busy years were good, and so they hope these years will be too. Men will encourage their wives to takes jobs or to participate more intensively in social, educational, or communal activities. Women in turn will encourage their husbands' careers and community interests. Neither feels threatened or rejected by the other's interests; rather, each feels the better for them, and each helps the other to understand the changes that are taking place in their lives and roles, and "you and I" become even more one.

In the later stages of married life, each spouse needs support from the other as sexual and physical activity declines and they gradually realize that one of them may some day have to cope with life alone. They accept the fact that their children are to be left free to build their own lives. They try to put aside as much as possible so that the children will not have to carry too much of a load when their parents finally reach old age.

The marital life cycle demands mature people who are committed to life and to their marriage. They marry for what they can each give to the other and not just for what they can get; they do not marry simply to attain happiness but rather for the joy of achieving a gratifying, strong, interdependent realtionship. There is a give-and-take in marriage, but taking becomes secondary to giving in the good marriage. To this end, ideally, a mature woman contemplating marriage to a particular man asks herself whether she will be able to fit into his way of life. Men are trained to be doctors, lawyers, ministers, policemen, firemen, businessmen, or whatever. Clearly, women do not come to marriage formally trained to be wives in the assorted ways of life that may confront them. The mature woman may go even further and ask herself how much she will be able to contribute to the fulfillment of her husband's professional potential. Indeed, will he willingly take her hand if she offers it? Will he help *her* to thrive? The mature man contemplating marriage to a particular woman asks himself whether he will be able to give her something of the kind of life she would like to have emotionally, economically, and culturally, and whether she will be able to be the helpmate and companion he needs.

In a good marriage, husband and wife use discretion and judgment to determine what needs doing in terms of their sense of responsibility to the marital relationship, to themselves, and to each other. Gradually, wisdom develops as intelligence and experience meet. The long-term goals that have been established between husband and wife give a sense of direction, and with self-control and responsibility, sensible, integrated behavior patterns can be achieved even at times when one spouse or the other does not really feel up to them.

In a good marriage, both partners have a feeling of adequacy and know their roles as man and woman, husband and wife, father and mother. They are able to communicate their thoughts and feelings to each other with a minimum of frustration and friction. Whatever anger is aroused is appropriately expressed at an appropriate time, and neither indulges in tearing down the other in front of outsiders. They have a private enclave—the private bedroom of marriage—into which only they can enter; its door is closed to everyone else, whether they be children, parents, relatives, or friends. Anxiety over their relationship is limited since each has faith and trust in the other and neither is ever threatened by the other with divorce or harm when things do not go well. That they have a positive outlook on life despite their problems does not mean they are Pollyannas; it means that they are able to push the negatives of life aside—without forgetting them—and to move ahead constructively. They are aware of life's difficulties, but they are not injustice collectors. Instead, they use judgment and discretion to cope as objectively as possible with the vicissitudes that arise, and they simply do not permit continued feelings of disappointment and anger to destroy their loving relationship.

## UNSUITABLE WAYS OF RELATING

It must always be remembered that when two people live together, there are bound to be occasions when they will respond to each other in an unsuitable or inappropriate manner, or at least in a way that seems so to one of them. Of course, not every unsuitable response by one spouse to what the other is saying or doing is necessarily a neurotic response (conversely, almost all neurotic responses are unsuitable). It may simply arise from ignorance or confusion, which play a tremendous role in marital difficulties but are not of themselves neurotic. A maladaptive reaction can also come from downright hostile intent, which again is not of itself neurotic, or it can occur as a result of differences in values.

Unfortunately, there is always the danger that a person's counterreaction to a partner's unsuitable reaction will be hostile. Hostility leads to hostility, which frequently causes a breakdown in communications, perhaps the greatest single factor in transforming marital strife into marital explosion. In a good marriage, such a breakdown is temporary, and husband and wife are quick to forgive each other and themselves and to try to understand what happened and why. In contrast, there is no forgiveness in the neurotic marriage, and the hostilities persist or go underground. Even if the partners in a neurotic marriage return to communication of a sort, they will have gained little if any understanding of what has happened between them. Neither forgives, nor indeed does he make any effort to forget.

Maladaptation in marital interaction is measured against what we believe should exist according to our conception of the human roles involved. Roles define how society believes one should act in a given situation in terms of an underlying ethic or ideal. When these ideals are carried over into marriage, they are a potential source of conflict if the values of the partners diverge to any great extent. A husband may feel his wife has not adjusted well to the marriage because he defines the role of wife in terms of housewife, while she prefers to concentrate on matters of more interest than maintaining a spotless establishment. Or there is the woman who measures masculinity in terms of earnings and believes that her husband should make a more determined effort to accumulate more money, even though they are living fairly well, while he has little motivation to increase his earnings and prefers to devote his time to reading or to being with the family.

A person who falls down in his various roles in a fairly consistent way may well be doing so for neurotic reasons. However, we must beware of the current tendency to label behavior neurotic simply because it deviates from what we have come to consider the typical or required pattern for a particular role. The marriage counselor must be careful not to inject his own feelings and values into a counseling situation, nor can he assume the role of judge or referee as he helps husband and wife to reach an understanding of each other's needs, expectations, and values. Rather the counselor, skillfully and insightfully, uses his feelings and values as tools in the process of gaining understanding of his clients and their interaction.

CRISIS

At a time of crisis, people who otherwise are fairly stable and can cope constructively with life may regress. Serious illness or death, adultery, separation, divorce, or financial setback, whether they involve a loved one or oneself, can engender temporary neurotic reactions. When such a reaction intervenes in an otherwise sound marriage, the likelihood is that the couple will eventually work it out on their own, though help may sometimes be needed to interrupt the tailspin into which they have been thrown. The situation is quite different in the neurotic marriage, where the never-ending treadmill pattern is intensified, often catastrophically, by a crisis. One of the most important phases of marriage counseling is intervention in and treatment of crisis situations, but for this the counselor has to distinguish between neurotic reactions to the crisis and inherently neurotic behavior patterns. The marriage counselor treats cases after the fashion of the doctor, who does not diagnose every stomach-ache that comes into his office as appendicitis in need of surgery.

# 8

## *Is What Is Going On Between You Neurotic?*

Marriages are not made in heaven or at the altar, but in the unconscious. Whatever the conscious reasons people may have for marrying, they make their choices on the basis of unconscious needs. There is little or no accident at this unconscious level. Although consciously we may seek someone different from ourselves who will complement our differences, unconsciously we tend to marry what we are, being fooled by differences in the way characteristics are dynamically expressed.

Intelligence tends to marry intelligence, for example, but a wife's devastatingly overwhelming feelings of inadequacy may prevent her from using her intelligence; she frequently feels stupid and is made to feel more so by the intelligence of her husband, who is able to use his brains advantageously, perhaps because he has cut himself off from his feelings or has a compulsive drive for intellectual achievement. Nevertheless, the husband's feelings of inadequacy are exposed when he is driven to make his wife feel stupid. A person with feelings of inadequacy and the need to depend on others tends to marry someone who also feels inadequate and is dependent—both are deceived by façades of adequacy and independence and differences in the way each operates.

In a neurotic marriage there is a failure by one or both partners to achieve the constructive give-and-take of the good marriage. Instead of mutual giving of self, there is mutual withholding, so that some needs may have to be met outside the marriage. There may be exploitation of one partner by the other, or destruction of one by the other, or these patterns may be carried out mutually to satisfy the need for punishment or to gratify conscious or unconscious death wishes.

In neurotic marriages, things are not always what they seem. The neurotic interaction plays into the negative, regressive tendencies and needs of husband and wife despite the fact that it frequently appears to be meeting conscious, rational needs and resolving life situations. Men and women are frequently irreconcilably disappointed after marriage when their conscious needs are not met, and yet they stay together. This is not out of commitment. They will give many rationalizations—children, money, parents, values, religion, or whatever—but the real reason is that, unconsciously, their marriage gratifies their neurotic needs and keeps them comfortable. These neurotic needs are usually exaggerations of normal needs about which the person is ambivalent. Consciously he says, "I want (to be close, to have sex, etc.)," but unconsciously he says, "I don't want"—or the other way around.

As long as the neurotic patterns of interaction continue their service, the marriages continue, and no one—whether he be professional or not—really has the right to judge them. Unfortunately, because the foundation is rickety, those marriages tend to break down. In contrast to the good marriage, wherein each helps the other to live to his own best potential, each partner in the neurotic marriage has the compulsive need to work out deep, unresolved feelings so that the marital interaction is based on such feelings as "give me" or "I use you." If each is satisfied to feed the other's neurotic needs and both are "happy," who is to say it is a bad marriage? It is only when there is dissatisfaction that the marriage goes out of kilter.

Most of the qualities we find in the good marriage are at a minimum or nonexistent in the neurotic marriage. Instead of maturity, we find immaturity with its many complexities. There is an inability to give; instead, insatiable demands are made. The self-involvement of at least one partner is so great that it frequently makes communication impossible. In their narcissism, men use women and women men. Lack of trust and faith not only in oneself but in the opposite sex paralyzes behavior and relationships. Independence is interpreted to mean isolation and not much is known of interdependence; the banner of dependence waves instead. Since the immature know little or no commitment to life, they know little or no commitment to marriage. Responsibility is at a minimum. The threat of abandonment or divorce hangs heavy and is frequently used as blackmail to gain satisfaction for needs. Fear, anxiety, and unceasing anger are the handmaidens of the neurotic marriage. There is little awareness of the future and no recognition of the ongoing pattern of life and its passing stages. Rather, life is anxiously and tensely lived only in the present, on a day-to-day basis. An everyday, loving relationship is not understood or accepted— only "being in love."

No marital relationship is based on the satisfaction of any one need. The following discussion of neurotically interacting husbands and wives I have counseled represents some of the many different neurotic patterns of interaction that occur. Each of these troubled marriages involved more than just the neurotic pattern considered here. All had the treadmill quality, described before, in which hostility begets hostility and anxiety begets anxiety.

ATTACKING, EMASCULATING WIFE
AND ANGRY, WITHDRAWN HUSBAND

Mrs. B, a presentable woman in her late twenties, had two children and was continuing to do graduate work. At times she played the role of a devoted mother and suburban housewife, while at other times she presented the picture of a college student who was still in her formative years and was not quite sure in what direction she was going to go. Repressed rage and hostility were quite noticeable. Since her intellect was more developed than her emotions, she tried to handle her emotional difficulties by intellectualization and rationalization, but she was not successful and felt frustrated and unfulfilled. Basically, she was afraid of men, with whom she tried to compete, and she felt herself a failure as a woman and experienced much sexual frustration.

Mrs. B had selected her husband for his quiet, benign, reserved personality, a seeming haven after years with two very angry, demanding parents. Unconsciously, Mrs. B had been attracted to her husband because he was weak and could easily be manipulated. Though on the conscious level marriage meant proof that she was a woman, her unconscious concept was that it would be a substitute for parental figures. The result was that she did all the things that a wife and mother should do, which enhanced her conscious feelings of superiority, but she could give none of the loving and warmth her husband needed because of her feelings of inadequacy and of being a little girl waiting to be loved.

Describing her general dissatisfaction with the marriage, she said her husband withdrew from her in every area, including sex, for weeks at a time, after which they would come together "in a good way." She would feel an overwhelming need for him when they were apart, but when they were together she could not approach him and waited in vain for him to approach her.

Mr. B, in his thirties, was a pleasant, soft-spoken, friendly man who had a strong need for acceptance and approval. He assumed a passive role rather than trouble to assert himself, but his passivity was really a defense against repressed resentments. In spite of the fact that he most often acted in an adult and responsible fashion, his unconscious concept of himself was that of a weak, ineffective, childlike individual under the control of other adult persons.

Mr. B had had a domineering mother whose demands and anger had never been directed at him but at his ineffectual father, who had meekly taken the barrage and slinked off. Mr. B's identification problem, in view of his domineering mother and ineffectual father, left him with doubts about his virility. He craved the protective surroundings of a close family relationship to assuage his loneliness and isolation. He had expected his wife to provide the warmth and love he needed, but she had given him cold intellectualization and rationalization or out-and-out anger instead. When he came to see me, he said he felt himself to be on the outside looking in and not part of his family.

Since Mrs. B expected her husband to be aggressive and to initiate their love-making, she would become angry when that quiet, passive man "showed no love" for her; again she felt unloved and unwanted, as she had in her parents' home. Her frustration and anger were so great as to drive her husband away, for it reminded him of his mother's anger at his impotent father. He would become frigid—that is, just not interested in sex—which, needless to say, did not improve his wife's disposition.

Both Mr. and Mrs. B wanted love, yet neither knew how to give it. Intellectualization and rationalization were Mrs. B's defenses against her deep-rooted feelings about relating to a man. Since she could not accept herself as a woman and take responsibility for herself emotionally, she could not accept her husband as a man. In her anger, therefore, she would emasculate him to avoid closeness. Mr. B, in his passivity, used cold indifference both as a defense against his fears of involvement with his wife and as a punishment for her emasculating anger.

Both Mr. and Mrs. B needed extensive individual counseling to help them with their feelings of anger and inadequacy. At the same time, much was accomplished in joint sessions to improve their communication and understanding of each other's needs and problems. They were highly motivated to help themselves but struggled with their hostility for quite some time before being able to translate insights into constructive behavior. Mr. B finally recognized that much of his anger resulted from the extent of his dependence on the opinions of his wife and mother to make him feel acceptable and worthwhile. He began to turn to himself for this support and became indifferent to his wife's opinions. This new-found independence left his wife feeling in limbo—her opinions, rationalizations, and intellectualizations no longer seemed to affect her husband as before—so she turned to herself for some of the answers to their unhappy relationship and gradually began to develop insight into her feelings about being a woman.

Emphasis on things intellectual is frequently a defense against feelings of sexual inadequacy. Despite brilliance and capability in intellectual areas, sexually inadequate-feeling men and women very often have no desire to comprehend the emotional needs of their spouses, for such comprehension would mean taking on more responsibility and involvement than they can tolerate. Instead, they develop different forms of distance maneuvers—among them intellectualization, verbalization, rationalization—to avoid the responsibility that would ensue if they did become involved.

There are many ideas that can aggravate marital hostility or make a neurotic marriage more neurotic. One of these is that every feeling should be made known and that spontaneously expressed feelings of hostility, such as those that manifest themselves during free association, are in every case a valid measure of true feelings and that suppressing such feelings can be harmful. This may be of value in a therapeutic relationship, but not in a marital one—one's spouse is not one's therapist and there should be no expectation that he play that role. If we revere such spontaneity as having complete validity, we can at times cause tact and politeness to be neglected and thereby aggravate angry feelings and disrupt social relations. A moment's pause, a bit of ordinary tact or politeness, can sometimes avert the harsh expression that can produce untold damage, particularly in a troubled marital situation. If husband and wife are encouraged to think before they speak, to be tactful rather than direct in tense situations, much unnecessary conflict can be avoided. To say in a fleeting moment of deep hostility, "I feel like killing you" or "I want to break your head" is not exactly the best way to bolster a sagging relationship; it is far more effective to pause for a moment and then say, "I'm pretty sore at you," and then to deal with the issue rather than the feeling.

## ATTACKING, CONTROLLING HUSBAND AND PASSIVE, DEPENDENT WIFE

Mr. and Mrs. C had both been married before and Mrs. C's child by her first marriage lived with them. Mr. C gave the appearance at first glance of being a remarkably well-adjusted person who was self-sufficient and highly capable of running his life and sharing it with his wife. Actually, he felt dependent, insecure, and inadequate, and had to be needed and to play the role of a father in marriage to feel like a man. He was intelligent and devised ingenious rationalizations to conceal his motives and put his behavior in the best possible light. He played the "good boy" to whom people did wrong, a device that helped to boost his self-esteem. He had not felt competent to start a family of his own and his marriage to Mrs. C provided him with a ready-made family. Her needs put him in the role of the needed father, which he wanted to play. When he appeared for marriage counseling, he presented a picture of his wife as an emotionally unstable person who did not keep her home well, was not too good a mother, drank too much, and smoked incessantly. Of course, he was without fault.

Mrs. C, a good-looking young woman, gave the impression of a person who had been kept off balance by adversity. She seemed to indicate that she would be able to cope with her life if only certain situations were cleared up. Emotionally, she was dependent, immature, and frightened—a little girl who had married Mr. C because she believed him to be a kindly father upon whom she could depend financially and emotionally for support against her first husband, who was threatening to take custody of her child. Her first husband had been difficult and demanding and her present husband was becoming the same.

After marriage, Mr. and Mrs. C had remained on fairly good terms as long as she stayed in the role of the dependent little girl who complied with her husband's demands and continued to need him to keep her going. As soon as she initiated any creative activity on her own, Mr. C's anger knew no bounds. He would impose harsh controls on her freedom and justified what he did by criticizing everything she tried to do—nothing she did was good or good enough. Then, having made her feel futile, he would withdraw in righteous silence. Mrs. C reacted by becoming defensive and anxious.

Mr. C had very little motivation to overcome his deficiencies. I saw him in joint sessions with his wife from time to time, but worked primarily with Mrs. C in individual sessions. With help she came to see that she had control of her own life; that although she still needed her husband in relation to her child, he actually needed her very much more than she did him on the emotional level. His insecurity and dependence were such as to compel him to control her and to attack her unjustly and then to rationalize his behavior. If she wanted to keep the marriage, the solution would lie in the extent of her personal growth toward maturity and independence, since his defenses were so strong that she could expect little change in him. Within reason, and in terms of her own sincere feelings, she would have to make him feel that he was high man on the totem pole and that he was very important to her. To accomplish this, everything she wanted to do would have to be done within the framework of the marriage; the marriage would always have to come first. In any case, mature, loving women who want to keep their marriages have always found this approach to be wise.

Since Mrs. C was highly motivated to help herself and keep her marriage, she moved slowly—albeit with difficulty—toward this role. Mr. C had difficulty accepting some of the changes in his wife, but as her anxiety and defensiveness lessened and she began to go toward him, he felt less threatened and his need to attack and control faded somewhat.

While the marriage counselor has an awareness of neurotic and psychotic behavior, he operates on the basically humanistic concept that many defects in behavior can be overcome since they are not always evidence of an unchangeable pathology—sometimes clients just need to recognize that they are doing things that are wrong. To counsel on the basis of the concept that people cannot change their obvious, conscious patterns of behavior is to undermine trust and responsibility in clients and has the potential for producing irrevocable wrong and hurt.

PASSIVE, DETACHED HUSBAND AND DUTY-RIDDEN WIFE

Mr. and Mrs. D entered a late marriage after each had had many affairs. After a few months of "heavenly bliss," misunderstandings of sufficient proportion developed between them in regard to his business, her career, and money to frighten them into seeking help for their marriage.

Mr. D, in his early forties, was a tall, well-dressed man who looked a lot younger than his age. In spite of his masculine exterior, he was effeminate, with much underlying passivity and a lack of inner strength. He was very angry but was detached from most of his feelings, having little awareness of self or others or the world. He had deep feelings of sexual inadequacy that he accepted with pessimism and a consequent lack of self-esteem. He felt burdened by adult responsibilities, particularly now that he was married, but was indifferent to establishing himself as an adult.

Denial was Mr. D's greatest defense. He felt that there was a lack of communication between him and his wife, but he denied that he had anything to do with it. Nevertheless, he was quite anxious about his failures and his inability to cope with his marital problems.

Mr. D was going into a new business at the time they decided to marry. He had little money and would not have married except for Mrs. D's strong assurances that she would help him get started. As long as things went the way he planned he was submissive, but he would turn aggressive when they did not. Fundamentally, he derogated women, tending to use them, drain them dry, and then throw them over.

Mrs. D, an attractive, pleasant, and dramatic woman, was able to talk freely on a superficial level but became very anxious and apprehensive when she had to face herself and reality squarely. There was a conflict between her thinking and feelings; she had good intellectual understanding, but emotional adjustment was difficult for her. Her idealized image of herself was that of a superior individual with self-confidence and efficiency, but she actually had deep-rooted feelings of insecurity and inadequacy, little self-esteem, and a sense of failure as a woman. She was overconcerned with questions of right and wrong and was governed by a hyperactive sense of obligation that prevented her from fully expressing her individuality. Her conformity was superficial, concealing an unconscious need to rebel, but she was so afraid she might lose control that she was unable to express directly any resentment or hostility she might feel.

Though Mrs. D was intelligent and sophisticated enough to recognize her husband's passivity and feelings of inadequacy, she had married with the determination to maintain the romantic aura of the honeymoon. She decided to do all the things she "should" as a wife, feeling that such behavior would prove she was a woman. She had always done everything she "should" do to be accepted as a woman and to defend herself against feelings of being inadequate as such. She had never known the feeling of accepting herself as a woman who willingly did what that role required of her. When she married, she felt that if she did all the things she "should" do in and out of bed, the marriage would be successful. She went so far as to say that she had felt that if she gave her husband his balls, he would be a man and she would then be a woman. She had proceeded on this premise, only to find her husband becoming more and more hostile after the first year.

The fact was that Mr. D resented having to measure up constantly to his wife's standards and values. After he felt more secure in his new business, he turned on her, demanding that he be in control of the marriage and punitively setting limits on their relationship and on her career and personal activity. Mrs. D, worn out by her unrealistic endeavors, became passive in the relationship, acceding to her husband's inordinate demands. Underneath, however, she was furious at having to compromise her personal values, but her sense of obligation held the marriage together tenuously until she could no longer tolerate her husband's punitive, compulsive approach to their relationship and sought help.

Much counseling time was spent with Mr. and Mrs. D individually and jointly. They would come in with crisis after crisis that, for the moment, prevented their looking at themselves in a realistic manner. After a time I was able to get through to Mrs. D sufficiently for her to begin to understand her unrealistic expectations of herself, her husband, and her marriage. As her ego gathered strength, the marital relationship began to change. She started to do what she had to do as a wife on a realistic level, emotionally supporting her husband without having the need to "give him his balls." Though her husband was able to appreciate the changes in his wife, he had a long way to go himself before he could do anything better for her in the marriage.

There are inadequate-feeling men and women who marry hoping that marriage will give them surcease from their constant nagging concern over whether they are indeed men and women. The women hope their husbands will make them feel like women and the men seek constant reassurance from their wives. Since the inadequate-feeling man is likely to marry an inadequate-feeling woman, their disappointment in each other is inevitable even when one makes an all-out effort in the hopes that this will confirm not what his spouse is but what he himself is.

Plainly, a man is first a man and a woman is first a woman, and then they marry—they don't marry to become a man and a woman—marriage at best can only enhance what is already there.

## THE CASE OF THE "BLACK AND WHITE" HUSBAND

Mrs. E gave the impression of being a sophisticated, highly intelligent, and well-educated woman who was caught in a conflict between family life and the strong need for intellectual and creative fulfillment. She voiced deep frustration and appeared nervous, tense, apprehensive, very anxious and depressed. She had a great deal of intellectual ability and vital energy but no proper outlet for them. Although she had invested all her energies in her family and home, they were not enough for her. Her conscious strivings were feminine, but unconsciously she had masculine drives, felt insecure as a woman, and had no clear concept of what it means to be one. She had a capacity for feelings but had been unable to make constructive use of this capacity in her relationships with her children and particularly with her husband.

She had hoped to go to law school but had married Mr. E instead. She considered her husband to be a brilliant scholar and professional man and was completely overwhelmed by his intellectual ability and prowess. After fifteen years of marriage, however, his intellectual abilities interested her much less than his coldness and his inability to give her love. Her anger over this was heightened by the realization that while her husband's professional success was due in part to his ability to show great concern for his clients and give them an overabundance of attention, her demands for love would be met only by further detachment on his part and withdrawal into his professional activity.

Mr. E, a cultured, well-mannered, intelligent man, was detached from his feelings, externalizing everything with much intellectualization and denial. He strongly resisted facing himself, and it was almost impossible to reach him emotionally on any level. He acted on the basis of a rigid set of values that he had assumed from his parents in early youth in order to be accepted by them, but he had never really made these values his own. He was frustrated, apparently unable to satisfy his emotional needs because of an exaggerated concern over the problem of right and wrong. The drive for achievement no longer seemed to give him the emotional satisfaction he needed. In spite of his calm façade, he was extremely anxious and feared a loss of control. He also felt insecure as a male and feared impotence; the resulting need to prove his masculinity produced an underlying compulsion to relate to a woman who would magically make him feel like a man. Someone had come along, but he struggled with the thought of any close involvement. His defense of blaming everything on his wife was beginning to break down, but his resistance remained strong and his motivation poor.

In counseling, Mrs. E became aware that, despite his intellectual abilities, Mr. E was a man for whom things were either right or wrong, that he saw everything in terms of black and white. He had had preconceived notions of what Mrs. E should do as his wife, and he had assigned her duties to her. When she did not meet his expectations, he was disappointed, she was wrong, and that was that. Because of his intellectuality, she had invested him with a third dimension of insight that he just did not possess when it came to their feelings and what it meant to relate to each other closely in marriage. Mrs. E's demands for love were just too much for her husband to tolerate and he asked for a divorce.

If Mrs. E had been able to fend for herself and had accepted the role of housewife her husband had set up for her, the marriage might have lasted. Unfortunately, she needed too much of the very thing he could not give—love and understanding.

A common behavior pattern in neurotic marital interaction involves the presuppostion that everything is either right or wrong, good or bad, black or white. This is an unfortunate exaggeration that some make, despite their intelligence and intellectual abilities. They fail to see that nothing happens or exists that is really one way or the other and that, indeed, while life is not perfect, it certainly is not a total disaster. It has been my experience that men tend to adopt this black-and-white approach more frequently than do their wives, who are able to see at least some of the shades of gray in life even if few are able to ever see the beautiful spectrum that life does hold.

In individual session, at an appropriate time, I explain a husband's deficiency to his wife by comparing his emotional condition to that of being color-blind. Every woman knows that if her husband was in fact color-blind she would have to drive their car. We then explore how she would continue to drive with her husband next to her, how she would feel, how he would feel. Then we go back to her husband, with whom she feels so frustrated and angry because he somehow sees no grays, no third dimension in life. In another individual session, I pick this up with the husband and point out his inability and explain how this frustrates his wife and what he can do about it.

Some time later, in a joint session, when husband and wife are having difficulty in communication, I crystallize the point as dynamically as possible. Once a woman really believes that her husband is not being spiteful, punitive, deliberately frustrating, or disinterested in what she is feeling or saying, her anger is dispelled and patience and understanding take their rightful place. Her husband, released from her condemnatory mood, is able to do what he can to better understand that third dimension of which she makes so much and, perhaps, even see one or two of the shades of gray himself.

## THE POWER STRUGGLE

A power struggle frequently arises between husband and wife when each feels deeply inadequate and needs to prove he is otherwise by gaining ascendency over his partner. Mr. and Mrs. F had come from financially and emotionally deprived homes. The most significant goal that each had was to get as far away as possible from his original family and move up the ladder of social and financial success, thereby to be acclaimed a person. While they shared that common goal, each was preoccupied with his own fantasies. Mr. F dreamed of how he would work and save enough money to establish his own business; the support he would have to give to his growing family never figured in this fantasy. Mrs. F dreamed of being a lady and never having to do anything as mundane as housework and taking care of their children; as a result, she gave little attention to either.

Neither spouse had ever been exposed to a loving day-to-day relationship that strengthens husband and wife and helps them toward their goals, so, not knowing anything better, each went his separate way. Mr. F was frequently out with the "boys" and would dole out whatever money his wife needed just as he did his love. Mrs. F, feeling more and more put upon by being made to be "just a housewife," became very frustrated when she did not receive the attention she needed. She began to compete angrily with the "boys" for her husband's attention, which made him even more withdrawn. Mrs. F then began to use the children against her husband, subtly weaning them away from him. Mr. F, who had more than the average feeling of concern and responsibility for the children, began to fight back, so that the children were being pulled one way and the other in the ensuing power struggle between their parents. Mr. and Mrs. F were like two babies in a playpen, too young to reach toward each other and yet wanting attention and love. One of them—it did not matter which—would have to grow up enough to be able to walk across to where the other was sitting.

After some counseling, Mr. F made some tenuous advances toward his wife, but she remained angry and sullen. He dramatically described how this made him feel: "I'm like a knight who rides up to the castle and yells, 'Throw down the drawbridge!' I stand there and wait, ready to enter, but all I get is darts." Since he was frightened of rejection and might have taken flight, more intensive counseling was given to Mrs. F, focusing on her refusal to grow up and take on the responsibilities of being a woman. Mrs. F had to replace her fantasy image of the lady of leisure with one more real and obtainable. Once this process began, the marital relationship became more constructive. The first step was seen when, instead of waiting for her husband to take her arm to cross the street, Mrs. F began to take his and he responded with loving attention.

People can only give what they have; if they have experienced little of an everyday loving relationship as they grew up, they have not much to give in that direction when they marry. On the other hand, they desire much and their demands can be great. Unfortunately, too often they marry people from whom they expect much but who can give as little as they—disappointment is inevitable.

Most of want love and power. While these needs remain slight, no conflict develops. It is when the desire for both love and power rises and becomes intense that one must take priority over the other. This is because it is practically impossible for the human being to strive with equal vigor for both.

## SADOMASOCHISTIC COUPLE

The G's took turns at hurting each other and at suffering. Mrs. G was the leader in her need to suffer, and her husband would always do her the favor of seeing that she did so. It was amazing how many negatives Mrs. G would find to achieve her goal, which, basically, was to gain the attention and security she wanted from her husband by having him make her suffer, since she could not seem to achieve attention and security in any other way. If Mr. G asked for her forgiveness after he had given her attention by hurting her, she had a new grievance, for his request showed how stupid and callous he was in expecting her to forgive him when he had hurt her so much. This in turn would cause him to feel even more guilty and victimized. So it went until, eventually, Mr. G would physically abuse her in sheer frustration, which seemed to satisfy his wife's need for punishment, and she would retreat for a while.

In counseling, both Mr. and Mrs. G were able to verbalize their needs. Mrs. G found it difficult to change her behavior. Instead, she had a "show me" attitude toward her husband— "show me you are a man and then I'll show you I'm a woman" was her theme. Joint sessions were kept at a minimum because of Mrs. G's compulsive need to use them to vent her hostility, only to complain about her suffering. Individual sessions allowed for this since within such a framework there was no chance of further disturbing the marriage. As her anger at her husband subsided, so did her hysteria, and she became reachable. Much time was then spent helping her to see her role as a wife. Eventually her anger turned on her children, which produced much anxiety for her, but she moved toward seeing herself more clearly, developing more awareness of reality, becoming less demanding, and beginning to be the initiator in her relationship with her husband. She began to think about long-range goals.

Mr. G spent his individual sessions exploring the reasons for his sadistic behavior toward his wife and the destructive manner in which he used his intellectual abilities. He developed enough insight to stop walking around "with a chip on his shoulder," but he saw his married life as a situation in which he would get off the merry-go-round although his wife would stay on, holding onto grievances she never could forgive or forget. He began to initiate sex and said he was trying to become the good one of the pair. His relationship to his wife did become better since he was able to control his need to hand out emotional and physical blows. As he became more benign to his wife and his ego grew a little stronger, his depression lifted and he began to think of establishing better goals for himself at work and at home.

In most neurotic marriages the interaction that takes place is a maneuver to maintain distance between husband and wife despite their protests for the need for closeness, affection, and love. In the sadomasochistic marriage, the partner who is acting out masochistically is often making a bid for attention that will carry with it no responsibility. Since the other partner complies with hurtful attention, the suffering spouse's feelings of guilt for not taking responsibility in the relationship are reduced.

### DEPENDENT, DEMANDING HUSBAND AND OMNIPOTENT WIFE

Mr. H, in his late thirties, was a weak, ineffectual man who made well-nigh insatiable demands on his wife for emotional support. He had married her thinking she was feminine, pink and white all over; she had given him the feeling that he was a man because he believed she needed his protection, particularly against demanding parents. He was unaware that he had gradually taken their place by making unreasonable demands for attention. Despite her appearance of being a weak creature, Mrs. H showed herself in marriage to be a capable, intelligent woman who manifested signs of strength in handling her weak, confused, and demanding husband.

Mr. H, who actually needed his wife's strength, would not admit it. He would ask for her help and would hate her when she responded. Every time she showed strength, he felt less a man. To avoid seeing himself as he was, he would accuse her of coldness and superficiality in everything she did.

Mrs. H, in her thirties also, had married thinking that she would be able to function in her career as her husband did. She had had no realization of how threatening this would eventually be to him as a man. She found that her own needs for emotional support were rarely if ever fulfilled by her husband; he was so self-involved that any demand she might make was angrily rejected. She reacted to him, as she had to her parents, by tuning him out and going her own way. She was able to find enough personal satisfaction in a return to school to further her education and in associations with other people, so that she did not have to ask much of her husband.

Rather than appreciate his wife's independence, her husband came to believe that she had no need for him at all. This made him feel even more worthless and led to his decision to take minimum responsibility as a husband and father and to his adoption of the role of a recalcitrant child instead. He labeled his wife an "omnipotent monolith" (a powerful pillar of stone), and while he resented her "strength," he continued to make many demands on it.

Long-term counseling helped Mr. H feel more adult, but his wife, with all her helpfulness, now became the stumbling block. It took many joint sessions before Mrs. H could recognize that her husband was not her mother and father and that she was no longer a child under the control of others and with the need to go her own independent way. She began to understand that independence does not mean isolation and that all the strength she had given to her difficult marriage would be of little avail unless she was able to incorporate her husband into the life of the family with kindness and warmth, giving him the pre-eminent position of husband and father in his own home. When she was finally able to make some small gestures in this direction, her husband's gratitude knew no bounds. She was rewarded by his gradual involvement in their family life in a responsible way, and slowly his demands on her began to diminish.

Particularly in the joint sessions, the marriage counselor shifts the focus away from the problems presented back to the feelings and the mutually provocative process that is going on. He is very structured when going into such feelings and behavior. A counselor can be very constructive, and sometimes rapidly so, by carefully dealing with the interaction of husband and wife and showing them how it reflects past experiences with parents and others they have known, and by helping them measure their interactions against the ideal of how they should interact, pointing out how they might live up to their own standards in this regard.

## "TWO FOR THE SEESAW"

When they were married fifteen years before, Mrs. I was eighteen and her husband was forty. Mrs. I's primary aim was to escape parents whom she felt she could no longer tolerate. Her father was a rigid, punitive man who gave a minimum of financial support to his family, and her mother was a withdrawn, quiet, martyr-like woman. There was little joy or comfort in her parents' home, and Mrs. I had frequently resorted to the fantasy that some day she would marry a man who would give her everything. She had married Mr. I despite the age difference between them because he spelled financial security. Having had little, Mrs. I was overly concerned with the sheer, primitive need for survival —nothing else really mattered.

Not long after the marriage Mr. I became quite depressed and disinterested in his business and stayed in bed for many hours of the day for four months. Fortunately, his partner was able to continue without him and Mrs. I showed herself to be quite capable. She nursed her husband, ran her home, and did a great deal to keep things going that she would not have thought of normally. Then suddenly Mr. I was fine; he was peppy and everything that had been so bleak seemed to have turned a golden hue. He went back to his business, told his wife just what to do and how to do it, spent more money than ever and gave her an expensive diamond pin—all of which pleased her very much.

Just about every year Mr. I would repeat this pattern of depression in which he needed his wife very much, and she would help and take over. Somehow she did not mind the depressions too much, for she liked running the show. However, she became upset in the periods in between the depressions when Mr. I was in control of everything. Instead of being grateful to his wife for her help when he had been ill, he would be derogatory and demanding. Mrs. I would feel very low, dissatisfied, and bitter at his high-handed manner and his inattention, but her concern for survival helped to stay these feelings.

However, as time went by she became increasingly dissatisfied with her life, even though she was more and more surrounded with the material things she wanted. Then, one day, after Mr. I had been in a depression for some time, the medication he had been receiving worked too well and he became overly elated. He thrust all their capital into a speculative venture in a single day and it was only through quick action by lawyers and the family that most of it was rescued. That did it! Mrs. I could not take such a threat to her security. She sought help. When her husband heard that she was working with a marriage counselor, he asked to participate, too.

Both Mr. and Mrs. I were exceedingly dependent people, with deep feelings of inadequacy, who placed primary emphasis on money. To Mr. I it symbolized power and masculinity. To Mrs. I it meant all the love and emotional security she was seeking, but most of all it meant survival in a world in which she felt very helpless. Mr. I, who was unable to give anything but money, liked the formality of being married but took little responsibility for his relationships to his wife and family. When he was elated, he was concerned about his business, felt omnipotent, and needed money; when he was depressed, he was concerned only with himself and his own needs. He had little interest in changing the status quo in his marriage. However, he was a shrewd man who had some insight into his dependent, childlike wife. He had always been able to comfort her with some extra money or gift. What he had not foreseen was her reaction when all their money seemed in danger of going down the drain.

With counseling Mrs. I became highly motivated to do something to really help herself, and she continued alone for some time after her husband left the sessions. She developed her own insight into the major pattern of her life and refused to be subjected to it any more. She gained enough ego strength to make plans for her future and that of her children. Her moods were no longer colored by those of her husband because she no longer depended on him so completely for sustenance. She now realized that she was the only one who could take actual responsibility for herself. She developed insight into the stable role she had to achieve in her marriage if she was to continue in it and not be influenced by her husband's ups and downs.

This case is labeled "Two for the Seesaw" because when one is up, the other is down. Just as every human being must achieve what Dr. Karl Menninger calls a vital balance,* so must every marriage. In this case, the wife's need for financial security motivated her finally to keep the marriage even though there developed a marital imbalance as she began to move on emotionally.

The fact that the case involves a seriously disturbed husband does not deflect from but rather crystallizes the point even more clearly.

---

Complementary neurotic patterns obviously are cause for misery and despair. Running through all the cases considered in this chapter are degrees of feelings of inadequacy, anxiety, dependency, hostility, aggressiveness, and passivity. Neurotic marriages show divergences in the extent of each negative quality, but the common treadmill pattern in the interaction between husband and wife frequently prevents them from seeing what is good in the marriage. Other factors which tend to aggravate neurosis and are frequently found in neurotic marriage patterns are panic, tension, and fatigue. The more panicked, tense, or fatigued a person is, the more readily will he react to stress with a primitive impulse to fight or take flight.

Not all reactions, severe as they may be, can be labeled in terms of deeply rooted pathology. Acute situational problems such as divorce, separation, death, a truly difficult and interfering mother-in-law leave in their trail depression and confusion that are not necessarily pathological. The marriage counselor can best help in these instances if he is aware of this and of the significant role time plays as a healer. Fatigue is not necessarily a psychopathological problem, but it may well create a marital problem. The fatigue of a young woman coping with her household duties and several children may well be assuaged in a joint

---

* Karl Menninger, *The Vital Balance*, Viking, 1965.

interview in which the husband is helped to see her need for physical assistance, reassurance, and support. The timing of incidents that cause complaint must be watched by the counselor; a truly tired wife who has no interest in sex is different from the neurotic who is either witholding sexual relations to punish her husband or is not interested in sex at all.

Troubled spouses need to consider objectively whether the debits outweigh the credits and, if they do, whether some of the debits can be reduced and some of the credits increased. To do this, therapeutic help is usually needed, not just on the individual level but on the marital level. Marriages do not seem to wait on the resolution of personal feelings despite the latter's obvious importance, but depend rather on what is going on between husband and wife at a behavioral as well as a feeling level. Intrinsic to marriage counseling is the counselor's concern with the problems raised by neurotic choices of mates and neurotic interactions in marriage—his concern is not as a judge but as someone able to bring warmth and objective understanding and help to troubled husbands and wives. The counselor helps them to understand how to use their individual personality traits to advantage in the marriage, not only by dealing with their inner emotional problems but also by furthering their understanding and abilities to cope with difficulties that are likely to arise in the marriage from particular traits in each spouse's personality. However, the reader is not to get the impression that marriage counseling is meant to be an easy guide to happy marriage, for there are no dogmatic rules for solving the many difficult problems that may arise between two people. Nor does marriage counseling provide any magic—there is only hard and earnest work on the part of husband, wife, and marriage counselor.

# 9

## *Who Are You?*

A recurrent theme runs through conflict in marriage nowadays: a profound confusion over what it means to be a man or a woman. At a time in life when men and women should long since have established who they are, a great many seek definition and determination of their actual roles. The misapprehension of roles is the single most important ideological reason for neurotic interaction.

Marriage, like any social phenomenon, is complex and does not function in a vacuum. It is hardly accidental that so many husbands and wives seek to know and understand their roles as men and women, as husbands and wives, and as parents. We have discussed some of the many reasons for the search for self in our fast-moving society—from the horizontal mobility that leaves rootlessness and loneliness in its wake to the mass culture and mass education that cast doubt on or even undermine the guidelines of behavior.

Although we are living in an age of vast and wondrous communication, few husbands and wives are able to converse with each other with the certainty that they will be able to make each other understand their ideas and feelings. This inability to communicate only compounds their difficulties. Frustration and anger are quick to come on the heels of misunderstanding and serve to widen the breach. No wonder then that in marriage counseling so much time and emphasis must be placed on helping people to communicate and understand each other. Once each spouse understands the other's problems, anger tends to diminish and each begins to help the other.

We speak idealistically of freedom and equality as every per-

son's right, but how many of us understand the deeper significance of such concepts? Time and again husbands and wives
confuse freedom with license. Freedom is a precious right that
exacts payment in responsibility, which in turn requires maturity. Where there is no responsibility, there is no real freedom,
only license. Freedom in marriage allows for the expression of
each partner's uniqueness and the development of individual potential, but it also demands a responsible awareness of the marital
relationship. When a couple's goal is to maintain their marriage,
they are content to find their personal freedom within its
framework.

As we have seen, equality is very often confused with sameness. The demand for equality is an assertion of the equal rights
of men and women to live their lives to their best potentials.
This assertion gives recognition to the differences among all
human beings; it does not mean that we must each be and
have the same thing. Rather it is that, being equal, we each
must be and have what is most suitable for us individually.
The marriage counselor educates and clarifies misconceptions
as to differences in roles that too often are obscured by the word
"equality," as though (as has been already said) equality means
sameness.

Still another source of marital breakdown is the belief that
husband and wife occupy the same status level in the family
unit. The status hierarchy that continues to be the backbone
of the Western world's family structure is headed by the husband's role, followed by that of the wife, and then by those
of the children in the order of their birth. The father's role is to
interact with the world, to support his family, and thereby to
represent the world to his family as well as represent his family
to the world. His most important task is to go upward in his
job and then to go down the hierarchical ladder of the family
to his wife, who is taking care of the children. Hers is a secondary, but not less important, role in the structure of the family.

We speak of love, but as Bettelheim has said, "Love is not
enough"—roles and limits must be defined. In the democratic
family, each person is aware of his determined role in the family
structure. The parents form the axis about which the family
revolves, with the major determinant of the movement being

the father within the framework of rules and law. The right to
dissent peacefully and give opinions when appropriate is not
confused with who takes responsibility for decisions. In the democratic family it is the husband who is seen as president and
the wife as family manager, while the children assume responsibilities only as they demonstrate their ability to assume them.
President and manager trust and respect each other and generally agree as to policy. However, where there is a difference
of opinion and a decision must be made, the president makes the
decision, fully aware of his manager's peaceful dissent, and the
manager accepts the president's decision with respect and without recrimination. The absence of a single head in any social
unit can seriously jeopardize the capacity to survive in times
of stress.

## WHAT IS A WOMAN?

Much has been written about women, their variety and diversity, their many problems, hopes, dreams and expectations, and
the phases and cycles through which they go. This is not too
suprising, since we are in the midst of a sociosexual revolution in
which the status of women is changing radically. The old ideali-
zations of women have been shattered, but no new images have
been firmly established in their place. In addition, her goal in
marriage has changed its focus from economic security to love
and companionship, a fact that has tended to produce further
confusion about the role of a woman.

There are large remnants of the old order in our society that
are not in keeping with the many changes that are continuing
to take place. These remnants only add to the confusion about
women. A woman still drops her father's name for that of her
husband. The law still demands that she follow her husband in
the choice of a home, and courts generally still recognize that
the husband, as the principal provider of the family, is to be
judge of where its home should be.

On the other hand, more and more wives and mothers are
working—many out of real necessity, a great number to improve
the family's standard of living, while others seek to gain financial
independence even though it may be at the cost of their feminine
appeal. The fortunate among them work at careers to which they

are dedicated. Though increasing numbers of women work, they usually are not legally bound to support the family, unlike their husbands, who have no choice about working. The question of choice about whether to work becomes crystallized in the divorced group, where women frequently find themselves catapulted into work out of necessity. Just when divorcées feel most insecure in their role as women, they must be both man and woman in their households. The divorced woman soon comes to appreciate the difference between choosing to work and having no choice but to work.

Women seeking help frequently express their problem as a choice between marriage and a "career." It is work with which men are involved, but for women it always seems to be a career. It would appear that some women seek self-esteem through their work even more than do men. Yet marriage continues to be of vital, primary importance to most women. It is because of this—their "career"—that they have to make all the more certain that they place their work well within the framework of the marriage.

The issue is not one of career versus marriage. The young wife who feels dissatisfied or stifled needs to gain a perspective on the span of life—a man's as well as a woman's. She needs to understand how each cycle of life is exciting and holds opportunities for furthering her potential, how each cycle can be a preparation for the next. The older woman whose children are grown and feels that her life is empty needs guidance to direct her energies outward to her community. She also needs to educate others by living as wisely and gracefully as she can on the basis of what she has learned from life and of her inner resources.

Woman's basic role has become more and more obscured by the many demands made upon her. One court has commented, "She wants but she does not know what she wants, and what she wants is out of feelings of rage and guilt." With political emancipation, legal recognition, and broad intellectual and educational opportunities, many women are confused about and limited in knowledge of their role in life. Perhaps we have become so "civilized" that women forget, or tend to denigrate, their basic roles of wife and mother.

What it means to be a woman is not easy to convey, particularly in marriage counseling, where for the most part clients have never, despite their years, resolved their relationships to their parents. Every marriage counselor should be able to define for himself what he has come to see as the role of a woman, primarily so that it can be used for clients to collide against, thereby to develop their own ideas and values. What follows is a personal view, which relies and expands on a concept of Margaret Mead. It seems to have helped women seeking an answer for themselves to the question of what it means to be a woman.

Every woman knows deep within that her primary role is to help nurture life. Her body tells her this; her womb is to hold life and her breasts are to nourish it. While women generally accept these basic facts, they know too that bearing children is not enough, that they must nurture those children for a long time. It is when women have to go on beyond the simple physical care of children that they frequently have difficulty fulfilling the complex demands of their nurturing role.

Ideally, a woman must be able to give "the milk *and* honey" of life to those for whom she feels concern. There are some women who cannot give even "the milk"; their children are lost souls. However, most women are able, at the very least, to physically care for and sustain their children. It can be likened to a cat giving milk to her kittens.

Since women need their husbands to support them, financially and emotionally, while they give their children sustenance, one would think that they would at least give their men the same care they give their children. Instead, many women apparently cannot do more than care for their children. In relation to their husbands, some manifest indifference and others hostility. Such women usually feel that men have it all, that it is a man's world, that men are frightening and mysterious. Their husbands, in turn, come to believe that they are low on the totem pole and they resent their wives and even their children.

Many women who are able to give "the milk" of life find it a struggle to give "the honey" to their children. The needs of children are greater and more subtle than those of kittens. Man's brain, which enables him to extend himself out of the immediate moment back into the past as well as ahead into the future, creates the need for greater fulfillment. He needs to be given, as part of "the honey" of life, help in learning how to live to the best of his human potential. To achieve this, he has to learn many things that, human psychology being what it is, can only be taught in the first place by a mature, loving mother. Such a mother will teach the child self-acceptance, self-esteem, self-discipline, and self-respect, and how to recognize and accept his limitations and potentialities. He will have hope, faith, and trust in self as well as in those about him and in life itself, because his mother knows such hope, faith, and trust. She can help him to experience the joy of achievement in making positive, close relationships with others as well as in work. She will teach him about the moon and the stars, and about the earth as well. He will gradually absorb the meaning of life from her, and how it is to be found in living in the world, with all its sorrows and disappointments and all its hopes and joys.

A woman can only give what she herself has experienced. Most women have received "the milk" of life; they have been taken care of physically, so they in turn are able to care physically for themselves and others. Few who are having serious difficulties in their marriage have ever received "the honey" of life —what they have never had they do not know how to give, so that they offer little or none of the joy of life. Their children in turn go through life empty and unfulfilled, searching for an unknown they are not apt to find and hence are unable to give to their own children. Therapy may temper this search, especially through the relationship between client and therapist, but at best this is a synthetic relationship; the client must come to the realization that what should have been cannot ever be and that she must now tap whatever internal and external resources she has to give herself the feeling of fulfillment for which she is searching.

This concept of a woman's role as that of nurturing—of giving physical care and helping people to live to their best potentials— goes beyond the woman herself, her husband, and her children to her community. Most women recognize this as part of their role, but immaturity—with its consequent irresponsibility and giving of self only with an expectation of return—hampers many women from accomplishing what they want to do and know they must do. A society in transition tends to confuse the immature, giving them opportunities for further rationalization for

evading responsibility. On the other hand, there are more opportunities than ever before for a woman to live a rich and satisfying
life. Often all she needs is a little support and guidance toward
them.

## WHAT MAKES A MAN?

Though comparatively little has been written in this vein about
men, at least until recently, it is apparent that men are struggling with as many difficulties, external and emotional, as women.
Just as women's social status continues to change, there have
been continuing changes in that of men as the old authoritarian,
patriarchal order has tended to give way to the egalitarian, democratic one. As long as men are able to maintain the egalitarian
ideal (and many a man does), we have the basis of companionate
relationships with women, particularly in marriage. Unfortunately, the demands of this position run some men close to the
edge; many who have failed to assume the new responsibilities
it places upon them are bewildered when they find they are
neither leader nor follower. Frequently they then tend to withdraw from the fray in anger, anger directed at domineering
women—particularly their wives.

Work is of primary importance to most men. Unlike women,
who almost always must fit whatever they do within the framework of their marriages, men require that their marriages fit
within the framework of their careers; for many of them, marriage runs at best a close second to work. It is not simply that
men are obliged to support their families; many seem compelled
to prove their manhood in this way. The kind of work a man
does and the extent of his achievement are taken as a measure
of his manhood and, of course, achievement is our society is too
often measured in terms of money earned and status attained.

Work often serves another deeper and less obvious need. It
can fend off the loneliness, isolation, and intolerable feelings of
emptiness that many men have. Extensive drinking, one-night
stands, or narcotics can do the same thing, but those remedies
are dangerous and temporary. Conformity, being like everyone
else—married, with children, a home, a car—so others will accept
him even though he does not accept himself, helps superficially.
Most men are likely to find this conformity not really satisfying,

for it is as an empty shell that leaves them basically unfulfilled. Work does a much better job of it, for it takes up much time and energy and leaves a man free to do little else. He ostensibly pursues it to give his family more, but the real aim may be to meet a gnawing need of his own. When he is successful at work, he feels alive.

Work and its pursuit give many a man an excuse to stave off any deep involvement with his wife and children. His superficial relationship to them may prevent any hostility from showing and may protect him from trouble, but unwittingly a gap grows between him and those he pretends to hold dear. When his wife, in desperation, seeks marriage counseling or a divorce, he displays fright and anger, for has he not been a responsible partner in the marriage, he asks.

Many of the externals that marked a man in a man's world have been taken from men nowadays. A man no longer moves about to conquer his natural surroundings in order to live. Instead, he tends to lead a sedentary life, and often he must master sophisticated but superficial relationships. He also has to master a variety of technical procedures to survive and support his family. Even this takes on less meaning if his wife succeeds at her outside work and needs his financial support less and less.

What then makes a man? Since the attitudes and behavior of the sexes are in flux, the only thing that is left unchanged is feelings. The feeling that one is a man results from a mother's nurturing and a close relationship with a mature father with whom a boy can experience an identifying process until such time as he feels in his bones who he is, stops identifying, and assumes his own identity. He not only knows he is a man, he *feels* he is a man. Absentee fathers do not help, for they are not there to be identified with. Angry fathers are often too frightening. Passive, weak fathers do not warrant a boy's respect. Mothers who overpossess and overprotect but fail really to nurture frequently stand between father and son, impeding the process of identification.

Nurturing is part of a man's role, too, but at best it is learned behavior. The male equivalent of the physical care women give is economic support. Accordingly, the increasing economic activity of women can cut into a man's feeling of masculinity. To the extent that their mothers were able to give them "the honey" of life and to the extent that they experienced the emotional support their fathers gave, men are able to give such emotional support to their families. Fundamentally, men recognize their responsibilities for financial and emotional support. Like women, men have comparatively little difficulty about "the milk" of life; usually they give financial support just as women are able to take physical care of those close to them.

To this limited extent, many men and women are able to give love. Paradoxically, few husbands and wives are content just to receive "the milk" of life. They seek "the honey" of life—the joy of life—despite the fact that they are often themselves unable to provide it. Too often partners in a marriage do not know what it means to live fully and responsibly, to accept the challenge of life, and to offer each other tender care, recognizing and accepting the other's uniqueness, respecting the other as a human being, and having understanding, faith and trust, and hope for themselves and their marriage.

## THE ROLES OF HUSBAND AND WIFE

As the ideal of marriage has changed from that of a basically economic venture to one of companionship and a loving relationship, goals, attitudes, and behavior have changed. Since feelings are slow to change, they tend to conflict with attitudes and behavior and so confuse what the roles really are. The result is that too many husbands and wives do many or all of the things they believe they should do, but resent the doing. They give, but they are angry because they feel they are giving in or giving up.

It is enlightening that even in Biblical times man sought and depended upon the ideal wife, who is described in Proverbs 31:

> A woman of valour who can find?
> For her price is far above rubies.
> The heart of her husband doth safely trust in her,
> And he hath no lack of gain.
> She doeth him good and not evil
> All the days of her life.
>
> Strength and dignity are her clothing;
> And she laugheth at the time to come.

She openeth her mouth with wisdom;
And the law of kindness is on her tongue.
She looketh well to the ways of her household,
And eateth not the bread of idleness.
Her children rise up and call her blessed;
Her husband also, and he praiseth her;
Many daughters have done valiantly,
But thou excellest them all.

If men reflected their women in times past, they tend to do so even more in the present. Much of what husbands do in marriage would seem to be a reaction to their wives' behavior. This does not make men less important in marriage; rather, it recognizes the responsibility of women to take the initiative. Taking the initiative means that a woman sets the tone of her home and her marriage. Her husband will respond to her warmth when she actively participates in their relationship. To participate actively does not mean to be aggressive; it simply means not sitting back and waiting for the first move to be made in every instance by the husband. Many immature, inadequate-feeling women, afraid of being rejected, tend to constantly wait for their husbands to act. They are unaware that their husbands are afraid of rejection themselves and tend to interpret their wives' inactivity as rejection, so that they become angry and then actually do reject their wives. Other such women who are afraid of being rejected unconsciously become aggressive in their marital relationships, demanding and controlling their husbands so as to set them up for emotional flight. By contrast, a mature, loving wife does not think or feel in the negative terms of inadequacy and rejection, but goes about her life in a constructive fashion, using her judgment and discretion to do what she knows needs doing for her marriage to be good, without complaint, resentment, or anger. And her husband's heart goes out to her and he has "no lack of gain."

Dr. Edmund Bergler* suggests that woman advances further than man in the maturation process, with man tending to retain more infantilism. Therefore, he says, every good wife must accept

---

* Edmund Bergler, *Divorce Won't Help*, Harper & Brothers, 1948, p. 214.

this and give her husband plenty of leeway. It generally takes two to make a bad marriage.

A good wife creates an atmosphere of real tenderness to which most men will respond. The "little girl" cannot create such an atmosphere since she needs to be the center of love and attention. If a man is mature enough, he may be able to communicate some of his feelings about this to his wife in the hope that she will understand and grow. Otherwise, neither goes toward the other and feelings of isolation dominate their relationship.

A good wife vents her hostility on her husband's enemies, never on him, and he reacts with loyalty and support in kind. The hostile wife who is angry at men in general and her husband in particular directs her aggression toward her husband instead of his enemies. Her husband's fury at her lack of loyalty and support always surprises her, but she can always rationalize her behavior.

A good wife knows how to be a sounding board, and her husband is grateful that he has one person to turn to with his problems and difficulties. He in turn will hear her out. The controlling wife who listens to her husband's troubles always feels she must advise and expects her husband to accept her advice. If he does not, she is furious; she simply cannot understand that what he wants is primarily a sounding board so that he can reach his own decision.

A good wife takes care of her husband's earnings and he trusts her, hoping the mistakes she may make will not be too big. The demanding wife who cannot get enough love frequently sees money as its symbol and uses her husband's earnings to buy unnecessary things to console herself and punish him. She is unable or refuses to comprehend what he must do to obtain the money she spends so freely. She frequently knows or cares little about the state of their finances.

To a loving wife, sex is joyful and is a wondrous way of communicating her love, and her husband in turn does not look elsewhere. The unloving, uninvolved wife uses sex as a marital weapon whenever things do not go her way. Sex is rarely a joy for her; rather it is something her husband wants and she tolerates. When her husband, in disgust, turns to another, she is enraged because, after all, has she not been the good wife?

A good wife accepts much responsibility in her marriage and her husband reacts with responsible action on his part. The immature woman cannot accept responsibility and waits for her husband to do everything first; then, she tells herself, she will do her share. In point of fact, she hopes that he will not take the initiative, for then she will not have the responsibility to do anything.

Only the mature man and woman can accept the reality that happiness is an elusive bluebird. Our forefathers recognized this when they gave us not the right to happiness, but only the right to the pursuit of happiness. The right to pursue happiness, elusive bluebird though it may be, is inherent in every marriage. More real and attainable is the joy of achievement, not just in work but in relationships with others. This can be particularly rewarding in the marital relationship when both husband and wife recognize their roles and responsibilities to each other and are motivated to carry them out in a loving and compassionate fashion.

## "BE A PERSON"

Most of us know right from wrong, but in recent years there has been much emphasis on feelings. What one does, does not seem to matter as much as how one feels. I remember a woman in a joint session trying to explain to her husband how she was gradually changing and trying to improve their marriage. The husband, who had been in psychiatric treatment for some time, remained cold and aloof and finally said that he would not do anything until he had a feeling that he cared for his wife. It was as though some magic had to be performed, some particular button to be pressed, for him to become involved in a marital relationship into which he had entered so many years before.

There is much confusion about feelings and there is a tendency to exploit them to avoid responsibility for doing what has to be done. "I must feel to act" is the theme. This is in contrast to what many of us learned at the hands of old-fashioned parents when they said, "Be a person." They did not plead or scold, they just said that and left it up to you. This meant doing what you knew you had to do, whether you felt like it or not. The implication was that you would know the significant feeling of being human and more of a person that would follow the deed. To become a person was not a question of conformity and hoping to be accepted if you did what everyone else did, nor was it a question of publicized achievement; rather it was deciding to do what you knew you had to do and doing it—*that* made you a person. It meant you were taking responsibility despite any negative feelings you might have.

Frequently the concern over feelings in therapy leaves patients with the impression that the heart (feelings) is the only thing that counts in the human being—the brain (attitudes) and the body (behavior) are of secondary importance. Ideally, I suppose, as the person in therapy develops insight into his feelings about himself and others with whom he has been or is involved, he must let this insight become absorbed into his very being, forgive himself and those others, and then do the right thing. However, in my clinical experience, I find that the process is not so orderly. Usually the person develops insight but is unable to move because his feelings are still in the process of growth or change.

Since marital relationships can be very tenuous, I tend to become somewhat directive at this point about clients doing the right thing and use the analogy of what it means to become a driver. A person may read all the manuals about driving, but we would all agree that this does not make him a driver. He will not ever be one unless he takes the wheel and begins to drive, despite his feelings of anxiety and inadequacy. At first, he will have to think of every step he must take—where the key goes, how to start the car, the use of the brakes, etc.; he will have to drive slowly and he might even have an accident or two, but with consistent effort he will become a driver. The day will come when conceivably he will drive as he walks and does many other routine things—with little or no concern about feelings or details. If anything, his feeling will be that now he is a driver, he is in control of where he wants to go.

What is true of learning to drive is true of rehabilitating a marital relationship in which much hurt has been experienced.

Now that husband and wife have achieved insight, they no longer can claim ignorance or confusion as the reasons for not taking responsibility in their relationship to each other. If their goal is to keep the marriage, they will have to go slowly and think of everything they say and do at first, but the time will come, perhaps several years hence, when this constructive pattern of behavior will become part of them and the negative feelings will subside as positive feelings begin to take their rightful place.

I am reminded of a bright, volatile, poorly educated foreign-born young woman who had been in individual therapy for some time. Her therapist sent her to me to explain to her what she might expect if she went through with getting a divorce. By the time she came to see me, events had taken a turn that was influencing her to reconsider. She was frightened and uncertain about how she might perform—in bed as well as out—in view of her earlier behavior, into which she now had some insight. It was obvious that there had been abundant therapeutic concern for her negative feelings, with little emphasis on those that were constructive. She was aware of what she had to do if she was to keep the marriage, but she was frightened of her initial feelings of inadequacy and fear of rejection. Since I was not to see her again, the only way I could think of to reach and help her was to say, "There is more to you than these bad feelings. You have a head with which to think, a heart with which to love, and a vagina with which to have sex. Go home and use all three at once and see how you feel then." I shall not soon forget her grin of understanding as she left me.

## LOVE AND LOVING

Perhaps one could say that love is a desire for fusion with another and a movement away from encapsulation within self. Love is the leaven of existence. How to achieve it has preoccupied man through the centuries. The definitions of love can be as varied as the persons attempting to define it. However, a distinction must be made between falling in love, being in love, and having a loving day-by-day relationship. Falling in love and being in love are too often states of receiving, not actual giving; "he makes me feel so happy" is the primary concern and not "how can I make him feel happy?" In a loving relationship there is no "giving in" or "giving up," but just giving with judgment and discretion and with the expectation of a return but no "contract" for it—there is just the joy of being able to give to the other and helping him do the same.

People burdened by immaturity and neuroses set out to achieve a fusion that cannot be said to be love, although they may find unconscious satisfaction for their neurotic needs in the relationship. Relationships involving masochism and sadism are examples of destructive fusion, as is the abuse of sex by the immature and confused who—in their isolation and self-involvement—use sex to help bridge the gap between themselves and others. In their profound unhappiness and their desire for closeness to others, they believe erroneously that sexual activity will prove their femininity or masculinity.

When I first saw Mr. and Mrs. J, I wondered how I could help them. Mrs. J was depressed and unable to function and cried all the time; she felt futile and inadequate; Mr. J was angry and almost ready to give up the marriage. No matter how much Mrs. J tried, she could not seem to meet the needs of her demanding husband. With help, she began to perk up and do what she had to do as a wife and mother, but she was still not satisfied. She wanted to go back to the work that had occupied her before marriage, but she was afraid that this would threaten her husband and increase his anger. Mr. J felt threatened by and hostile to his wife's desire to work, but he gradually realized that she would be a happier person if she worked at least part-time.

Mr. J's anger slowly abated as things became better at home. At one session something he said made me comment, "When you came in here you were way out because of your anger. Now you have come in toward the middle ground. This is good but not enough; you will have to do something for your wife to show her your feeling for her. Give her something—it does not have to be much—give her a rose." At this, Mr. J became tearful and pulled from his pocket an envelope that bore my name. It was St. Valentine's Day. The envelope contained a card with a single rose on it. I knew that Mrs. J would be getting a rose too.

---

Helping professionals talk of the need for therapists to give love in marriage counseling as well as in other therapeutic relationships so that clients may come to experience its meaning. Personally, I feel compassion to be a far more suitable and all-encompassing word. As I see the anguish and suffering of those in marital distress, humility and compassion have come to mean very much more than love and loving. In marriage counseling, compassion spells for me an understanding of and a deep feeling for every client's struggle for life. Compassion is based on an awareness and acceptance of each person's desire for the good life despite his hostility, anxiety, and guilt. Husbands and wives who learn what compassion is can better help one another to live to the best of their abilities.

# 10

# *Fantasy, Reality, and Faith*

Among the many things that can be said about marriage, one is
that it does not, in and of itself, create happiness and mutual
understanding. For that matter, it does not, of itself, really create
a new way of life because it represents a culmination of the
psychological development of the partners. Ideas and feelings
that were planted long before grow during childhood and adolescence and eventually crystallize in the marital and parent-child
relationships. This raises the recurrent likelihood that a deadly
cycle will be established. Parents who, because of their own
emotional struggles or upbringing, are unable to establish a
happy family life are bound to bring up children who, in turn,
will consciously or unconsciously relive with their children what
they experienced with their parents. So are the sins of the fathers
visited upon their children. The way to break this cycle is
usually by therapeutic help, although there are times when people
who are highly motivated are able to achieve a breakthrough on
their own.

## THE FIFTH COMMANDMENT

Time and again in marriage counseling one sees people conflicted by their unresolved feelings of hate and anger for their
parents. "Don't expect me to love my parents, I can't even respect
them. How am I supposed to feel?" is a recurrent theme. These
feelings have a way of subtly repeating themselves in many
ways in the marriage.

The Fifth Commandment established the relationship of parent and child; it says, "Honour thy father and mother." I tend to interpret the commandment to mean that one must give father and mother esteemed acceptance of the sort the Chinese give their ancestors, but without engaging in ancestor worship. The commandment does not say love thy father and mother, or obey or respect them. Love, obedience, and respect have to be earned by parents as well as by anyone else. When parents, like Chinese ancestors, are given esteemed acceptance, it does not much matter what they have been like as one grew up because such acceptance does not have to be earned. It is far more important that their children be able to give that acceptance so that the answer to the all-pervasive question "Who am I?" has substance. Parents cannot be ignored, denied, disposed of; they are a reality, and should be forgiven for what they have done and given at least esteemed acceptance by their child, now that he is an adult, for what they did give to him that was good once upon a time. Such acceptance of parents is the first step toward accepting oneself.

Ironically, children find it initially very easy to love, respect, and obey their parents. A child begins to rebel when he intuitively realizes that his parents' needs are superseding his own, as when parents refuse to recognize his growth and ability to take responsibility. The child rightfully sees his parents then as taking the easier way out in meeting their own needs rather than his. Children are keenly intuitive and easily sense the feelings behind the good words and good intentions of their parents. The circle tightens when children grow up in an atmosphere in which they are frequently disappointed in their parents and in what happens in the home. They turn to magic, fantasy, and daydreaming to avoid becoming involved with disappointing reality, and later refuse to give these defenses up for the mature, adult state, in which they would have to cope with reality and take responsibility for their decisions. Magic is appropriate when one is five years old, and fantasy is an appropriate tool for the adolescent as he comes to grips with what and who he is and will be, the kind of work he would like to do, and the kind of person he will some day marry. Magic and fantasy are not appropriate for the mature adult.

## FANTASY VERSUS REALITY

The difficulty for many who marry is that their daydream and fantasy life has continued into adulthood and interferes with their acceptance of the realities of marriage. Things they found unacceptable as they were growing up were overcome in the fantasy that after marriage all difficulties would end. This led them to the mistake of viewing marriage as an end in itself instead of seeing it as a link between what has gone before and what will be. Now that they are married, they continue to find fantasy and daydreaming far more acceptable than disappointing reality, for in the world of fantasy nobody intervenes in their domain, there is compensation for every disappointment, and they can push problems off into the future.

When a daydream about marriage is not borne out by reality, what can the entrenched dreamer do? Unable to cope with disappointment, usually having little faith in anything, frightened and seeing only the negative aspects of his marriage, he tends to do only what he knows how to do—establish another set of daydreams to protect himself anew from the impact of reality. This only serves to create more misunderstanding and confusion in the marriage, because the new fantasy, when acted out, makes new demands again—without too much relationship to what is going on. Those who lead this fantasy life make no attempt to see their spouses as they really are because they fear disappointment and frustration. They go from one fantasy to the other rather than take responsibility for what actually exists. Having little or no faith in themselves and others or in the constructive possibilities open to them, they find the thought of accepting their marriages as they are intolerable.

The wonderful thing about being human is that it offers the opportunity of choice. A person can choose either to retreat into the world of daydreams and fantasy or go forward into the world of reality. Confusion and tensions arise when one does not make such a clear choice and straddles the two worlds, seeking the irresponsibility and pleasantness of the world of fantasy to fight off taking the responsibility he knows is his in the world of reality.

Mr. and Mrs. K struggled with their marriage for twenty years before they sought help. Although divorce had crossed their minds, each declared that he did not believe in divorce and used his religious background to back him up. As counseling proceeded, it became apparent that Mr. K was quite badly off emotionally, with little potential for a real marital relationship. If anything, the marriage for him was only a safeguard against a break with reality. Mrs. K was immature and had escaped into fantasy all her life rather than face reality. With help, she came to see how sick a man she had married, but she was unwilling to accept the compromise of divorce to terminate a marriage that she knew was highly destructive to her. To divorce, she would have had to discard her last fantasy—that she was an omnipotent queen who could endure anything and, above all, could eventually even make her husband well. Her fantasy helped her escape from reality, in which she felt herself to be an inadequate woman, incapable of taking responsibility for the marriage she had made or, for that matter, any other marriage she might make if she were to divorce.

For these people who cannot compromise their fantasies, there is no middle ground and so, when reality is finally forced upon them, they frequently turn to their children for relief, saying, "My son will not be like his father." Mrs. K kept repeating this theme. She was suffering from a marriage to a man whose mother had turned to him and stood between him and his father, yet Mrs. K found herself doing the same thing with her son.

The attachment of the parent for the child of the other sex may start long before the child is born and has its beginnings in the fantasy in which the child will make up for all that is lacking in the spouse so that the child becomes the donor-recipient of all the parent's feelings that the spouse has not fulfilled. The child is not perceived as an entity in its own right but only as a continuation of the parent's daydream. This results in overprotection, domination, and overemphasis by the mother on the child's obedience and in absenteeism by the father—all ways of expressing the parent's disappointment in self and in the spouse. Reality did not meet the fantasy for the parent; the child, unable to cope with what is going on, takes his place in the world of fantasy, and another cycle has started.

## IMAGINATION

In helping distressed husbands and wives who find it hard to cope with the reality of the marriages they have made, I like to say, "If you would take the magic of the five-year-old and the fantasy of the fifteen-year-old and mix them with the reality of life, you would come out with a much more wonderful way by which to live, and that is through the use of imagination." With imagination, the adult can project himself in time, and this helps him do many things. First, he is able to set long-range goals based on a realistic appraisal of his prospects. This enables him to follow through with short-range goals that will pave the way toward accomplishing the long-range ones. I frequently ask a troubled husband and wife how they see themselves five years hence. Their answers reveal how much imagination they have working for them. The more emotionally troubled are quite likely to be living from day to day, with no eye to the future.

If a person's decision is to keep his marriage, for whatever reason, then he has to imagine what he must do, how he must behave, and what his expectations should be. If he is able to do this, he might then accept a compromise between his fantasy and reality. To accomplish this, he needs to have faith, love, and hope.

## FAITH

There is a need for mutual trust between husband and wife if they are to rehabilitate their marriage successfully, free of magic and fantasy. Too frequently trust has to be built step by step in the counseling process. Significantly, those who do not trust seem always to deny having faith. They ask: "Faith in what? The supernatural? God? Mankind? Self? There are no facts to go on!"

A distinction needs to be made between a belief, which implies some facts, and faith, which implies none that one can go on. Yet faith has some relationship to facts in that it transcends and redefines them. This is far different from living apart from the facts, as is the case in magic and fantasy.

There are those who look only for facts, thereby to see more clearly the destructive side of life and their marriages. They have no awareness of how to look for the constructive—their marriages go from bad to worse and they do not know why. Others scrutinize the facts and can see the bad but somehow they are able to let it go and, with courage, see the good, the favorable factors and potential in their spouses. In their faith their marriages blossom. To be able to select the essentials of both good and bad depends on an individual's faith and his philosophy of life as well as his perceptive powers and judgmental abilities.

To the extent that religion is a way of life in which one moves out of self and places reliance upon the intangible unknown, faith in God may assist a person to have faith in himself and in his spouse. In terms of reality, religious faith can take the place of daydreams and fantasy, but it must not be used in a dependent way, as the immature would use it. Rather, if it is used by those who are mature and independent in spirit, it can be helpful in reinforcing faith and trust in self, in others, and in life. There is a difference between blind faith and mature faith. If faith is blind, the individual leaves everything to God like a trusting, naïve child; blind faith in Providence or a spouse may be easily shattered. The mature person who has faith in a purposeful universe understands that his faith is not a substitute for cooperative action and the art of loving.

RELIGIOUS RITES AND RITUALS

If we look to the meaning of the family, love, and sex in the theological context, we observe that the continuity of the generations is the tie between the individual and something far beyond the individual, namely, life itself. In this framework, sex can be seen as the link between the individual and mankind; sexual intercourse is something that can carry the individual beyond himself.

When a religion teaches that a person is not the goal in himself, but rather a tool toward the goal—namely, the continuity of life—it begins to give an indication of the true role of marriage, love, and sex. Confused husbands and wives are too self-involved, too tied to the problem of the day to accept such a concept off-hand. They must be helped toward it if they are to preserve their family unit as a part of the continuation of life on earth. Within this context, troubled husbands and wives have much to gain when they realize that love and sex are complementary elements in the search for unity with mankind. The two sides of mankind, the two sexes, seek unity, and in their attraction to each other lies love's potential. Sex becomes an exchange that goes beyond the boundaries of the individual but remains within the boundaries of the species. From such sexual experience is derived the strength of the family unit, which preserves the continuity of the roles of people on earth.

Religion takes on special significance for parents who understand and feel some of what has just been said. They give vent to their feelings by way of symbolism. The symbolism of religion has much significant value, but it must be made manifest within the family when the child is very young. The young child sees his parents as omnipotent beings who fill his whole world. To cope with his inevitable disappointment later, he needs to see at an early age that there is something beyond those omnipotent parents—something to which they themselves turn. It is of great importance to the child that he become aware that his parents are not the pinnacle of power. He understands this when he observes them kneeling before the Crucifix or praying before the Sabbath candles.

The young child cannot think in abstractions; he only feels. "Be kind to animals" means nothing when he is two, but having a cat or dog does. When he is eight or ten years old, he can absorb the concept and link it to a feeling established a long time before. In the same vein, the child at Sunday school who already is aware of something beyond Daddy and Mommy is ready to accept and absorb the ethical concepts he is being taught.

Through rites and rituals, the generations pass on what they have felt and learned. Rites and rituals appeal directly to feelings, and the child who is properly exposed to them at an early age develops a basis for future learning. Parents who can express their positive feelings about life and themselves by a meaningful —but not compulsive routine—use of rites and rituals develop a rich atmosphere in which they and their children thrive. So, rites and rituals become important in family life.

Mr. and Mrs. M were a young Jewish couple with two little children. Mr. M was a benign, passive man who had a great need for the warmth of family life. He had married a bright girl who knew far more about their religion than he did. When they married he hoped, through her, to establish the kind of Jewish home he had dreamed about but not really had as a boy. Unfortunately, he had not counted on his wife's internalized anger. She not only suppressed her own feelings about the observance of Jewish ritual in their home but, as Mr. M put it, broke down and took away whatever little faith in God he had.

After a number of sessions with Mrs. M, it became apparent that she considered any expression of religion in the home to be a destructive force. She said she had had several traumatic experiences with her parents whenever she had tried to express her deepest feelings. She had been active in Jewish student affairs and once had bought brass candlesticks with her pocket money and taken them home for Sabbath observance. Her parents laughed at her and refused to let her use them. They had long since declared their lack of interest in religion and were unable to comprehend her need. When she insisted, their anger was overwhelming and she never used the candlesticks.

One day she told me how much she wanted to make her children's life meaningful. As I have stated in the introduction to this book, I do counseling in my home. I showed her our Sabbath challah cloth which covers the twist bread on our dinner table each Sabbath eve. My father had designed it. My husband had selected the Hebrew wording and I had embroidered it. My husband's name and mine, with the names of our children, are embroidered in Hebrew around the cloth. As each child marries, we add the in-law's name and as the grandchildren are born, their names are added. The cloth is extremely meaningful to our children and to us.

Mrs. M and I discussed the Sabbath and what Friday night can mean to a Jewish family as they sit down for dinner, how it could establish her husband as king in his home, and how this meant she would then be queen and their children princes. We talked of how their children would begin to see that there was something more than just the everyday aspects of living, for on Friday night, somehow, something special happens that goes far beyond Papa and Mama.

The young woman burst into tears. This was a turning point. As time went on she bought all the ritual objects for observing the Sabbath. Only one thing was omitted: she found it impossible, somehow, in the big city of New York, to find a ritual skullcap for her husband. They started to observe Friday nights and Mr. M was happy to cooperate, but he waited for his wife to buy him the little hat. For him it meant her recognition at long last that he was the man of the house. He could not appreciate for some time that first Mrs. M had to accept herself as a woman before she could give him any overt recognition as a man. Neither was he ready to give himself that recognition and buy the hat himself. Mrs. M struggled with herself for a long time, but finally she did buy her husband his skullcap. When last I heard, observance of the Sabbath had become part of their way of life and they had become members of a synagogue.

---

Religion is as much a part of reality as anything else. The parent who reads Bible stories to his child along with those about Columbus, Winnie the Pooh, and Dr. Doolittle welds family and religion together. The child grows up with the idea that some day when he has a family of his own, it will spell the continuation not just of a daydream but of a faith in which he has participated. This faith has given him the feeling of being part of the generations that have come and gone and of those that will be, and of time—the centuries past and future. He has not been exposed to compulsive, meaningless mumbo jumbo that his parents went through to ease their consciences. Instead, he has been exposed by his parents to their feelings about life, to their love and faith, and to reality's significance. Above all, he has been given an awareness of the flow of time. Some day he, as others have done before him, will use those rituals to transmit to his children the wondrous feeling for life that he received from his parents a long time ago.

# III

# *Marriage Counseling Can Help*

# 11

## *Inside Marriage Counseling*

Marriage counseling is an answer to a major problem of the times we live in. It is not the only answer but it is an answer. It is a product of the times that there be professional assistance in the promotion of more adequate marriages. We find that although family life is difficult today for many people, most everyone earnestly desires it. What better evidence is there for this than the fact that, although the divorce rate remains high, the active search among the divorced for new marital partners is extraordinary and remarriage is increasing. Marriage counseling, as it has been developing in the past twenty-five years, is an attempt to help meet the need for a more comfortable and constructive marital relationship and family life.

Marriage counseling is an art, a professional technique that gives indication of one day being a profession. It is practiced at various levels and employed in different ways by persons whose basic training is in an established profession—the ministry, medicine, psychiatry, the law, psychology, education, or social work. Many people practice in this budding professional area within the framework of their own professions. They usually have some psychological knowledge, formally obtained or otherwise, but few have had supervised clinical experience or education. They can be said to be ministers, doctors, lawyers, etc., who employ marriage counseling techniques when they find it useful. It is being gradually recognized that these professionals should be distinguished from those who in fact leave their basic professions, get clinical experience and knowledge, and then devote all or, at least, the larger part of their professional time to marriage counseling on a private and/or clinical basis. Only the latter are entitled to be known as marriage counselors—perhaps they should be called clinical marriage counselors.

Because marriage counseling is a very young profession, it is still struggling to establish standards of professional competence. Exceedingly demanding professional requirements for membership have been set by the American Association of Marriage Counselors in a strenuous effort to elevate marriage counseling to the level of the other helping professions. A few states have passed legislation imposing educational prerequisites for and restrictions on the practice of marriage counseling; a number of other states are considering such legislation.

To explain what marriage counseling is, what it can accomplish, and where it stands in the hierarchy of therapeutic techniques, it becomes necessary first to define and distinguish it from education and psychotherapy; and then, to understand the various therapeutic techniques that are being used to help marital distress and how they differ from that of marriage counseling.

### EDUCATION, PSYCHOTHERAPY, AND COUNSELING

Education can be said to be a learning process that focuses on the potential for healthy growth within an individual's capacity for social adjustment. It directs itself to the healthy, positive, conscious aspects of the personality. The goal is to influence change and, if possible, to help further define the individual's social roles. To accomplish this, education may concentrate on one specific role (such as that of being a husband or a wife) that is involved in a variety of roles with which the individual may be concerned (such as being a good sexual partner, a good parent, a successful professional, etc.). Professors and teachers are identified with education; those who do therapy also educate.

Traditional therapy largely focuses on the unconscious, placing primary emphasis on the inner self in relation to the many roles the person has assumed. As a result, in such therapy the individual's needs as husband or wife are often given secondary emphasis. Psychiatrists, psychotherapists, psychologists, and counselors with clinical backgrounds utilize the concept of transference for this kind of therapeutic experience in varying degrees of intensity. Transference is the process by which the patient attaches to the therapist attitudes and feelings he has toward important persons in his past, for the therapist to interpret, giving the patient insight into his present behavior.

Counseling straddles the conscious and the upper layers of the unconscious. Because of this, it comes closer to education at times, yet there are differences. While education aims to define a specific role within a variety of the client's roles, directing itself to the parts of the ego that are undisturbed by conflict, counseling selects an area out of the total personality and endeavors to help it, giving therapeutic attention to those segments of the ego that are disturbed or in conflict. Counseling is concerned with the social, interpersonal aspects of the client's problems and tends to deal more deeply than education with his hostile or negative attitudes, probing the upper layers of the unconscious if necessary. The counselor, like the educator, does not aim to deepen the transference; however, the counselor may more openly recognize and more directly deal with transference than does the educator. The counselor is generally more concerned with the establishment of a dynamic relationship with his client in which a working rapport can be developed. Counseling, therefore, can be said to straddle not only the conscious and the unconscious but also education and therapy.

## VARIOUS THERAPEUTIC TECHNIQUES
## FOR HELPING MARRIAGES

Therapeutic techniques for treating marital distress vary from intensive therapy to supportive therapy. Intensive therapy may take a number of forms. The classical form of psychoanalysis focuses its attention on the individual, and the marriage is incidental. Other intensive therapeutic techniques reflect different degrees of concern for the marriage as such. Marital partners may be treated individually by two therapists who are in communication in an effort to maintain the marriage (collaborative). Husband and wife may be treated individually but during the same period of time by the same therapist who never brings them together in joint session (concurrent). They may be treated together in the same session by one therapist who never sees them individually (conjoint). Lastly, a combination of these techniques may be used (eclectic). Some therapists use analytic family therapy, others are expert at group psychotherapy. The determination of technique to be used for helping a distressed marriage usually depends largely on the orientation of the particular therapist. These techniques differ from marriage counseling in that their purpose in varying degrees is primarily to change the individuals who compose the disturbed marital relationship first, and thereby to change the relationship itself. Marriage counseling, on the other hand, is based on the theory that although a disturbed marital relationship might be but a symptom reflecting the inner conflicts of husband or wife or both, a disturbed marital relationship tends to perpetuate and intensify those conflicts causing even more personal difficulty—it is a treadmill from which husband and wife can be more readily extricated by having their marital relationship treated first. The marriage counselor attempts to make the relationship more wholesome so that husband and wife can be freed to help themselves and each other.

MARRIAGE COUNSELING

In essence, marriage counseling focuses particularly on the interpersonal relationship within the marriage or in the premarital state. It is a therapeutic process that deals primarily with the psychosexual relationship peculiar to husband and wife. Like education, it emphasizes the constructive, healthy, unconflicted aspects of the egos of husband and wife, using, among others, directive and guiding techniques. Like psychotherapy, it probes the unconscious, but only if necessary to resolve hostile and negative attitudes and feelings that prevent the marital relationship from flourishing.

The educational technique involved in marriage counseling is frequently employed by professionals in various fields who have some psychological knowledge and insight but are limited in clinical experience. They find the technique expedient within their professional frameworks, and this can be worthwhile if limitations are recognized and referral is resorted to when necessary. Psychotherapeutic techniques as well as educational are used by professionals who have had psychological and psychiatric education and intensive clinical experience. Such professionals are clinically prepared for probing unconscious needs, but know their limits and are prepared to refer if the depth of pathology is greater than they can cope with.

The *hope* of marriage counseling is to keep troubled marriages intact if at all possible. The general *goal* of marriage counseling can be said to be that husband and wife gain enough insight into and understanding of their personal and marital conflicts and difficulties, and enough emotional strength, to deal more adequately with their relationship and their problems. Their gain in individual emotional strength should be enough so that each can make a conscious decision, whether it be for the marriage or otherwise, and take responsibility for that decision.

The *focus* of marriage counseling is always on the marital relationship, which is a third entity, different and apart from the two persons who make it up. The focus on the interpersonal level implies that although there is therapeutic concern for the problems of the individual spouses, this is secondary to the concern for the problems besetting the marriage itself. Of course, there may be times in marriage counseling in which the primary therapeutic effort is devoted to the husband or wife, or both, as individuals, but the focus returns eventually to the marital relationship.

This approach makes for the difference between marriage counseling and personal therapy, in which the therapeutic focus is on the reorganization of the personality structure of the individual spouse and the marriage is incidental. Marriage counseling differs, too, from family counseling because it focuses particularly on the psychosexual relationship peculiar to husband and wife, whereas family counseling focuses on parent-child relationships and sibling relationships, with a parallel concern for the husband-wife relationship.

Confusion about the significance of marriage counseling seems to stem in large part from the problem of *focus*. Most training programs for therapy emphasize the individual's past experiences and feelings that have their origins in the past. Training programs in marriage counseling, on the other hand, concern themselves primarily with the here and now and the feelings caused by present difficulties in present relationships. In marriage counseling we look at once for what ego strength may exist in each spouse and put it to use rather than immediately setting out to explore deep-rooted feelings or furthering the narcissism of the individuals involved. The primary focus of marriage counseling on the situational and on the interpersonal relationships does not intend, however, to exclude the traditional therapeutic focus on the individual but recognizes that the urgency of marriages in distress does not allow for the time-consuming exploration characteristic of traditional therapy—the urgency demands marital stabilization first and therapeutic exploration of the partners later, if necessary. Marriage counseling has much to offer by way of the exploration and testing of reality, with its ensuing directive, conciliatory, guiding, supportive, and educational techniques. These techniques, combined and appropriately fused with others more traditionally recognized, can only serve to enhance the help given to the maritally distressed. No technique should be used exclusively, for obviously no one technique can always prove satisfactory or sufficient. Again, one focus does not exclude the other, there is no dichotomy—rather, both are to be employed, depending on the needs of the clients and the clinical abilities of the counselor.

It takes an experienced and sensitive counselor to diagnose pathology, know his treatment limitations, and explore what strengths are there and what can be done to alleviate the suffering and distress that marital partners inflict on each other. The marriage counselor's techniques can run the gamut from superficial, if you will, directive advice in crisis intervention to intensive nondirective exploration of the very depths of each spouse's personality and feelings. To know what techniques to use and when, and to be able, if indicated, to interweave them with one another, is an art—a necessary art—if marriages are not to be destroyed as a result of the exclusive worship of pedantic psychoanalytic and psychiatric techniques.

There is much hurt and distress in the world and many can help in many ways. Help cannot be enhanced by attempts at theoretical exclusion. Help can be enhanced by an awareness of and respect for the role each professional has to play as part of the whole helping team.

While psychotherapists generally stress growth and change by way of transference, marriage counselors stress change and growth by way of dynamic relationship and rapport. Transference, as used in Freudian technique, involves the displacement of the libido from the patient's infantile love objects (usually the parents) to the therapist in the course of psychoanalytic treatment. This redirection of desires and feelings, conscious and unconscious, may be positive if they are warm, friendly, and affectionate, or negative if they are unfriendly and hostile. Marriage counselors do not generally speak in terms of transference. They speak rather in terms of relationship and rapport. Generally speaking, all therapists are coming to recognize that the relationship between counselor and client or therapist and patient is central in the counseling or therapeutic process.

The term "relationship," as used here, refers to the interaction between counselor and client that becomes for the client a motivating force for change and growth. Consequently, the marriage counselor's personality, philosophy of life, and value system, his belief in what marriage counseling can do, his willingness to be firm and honest, to persevere, to support, and have compassion for the parties involved, and his faith in and respect for other human beings are all most important.

The marriage counselor tries to remain within the framework of present events so that, although he is aware of the client's transference and his own countertransference, he rarely uses them, since he wishes to avoid having the client regress to earlier stages of psychic development. He keeps his helping relationship with both partners oriented to reality, focusing on the fact that he represents the marriage and is trying to help them as one human being helps another. A client, who told me she thought of me as "the Hollywood mother" she had always dreamed of had to be informed in no uncertain terms that I was no fantasy but a real person who, with all the limitations that a real person can have, was trying to help her help herself. The client who felt that I was her mother and sought to become even more dependent on me than she already was had to be told that this could not be permitted—at best, it would be a synthetic relationship in which she would feel a kind of synthetic love to make up for something she should have experienced years ago and which cannot be expected to be found at so late a date. It would be far better to view me as a human being trying to help her in her present difficulties and to gain enough strength to seek for herself real and more appropriate sources of satisfaction. In this way the marriage counselor searches for the client's ego strength and uses the positive, constructive side of the client's personality to help overcome the negative, destructive one.

This is not to say that transference never is used in marriage-counseling cases; it is, but if the marriage counselor is treating both husband and wife, it is inevitably diluted. However, it is not unusual for the marriage counselor to deal with only one spouse, in which case a transference may flourish.

The formation of multidimensional relationships often become necessary in marriage counseling. There is the relationship of the counselor to the marital partners, individually and together, which is basic to the process, but the counselor may go beyond this to establish a relationship with the children and the family as a unit of interacting personalities. The counselor must keep this many-faceted relationship constantly in mind to stimulate its development to its fullest potential and to utilize it for the growth of the personalities involved.

The term "rapport" as used here is different from "relationship." The marriage counselor develops a relationship with the client to achieve dynamic changes and growth, but hopes to achieve a rapport with him that will constitute a framework for working purposes. "Rapport" refers to the positive, cooperative association of two persons that makes confidential, sympathetic understanding possible so as to help the counseling process. The establishment of a good working rapport makes the client-counselor relationship constructive.

Mrs. A, a young woman whose appearance was a cross between Alice in Wonderland and a beatnik, had married another student while at college and they had had four children in as many years. Her husband had been in treatment with another therapist for about a year when she sought marriage counseling. I was able to establish a relationship with Mrs. A after a few sessions, but it took considerably longer to achieve a working rapport because of her feelings about women, which exploration indicated had much to do with how she felt about her mother, whom she saw as cold, removed, efficient, and able but not to be trusted very much. Once it was established that the projection of her feelings onto me was preventing us from going ahead to deal with what was troubling her, rapport began to develop and Mrs. A began to make some positive gains.

She had a chronically difficult marriage with a man who gave her little pleasure, little money, and much trouble. She had considered divorce, but she realized that this would mean being worse off financially than she already was. With her permission and that of his therapist, I asked Mr. A to come in for some joint sessions with his wife. His resistance and anger were apparent from the start and never abated in the six joint sessions that followed, during which the focus was on the serious limitations of his relationship with his wife and the difficulty in her continuing to live with him. It became obvious to Mr. A that he was being called upon to determine which was more precious to him, a stable family life or a life of satisfying his personal needs. His personal therapy appeared to be a way of satisfying those needs, for while he was helped to explore his feelings, he sank deeper into his self-involvement, to the exclusion of his marriage—after all, he said, he was having so much difficulty that no one could expect him to take on any more responsibility. Marriage counseling, on the other hand, represented to him what he knew he must do if he was to achieve any marital stability and be a man, a husband, and a father. The joint sessions put him on the spot and acted as a catalyst to push him on for further resolution of his dilemma—and he hated my guts! It can be said that a relationship of a negative character was established between Mr. A and me, for change and even a certain amount of growth did take place. However, a rapport between us can hardly be said to have been established—Mr. A was just too angry at what I symbolized.

For some time after the joint sessions Mrs. A continued to consult me while her husband continued with his therapist. Despite this arrangement, the case remained a marriage-counseling one since the focus remained on the marriage. Mrs. A began to accept the limitations on what she could expect from her marriage, recognizing that she and her husband would probably never come very close to each other, but she hoped that some day they would be able to go along at a more or less even keel and not drag each other down, as they had. Neither wanted deep involvement; rather, they wanted companionship with distance. Mrs. A was helped to do many things for herself as a woman, to further her education and to move toward the work goals she set. The counseling goal was to help her to gain enough ego strength and assurance so that if she should ever want to consider divorce again, she would be able to make her decision out of strength, not weakness.

Had Mr. and Mrs. A originally appeared for marriage counseling together, a relationship and rapport might have been established with them, individually and together, unhampered by other therapeutic relationships, that could have led them to a stabilization and rehabilitation of their marriage. Then, after this was accomplished, if Mr. A needed deeper therapeutic help than I felt I could give, another therapist would have been recommended to him while I continued with Mrs. A, able, when necessary, with his therapist's knowledge and consent, to call Mr. A in about the marital relationship. This is a workable procedure that both spouses usually understand and accept. The procedure in this case only set the stage for Mr. A to become even angrier since he consciously believed, however mistakenly, that the marriage counselor did not like him and saw the marriage only through his wife's eyes; unconsciously he was enjoying his regression to the narcissistic level too much to put forth much effort in his marriage

Any process by which people are helped to live more constructive and satisfying lives—that is, the *what, how,* and *why* of the help given—must be accomplished within the framework of a philosophy that is itself dependent on *who* is helping *whom* and *where.* In any given case the marriage-counseling goals, the techniques that are used to achieve them, and the theory behind it all depend upon who the marriage counselor is, whom he is helping, and the setting in which he is giving the help.

## WHOM DOES THE MARRIAGE COUNSELOR HELP?

Marriage counseling help seems generally to appeal to the more educated and intelligent, but their expectations and needs vary as do their age and length of marriage. Some seek magic; they think that somehow just appearing for counseling will be enough and then, without any real effort on their part, what was wrong will right itself. Many seek professional intervention in a crisis in which they feel helpless. Others, consciously or unconsciously, try to use marriage counseling to ease their way out of marriage—after all, they can always say they tried. Still others come seeking conscious, structured, directive help for their marital problems. They want short-term help and are not interested in a long-range program of therapeutic treatment since they do not feel that anything is wrong with themselves, only with their marriage. At best, they feel that any long-range program should be applied to their spouses, with whom everything is wrong.

Many appear in the marriage counselor's office because they have been told to do so by some other professional person to whom they have turned for help. They come as children to a parent seeking relief from their anxieties, tensions, and burdens. Frequently they refuse out of hand the suggestion of psychiatric help—unfortunately the psychiatrist is still a frightening "head-shrinker" for many people. They find the marriage counselor far less threatening, since they expect him to be an arbitrator and to help them not with themselves but with something they consider outside themselves—the marital relationship. For all that, it must be remembered that it is possible for people to have difficult marital problems and not be in need of intensive therapy.

## WHO IS THE MARRIAGE COUNSELOR?

Marriage counseling is interdisciplinary in character, and since a marriage counselor may come from any one of a wide variety of professions, his philosophy of marriage counseling is substantially colored by his particular profession since professional disciplines vary in their philosophies of the way people can be helped—from the directive approach of the lawyer to the psychoanalytic, nondirective, soul-searching approach of the psychiatrist; from the crisis-oriented social worker to the ego-building clinical psychologist. Marriage counselors who come from the law, education, the ministry, and medicine are particularly geared to the conscious and behavioral aspects of the interpersonal marital relationship. This fact serves, perhaps, as their special contribution to offset the traditional clinical concept of counseling and psychotherapy. At no time, however, is concern for marital interaction intended to exclude or take the place of concern for the unconscious motivations or pathology of the individual spouses. A competent marriage counselor is able to diagnose pathology in the individual spouses and their relationship in order to determine treatment or referral.

The philosophy of marriage counseling demands that the interpsychic relationship and interaction in a marriage be evaluated differently from the intrapsychic difficulties of an individual. The many-faceted marital relationship goes through a number of stages in its lifetime, so that the counselor is always aware of the impact of time on the relationship. Time and timing play a tremendous role in marriage—things happen, people are hurt, and in anger and righteous indignation they are likely to make statements and decisions that they really do not mean or are sorry for later. Beyond this, people's needs change, so that what seemed so important at one time has little significance at another. The marriage counselor has to have a feeling for the broad sweep of life and its many phases to be able to help a troubled marriage at the particular stage in which it is when help is sought. Emotional exploration and therapeutic guidance and support of both spouses, with an awareness of the healing nature of time, can establish the foundations for a rehabilitated marriage that may be far more real and satisfying than the original marriage ever was.

The extent of the counselor's psychological education and clinical training in marriage counseling plays an important role in his philosophy. The demands of counseling people in distressed marriages in a complex society require the counselor to be broadly educated as well as clinically trained. He has to have knowledge of marriage and family life from a wide legal, religious, social, and cultural perspective in order to apply his clinical knowledge, insight, and training more wisely to the case at hand. To cope with marital interaction he must have clinical knowledge of pathology and personality development.

Actually, it is the marriage counselor's concept of personality that will do much to determine the kind of treatment in which he will engage and the treatment goals he will have. If he views personality as static and bound by the past, then his expectations and goals in regard to his troubled clients must be limited; if he believes in the growth of personality, he will have broad goals in treatment and endeavor to help his clients toward establishing and achieving such goals. Though the clinical diagnosis for the partners and their marital interaction may indicate much that is negative, the counselor brooks little negativism and despair if he has a dynamic concept of personality growth. When he sets out to help two human beings and their marital relationship, he is aware of the negatives, which he is able to treat if necessary, but he does not concede to those negatives and places them in a secondary position when feasible, in favor of the positives that he discerns in the partners and their relationship. There is great potential for personality growth in a marriage once the relationship is stabilized and begins to be emotionally rewarding. Husband and wife may need to grow for the marriage to become stronger, but as the marriage begins to gain strength and momentum, it is able to encourage their personal growth in turn, so that marriage and marital partners become mutually helpful in the therapeutic process.

A marriage counselor who accepts the concept of dynamic personality growth, who believes in the marital relationship as potentially constructive, affecting not only husband and wife but children, families and friends, the community in which the couple lives as well as life itself, and who views marriage as a benign expression of God and man's humanity, can do much toward helping to heal the wounds. People can live a good life together with scar tissue, for such tissue sometimes is even thicker and stronger than the original flesh; they cannot if the wounds are prevented from healing by persistent picking and scratching. So does the marriage counselor's own philosophy of life and values combine with his clinical insight, objectivity, and empathy to affect his philosophy of the helping process in marriage counseling.

## THE CLINICAL MARRIAGE COUNSELOR[*]

As marriage counseling emerges as a profession in its own right, among its practitioners is a new professional person able not only to intervene in situational crises and stem the flow of neurotic interaction but also to treat the interpsychic conflicts between husband and wife as well as their individual intrapsychic problems.

The clinical marriage counselor believes that personal and interpersonal conflicts tend to exist simultaneously, but that not every stomach-ache warrants the diagnosis of acute appendicitis and consequent surgical intervention. Just as the general physician must diagnose and then determine to treat and watch the response to treatment before referral to the surgeon, so the clinical marriage counselor sees his role as diagnostician and therapist and is prepared to refer to the psychiatrist when necessary.

The clinical marriage counselor comes from one of the helping professions and is devoted to the practice of the new specialty. He draws on psychiatric, psychological, sociological, anthropological, and educational knowledge, and brings clinical insight into personality and marital dynamics along with an intensity of supervised clinical experience as well as life experience. He is crisis-oriented, is able to focus treatment more intensely on the disturbed interpersonal relationship in an effort to make it more constructive, and yet able to deal, if necessary, with the individual problems of husband and wife.

Marriage counselors who intend to practice privately as clinical marriage counselors must, I believe, have undergone personal therapy themselves to become aware of and resolve their own feelings about themselves and their marriages as well as to experience therapeutic process at first hand. Admittedly, there are talented, adjusted marriage counselors who may not need

---

[*] The clinical marriage counselor's philosophy and therapeutic techniques described here and throughout this book have evolved from a long and intensive personal counseling experience with troubled husbands and wives in distressed marriages.

to comply with this suggestion. Still, assuming the adjustment to be there, one must evaluate the talent for insight in each therapist. Insight is the counselor's ability to integrate his clinical and general knowledge with his observations of the behavioral patterns of interpsychic conflicts in a marriage together with the intrapsychic conflicts of husband and wife so as to get at and, if possible, treat the problems behind the problems presented. I suppose one could liken the talent for insight to that of sight singing in the musical world. Some people have a talent, others have to be taught, still others can spend years in training and never be able to sing on sight. In a certain sense, therapists cannot really be trained, because therapy is an art. There are those who have had many years of therapy and training who might become good writers or speakers, but they will never be good clinicians. Insight, a good sense of values, a sense of humor, the ability to put things in their proper perspective, the ability of the counselor to use himself effectively in the counseling process are essentials in the art of marriage counseling.

Clearly, counselors must have many qualifications as persons, but personality in itself is not enough. They must also have a clear conceptual framework, and this presumes considerable skill and knowledge. They must have the education in psychology and psychiatry that underscores personality development, plus years of clinical experience and supervision. Generally, the techniques marriage counselors use fall somewhere between directive and nondirective counseling. Marriage counselors may range from being temporarily directive to help clients solve their problems, with the clients passively receiving the benefits of their wisdom and experience, to being catalysts, particularly in individual sessions that precipitate clients into becoming active in the diagnosis and resolution of their problems. The techniques for obtaining a conceptual framework have been established by the various professions for themselves. As these are merged to meet the goals of marriage counseling, something very worthwhile is developing to help those in marital distress.

Clinical marriage counseling is done at several levels of intensity. The first level is crisis-oriented, dealing with immediate

situational distress in the here and now. Since a somewhat directive technique is needed to resolve situational crises, marriage
counselors have to be aware of underlying dynamics to accomplish the resolution without harm. At the same time, supportive
therapy is given.

Supportive therapy deals with the "here and now" situational
problems within the framework of sociocultural forces. It attempts to ease the client through a threatening or unbearable
situation until he has gained enough strength to be able to go
it alone or, if not, to undertake a search for the causes of his
distress.

In marriage counseling, supportive therapy may take various
forms, including the directive, authoritarian, reconciliatory efforts
characteristic of the matrimonial lawyer and the guiding, educational techniques of the physician within the framework of their
professions. When such counseling is carried out with awareness
of professional and personal limitations, it serves a very real
purpose. The clients' presenting problem for the marriage counselor is like the bleeding wound that the doctor hurries to treat
after an accident. Like the doctor, the marriage counselor makes
every effort to stop the bleeding, and just as there is time enough
after this is done for the doctor to examine the patient further,
so there is time enough for the marriage counselor to look for
deeper causes.

In crisis counseling, the marriage counselor is in the role of
the good, authoritarian parent upon whom clients can depend
and to whom they can pour out their feelings with an assurance
of sympathy, understanding, and privacy. This accomplished,
the counselor reviews with husband and wife what is going on
and where the trouble lies, and helps them change what they
can of the discordant elements in their life situation. In this
first phase of the process, the counselor draws on what is constructive in the couple's personalities, their relationship and life
together, but makes no attempt to resolve either the conflicts
between them or their personal problems.

The client who seeks help for his marital problems is frequently not interested in or amenable to pursuing any search
into the sources of his difficulties. He wants active help—information, guidance, advice, direction—in dealing with what is

happening to him right now. He may or may not be aware of or accept the fact that something is wrong with him, but he "knows" that something is very wrong with his spouse and, therefore, with that third entity, their marital relationship.

It is not always necessary, or indeed wise, to start intensive therapy immediately in marital distress. Man and wife want relief from whatever it is that they believe is hurting them most, be it a crisis due to a breakdown in communication, adultery, financial difficulties, children, or problems resulting from separation and divorce. In helping them to resolve the immediate issues, the marriage counselor has the opportunity to assess the strengths and weaknesses of the marriage and the ego strengths of the spouses. Often what appears to be a simple presenting problem will be found to conceal unexpected complexities, while an apparently complex marital situation may yield to a short-term and more limited therapeutic approach.

There is usually an urgency about the troubled matrimonial relationship—particularly in cases referred by lawyers—that no other troubled relationship seems to have. There is frequently just no time for intensive therapy of any kind until things quiet down. An underlying element of permanence exists in the relationship between parents and children that generally tends to hold time in tow when a serious problem arises, but this is not true of the marital relationship—witness the many divorces today. A marriage, a family, is on the brink of disintegration and annihilation and attention must be paid to it. Somehow the marriage counselor must achieve a cease-fire in the hostilities. In the comparative quiet of the "false peace" that ensues, husband and wife may be able to gain some perspective on how they act, react, and counterreact to each other; perhaps during the moment of truce they can be helped toward reconstruction of their marriage. After the marriage has been temporarily stabilized, the marriage counselor turns to more consideration and intensive treatment of what has been going on in the marital relationship and, if he deems it necessary, in the individuals. In individual sessions, however, he never loses sight of the marriage, for the marriage can help the husband and wife as each can help the marriage. Joint sessions for treatment of the marriage may or may not continue. At some point in the treatment, the marriage counselor may decide to refer one or both spouses to another therapist—perhaps because of the marriage counselor's professional limits, or because there is a persistent adultery, unknown to one spouse, that the marriage counselor cannot be aware of and continue to treat the marriage and the "innocent spouse," or because one of the spouses has traits that prevent him from trusting the marriage counselor to handle both him and his spouse.

Differences in therapeutic technique lie in differences in philosophy, orientation, and experience of the counselor. The marriage counselor tends to deal with the conscious problems and surface realities of the marriage first and, if clinically trained, may then determine whether it is necessary to treat the individual spouses' unconscious feelings and motivations; or he may, if necessary, treat all at once, using individual and joint sessions. This process is in contrast to that of therapists who are primarily concerned with intensive therapy. The latter will tend to deal with the unconscious first, in an effort to reorganize the individual and eventually come up to the level of consciousness and reality later. I believe that marriages are not always able to survive this approach. However, the two techniques are not mutually exclusive and both can help if used appropriately to meet the needs of clients.

One cannot satisfactorily evaluate a marriage from one partner's point of view in the classic analytic tradition. The individual spouse's complaints may be accurate enough from his perspective, but they are almost invariably an incomplete description of what has been happening in the marriage. The marriage counselor, trained to help both spouses individually and jointly, is in the advantageous position of being able to get a more complete description of what has been going on and to help husband and wife to recognize what they are doing to each other. Inevitably, the accounts given by both spouses in individual sessions are filled with divergences and contradictions. When these become marked, I tend to ask the partners in joint session whether they were at the same place at the same time. Frequently one partner says the other is "lying," a word that is inappropriate between husband and wife and most often is not a fair judgment. Each has to gain insight into and understanding of how the other perceives the marriage and events. Two people facing each other in a room do not necessarily see the whole room. One sees one end and the other the other end. Neither is lying when he differs from the other in describing the room. The marriage counselor, representing the marital entity and reflecting what is going on in it, is able to see more of the whole by putting both descriptions together and so help husband and wife gain an understanding of the differences in their perceptions.

The clinical marriage counselor is a moral person because he hopes to save and keep marriages. Religion and society— that is, church and state—are for marriage; and so is the marriage counselor. This does not mean that the marriage counselor is a zealot who is out to save all marriages without regard for human needs. Rather, it is that the marriage counselor hopes to save a marriage if it is possible. He is enmeshed in the reality of marriage and is constantly aware that clients do not live in a vacuum, that there is a world beyond the marriage counselor's office to which clients go. His concern for them when he undertakes to help them and their relationship inevitably labels the marriage counselor as a moral agent, but this does not mean that he ever acts as a moral judge. One of his aims, in fact, is to offset the confusion that may exist in moral values and standards of behavior. Therefore, he needs to stand for life and hope—and, in addition, for the values he has evolved for himself—if he expects to be successful in dissolving confusion in his clients. Having developed a system of values as a way of life for himself, he has no need to use that system in hostile judgment of others. Rather, since he has integrated those values into his life style, the marriage counselor becomes a trustworthy sounding board on which the client can test the validity of his own values. The outlook here defined is in contradistinction to that of therapists who insist that they do not inject morality into the therapeutic situation and are concerned only with the client's psyche.

Nowhere is the counselor's philosophy of life more poignantly conveyed than in marriage counseling. The counselor's value system cannot be imposed on a client, but whether the counselor states those values or not, they inevitably come through in the counseling relationship, giving the client something to confront and work with. Therefore, the marriage counselor has to come to grips with his personal value system, be aware of it, and be able to reassess it from time to time. Whatever may be the motivation of anyone who undertakes to do marriage counseling, self-awareness and self-understanding are imperative. Marriage counselors, being human, must make an honest attempt to understand the dynamics of their own marriages.* If the marriage counselor should not be a zealot, consciously or unconsciously seeking to keep all marriages, by the same token he should not seek, consciously or unconsciously, to destroy marriages.

---

* One cannot escape the feeling that a marriage counselor should have been married—at least once.

# 12

# The Clinical Marriage Counselor
# and the Helping Professions

As we have seen, marriage counseling has been changing rapidly from an art long practiced by a variety of lay and professional people to a technique used by various helping professionals within the framework of their professions. Moreover, this old art and new professional technique has begun to display a potential for development into a profession in its own right. No wonder then that there is confusion and skepticism as to what marriage counseling is, what it can accomplish, and who, indeed, can be expected to accomplish it.

The first step toward clarification is to recognize that there is a considerable difference in therapeutic depth and goal between the marriage counseling done by members of the helping professions not clinically trained for it and that done by the clinically trained marriage counselor. The clinically untrained lawyer who, through directives, attempts reconciliation when divorce is being considered; the physician who explains only the physiological processes of sexual behavior in answer to his patients' questions, with little or no comprehension of their feelings;* the minister who intervenes at the time of marital crisis with little understanding of the dynamics of marital interaction—all these helping professionals are doing a limited kind of marriage counseling within the framework of their professional practice. Such counseling has merit but it is not to be confused with the more extensive

---

* Ethel M. Nash, et al., *Marriage Counseling in Medical Practice*, Chap. 2, "Sexual Symptoms in Presenting Complaints," University of North Carolina Press, 1964.

clinical marriage counseling offered by those who have had years of clinical supervision and training and who make marriage counseling their full-time profession.

The clinical marriage counselor, as has been indicated, not only is concerned with all the situational and educational aspects of marital distress, but is clinically competent to cope, concurrently or in sequence depending on the need, with the dynamics of marital interaction and the interpsychic relationship between husband and wife that result from and therefore involve the intrapsychic problems of each.

Secondly, there is a real need for professionals of broad experience and knowledge to bring the specialties together into an integrated whole for the benefit of those who seek their help. In this respect the clinical marriage counselor stands in a tenuous and difficult but highly desirable position professionally. Coming from one or two of the recognized professions, spending his total working day in counseling and in contact with other professionals, the clinical marriage counselor has the potential for bringing the different professions together not only for the benefit of the individual but for the marital entity. It is one of the purported duties as well as ethical standards of such a marriage counselor to know his professional limitations and how to use other helping professionals in the treatment of a client and when and to whom to refer.

Louis Nizer, an attorney with much experience in matrimonial law, says:

> Orthogamy is the science of straightening out a marriage that has gone wrong. The orthogamist must combine the skills of a marriage counselor, psychologist, psychiatrist, pastor, doctor and lawyer, or at least he should have had their talents available to him.*

I would substitute for the orthogamist the clinical marriage counselor who is trained to enlist the services of the many professionals as needed to help the distressed matrimonial client: the psychologist, for a more thorough comprehension of the client's pathology; the doctor, for the client's physical well-being; the lawyer, for the client's legal protection; the psychiatrist, for

---

* Louis Nizer, *The Jury Returns,* Doubleday, 1966, p. 168.

medication and hospitalization, for more intensive therapeutic help than the marriage counselor may be equipped to give, and for the counselor's own supervision; and finally, the minister, for aiding the client in redefining his values and his attitudes toward life within his own religious orientation.

No one human being can be all things to another. The various helping professionals and marriage counselors who recognize their respective capacities, limitations, and skills can jointly and co-operatively perform a welcome and useful task for the disturbed matrimonial client. The helping professionals must not practice marriage counseling and marriage counselors must not practice in their fields of endeavor. Yet it is to be expected that they may find it necessary on occasion to touch on one another's provinces.

The psychologist and psychological testing will be considered in the next chapter in connection with a review of the process of marriage counseling. The relationship of the lawyer and the marriage counselor will be appropriately discussed in the chapters on divorce. The discussion that follows concerns the interprofessional relationship of the marriage counselor with the physician, the psychiatrist, the minister, and the social worker. The purpose is to explore what these professionals can do about marriage counseling and what their potential might be in the field. To this end, the following questions are asked: What is their role in regard to cases that call for marriage counseling aid? What do they do and what can they do to help stabilize marriages? When should they refer to the marriage counselor? How and when should a marriage counselor refer his client to a particular professional? Can such referrals prove to be cooperative ventures in helping clients? Should marriage counseling training be given in the various professional schools?

## THE PHYSICIAN

With so much emphasis placed on the psychological origins of distress, the marriage counselor, like all nonmedical counselors, must be particularly aware of the need to have a client's physiological complaints explored. Counselors should beware of attempts at medical diagnosis. Although most persons have their own physician, the counselor should be able to recommend one if necessary. More frequently used in marriage-counseling cases is the obstetrician-gynecologist. Attitudes, feelings, and behavior in regard to sex can rightfully be explored by the counselor, but he must know when to refer to the physician such problems as premature ejaculation, frigidity, and sterility. In matters of contraception, where feelings have been explored and a decision has been made as to method, a discussion between the marriage counselor and the gynecologist about any pertinent emotional problems can be valuable to the client.

In recent years physicians have become increasingly aware of the need to consider emotional factors in treatment. This advance is being furthered recently by the exploration of the potential of the various forms of counseling, including marriage counseling, being employed by physicians within their medical practice. The following observations emerge from my discussions and experience with obstetricians and other members of the medical profession.

The doctor does some form of marriage counseling almost every day, and the questions are manifold. Marriage counseling may well start at an early age. The general physician, and the obstetrician-gynecologist in particular, has the opportunity to reach teen-agers so that they can experience an introduction to premarital and marital counseling.

The unmarried mother-to-be is not an infrequent visitor. The concerned obstetrician needs to listen, evaluate, and advise. The questions are many and serious: Should I marry the boy? Should I keep the baby? If I keep the baby, what will happen? If I don't, what will I feel? Unless doctors are trained in counseling, how they handle these questions frequently depends on their personal feelings in regard to unwed mothers. Such feelings necessarily influence the girl's feelings and actions for her entire life, so that the doctor needs to be very cautious with his advice.

Another question that frequently presents itself is what to say to a couple seeking a blood test in preparation for marriage. Doctors have a wonderful opportunity to do some educative premarital counseling. However, many still do no more than give an elementary lecture on sex. If couples ask for contraceptive advice, they give it. Physicians with more awareness—and time—will expound their philosophy of life and of marriage, but even these doctors often give little consideration to the real feelings of those to whom the advice is being given. One wonders at the paucity of insight and education that produces such a situation. One can only say that the motivation is there. Unfortunately, doctors have not been trained in marriage counseling. To their credit, more doctors are becoming aware of their professional limitations in this area and are referring patients for counseling.

The young woman who complains of her inability to reach orgasm is likely to appear in the doctor's office. The doctor's duty is to resolve distressful physiological elements, but after this comes the investigation due psychosomatic ills. There may be a need for much time-consuming counseling that the busy doctor may not be ready to give even if he is equipped to go into feelings with any depth.

Prepregnancy and predelivery counseling is another phase of marriage counseling doctors do. The girl who comes in for examination to find out if she can have a baby wants to know many things about the phenomena of having a child and doctors usually take some time out to educate her. The next step is predelivery counseling, which should include both husband and wife. The advent of the first child is one of the major crises in marriage, yet few physicians discuss with the parents what is happening in the pregnancy itself from month to month, what labor is, how it happens, how it is maintained, and then what will happen at the delivery. The number is limited, although perhaps more obstetricians today do tend to discuss the delivery itself. However, only a few talk of what is going to happen to the couple when they go home with the tiny intruder into their life together.

By and large, most marriages become solidified after the delivery of the first child. Yet, many husbands and wives suffer when they are faced with the responsibility for this new life. The man needs to be mature enough to withstand his wife's attention being focused primarily on the baby—he no longer can expect all her attention to be focused on him, he is no longer first and, what is more, the freedom that they originally knew is gone. Most husbands resent this and can carry their resentment to the point where the marriage is weakened. On the other hand, young wives must be made aware that they need to nurture not only their child but their marriages too. The young mother enthralled by this new life frequently forgets to nurture the one on whom she depends to help her succor her baby—the one who hopefully will remain when her child is raised and gone. If a doctor sees such immaturity in his patients, he should refer them for counseling unless he is equipped to give long-term counseling help.

The obstetrician-gynecologist and the general physician are frequently confronted with the woman patient who says, "My husband is cheating on me. What shall I do?" This is a tremendous problem, yet the physician must do something—and he would be wise to refer immediately to a clinical marriage counselor rather than touch what might well be a hornets' nest.

Infertility can create marital problems. If the infertility can be corrected, the condition is surely a problem for the doctor. If the infertility cannot be corrected, the question is a difficult one for most doctors to handle, and they should consider referral for counseling.

Patients' problems with their parents present themselves from time to time to intrude upon the relationship that the obstetrician wishes to build with his patient. He has to be able to break through a mother's overinvolvement with her daughter to achieve this. Postpartum psychoses seem to appear more often where the girl is overly dependent upon her mother and is overwhelmed with the new responsibility which she feels incapable of handling. The doctor needs to question how far he can go in helping such a girl emotionally.

The fact is that the busy physician can do little marriage counseling as a practical matter, though he may be motivated and knowledgeable. The busy doctor cannot devote an hour to one patient and ignore the needs of others who are waiting. Indeed, it is questionable whether he should, considering the present shortage of doctors. On the other hand, he may devote half a day a week to dealing with special problems; at most, he takes on the role of traffic director, sending patients to other physicians, psychiatrists, or marriage counselors.

Until now, few medical schools have attempted to train their students in marriage counseling or any other kind of counseling. Recently, in some schools, curriculum changes are being undertaken to make room for the behavioral sciences. What is more appalling and not very widely recognized is how little many physicians know about the psychology of sex. They can teach the physiology of sex but few have any knowledge of the feelings involved. Dr. Sophia Kleegman, a pioneer in modern marriage counseling and an obstetrician-gynecologist on the teaching staff of the New York University Medical School, sought for years to give a course there on sex in marriage before she was enabled to do so. Her battle cry is a good one: "Educate the educators."

The doctor, at best, has little counseling training, little time to spend on counseling and, no doubt, little interest in protracted marriage counseling. As one of a team of professionals involved in keeping people healthy, he cooperates with psychiatrists, analysts, marriage counselors, ministers, and social workers. The more knowledge of counseling he gains, the more able he will be to know when and to whom to refer. The physician, as a completely authoritarian figure to the patient, has the responsibility of helping him find the many roads to health. If the physician cannot take responsibility for a marriage and follow that responsibility through, he is obligated to refer the patient. The marriage counselor, to whom he refers, must cooperate and know his own limits and role.

THE PSYCHIATRIST

Whereas the focus of marriage counseling is on marital interaction and interpsychic problems, that of psychiatry is on the individual's intrapsychic life. It is apparent that treating just the individual problems of husband and wife can in many cases be as limiting as just treating the marital interaction. A much better solution would seem to be to treat what a client is complaining about plus what other problems he may have that may be destructive to his well-being. As the number of psychiatrists oriented to marriage counseling increases (it is growing slowly), the treatment opportunities for troubled couples will be that much greater.

Free association is an essential element of analytic theory, the cardinal rule being that the person says whatever comes to mind, however shaming or embarrassing it may be. Traditional psychoanalytically oriented psychiatrists generally believe that joint sessions serve to add a dimension to the individual spouse's resistance to free association, inhibiting him from freely disclosing feelings, attitudes, and fantasies that most intimately concern himself and his marriage. By holding joint sessions, the therapist, in effect, has joined with the patient-spouse to fence in certain dimensions of the latter's pathology. Furthermore, if the therapist does succed in drawing out important material, it may help the patient but harm the marriage by making his spouse aware of his hostile attitudes, adulterous fantasies, and the like. Psychiatrists, therefore, feel that an inherent conflict is set up in the treatment situation so that the therapist is unable to help both patient and marriage.

This difficulty that psychiatrists find in treating conflicted marriages would appear to be self-generated. The clinical marriage counselor's experience indicates that there does not have to be this either/or approach, but that generally both the joint session and the individual session can be used, depending on need. Aside from using the joint session for treatment of marital interaction, the therapist can gain more insight into underlying attitudes, noting behavioral effects between husband and wife that cannot be seen clearly in individual sessions.

If spouses develop a trusting relationship with the counselor, there need not be much fencing in of pathology, if any—pathology can be explored and treated, if necessary, in individual sessions on the basis of the rule that what is said by one spouse is not to be repeated to the other. In contrast, the rule of joint sessions is that what is said should be constructively discussed by the couple when they are alone. Obviously, the marriage would be damaged if every feeling and fantasy were permitted to be aired in the joint session. Many people marry with the mistaken idea that they have gained a confidant to whom anything can be said, only to find that this does not quite work out. Indeed, where is it written that every feeling or fantasy has to be expressed just because it comes to mind? In marriage counseling, the joint session is for constructive use, not for the venting of wrath, and can serve as a model for behavior. The marital relationship, being more intense than any other social relationship, requires controlled behavior if it is to be successful—behavior that many people have to learn. Narcissistic feelings must be restrained in favor of feelings of affection and concern for others. Much help may have to be given in this direction in individual sessions, and the joint sessions can be used to crystallize the point dynamically.

This intense intimacy that spouses desire and expect often prevents them from recognizing that one of the factors that can facilitate a marriage is the right of privacy—there has to be space in togetherness. This too can be pointed out in the joint session. I remind them of what Kahlil Gibran has to say about marriage in *The Prophet*:*

> Give your hearts, but not into each other's keeping.
> For only the hand of Life can contain your hearts.
> And stand together yet not too near together:
> For the pillars of the temple stand apart,
> And the oak tree and the cypress grow not in each other's shadow.

Marriage counseling, it is sometimes said, is not therapy in depth. As already observed, this depends substantially on who the therapist is as well as the client and the kind of setting in which it is being done. Perhaps it should be noted further that intensive therapy does not always have to do with the unconscious but rather the amount of stimuli the counselor can create and tolerate in a session. The reason that many therapists do only individual therapy is that there is a limited amount of affect involved in dealing with one person. Some can do very well with just one person but are unable to handle the stimuli aroused by the number of persons in joint or group sessions. Therapists who are not comfortable in such sessions may develop the rationale that dealing with two people jointly is not work in depth.

There is a pragmatic question that needs to be asked in every case and that is: "How can *this* person, marriage, or family be treated?" If the therapist first consulted cannot deal with all that is necessary, then he must consider referral. The psychiatrist who is not interested in doing marriage counseling should be able to

---

* Kahlil Gibran, *The Prophet*, Knopf, 1964, p. 16.

say to a husband or wife whose marriage is disturbed, "See if your marriage can be stabilized, then come back and we will proceed." This is the counterpart of the marriage counselor's referral to the psychiatrist.

There are at least four instances in which it is clear that the clinical marriage counselor should refer to the psychiatrist: first, if medication is seen as a necessary part of treatment; second, if either spouse needs hospitalization; third, if the client presents serious psychosomatic symptoms; fourth, if there are suicidal gestures on the client's part. The psychiatrist is in a much better position to deal with the suicide problem because his role is more culturally defined and he is legally protected, by and large, whereas the marriage counselor is not. The marriage counselor needs to be as secure as possible in regard to any gesture a client may make if he is to benefit the client. Since suicide will create an uncomfortable situation for the marriage counselor, too much anxiety may be created in him by a client's suicidal gestures for the marriage counselor to be of any help, and so he should refer.

As a clinical marriage counselor, my relationships with psychiatrists indicate that psychiatry and marriage counseling can be a successful joint venture, depending on the philosophy of the psychiatrist and the marriage counselor. A good marriage counselor seeks psychiatric supervision. The psychiatrist's supervision of the marriage counselor gives the latter a depth of insight and clinical awareness that can only be beneficial to clients. As a practical matter, psychiatric supervision serves to protect marriage counselors legally in states where they are not licensed.

Where the marriage counselor is able to obtain a psychiatric evaluation of clients, it can prove valuable in planning treatment. However, timing is important, and clients should be sent for psychiatric evaluation only after their relationship with the marriage counselor has been established.

When it becomes necessary to refer a client for psychiatric treatment, the marriage counselor might do well to have an established professional relationship with several psychiatrists whom he knows will cooperate with him in terms of the marriage and not put the referred spouse into therapeutic isolation. Since the marriage counselor is continuing with the other spouse, he needs to feel free to confer with the psychiatrist and be able with his consent to call the referred spouse in for occasional joint sessions to further the resolution of the problems of the marital relationship.

## THE MINISTER

Historically, the minister was expected to help the members of his congregation with their personal and marital problems. His basic model of operation required that he go into the homes of those with whom he was concerned in order to help in times of crisis and distress. The modern minister continues, because of this, to have the advantage of a natural entrée into the homes of his congregants since their image of him is still that of one who will help them in their times of trouble.

According to Harrop A. Freeman, approximately 50 per cent of the troubled turn to their minister for all kinds of help, so that he spends 40 per cent of his time counseling, has few men clients, prefers to see and has the greatest success with twenty-five-year-old to fifty-year-old women, particularly if the latter are younger than he. The problems that present themselves to the clergyman predominantly concern the family and marital relations.*

As previously discussed, the first and more obvious dimension of marriage counseling focuses on intervention in the crisis and the temporary stabilization of the marriage, during which a certain amount of education, guidance, and support may be attempted. Whereas the clinical marriage counselor sets out to accomplish this "false peace" with the purpose of temporarily freeing husband and wife to probe more deeply into their marital and personal conflicts, ministers with little or no clinical training tend to make this temporary truce their ultimate goal.

Many ministers are successful in intervening in crisis situations because their general training orients them to situational and educational help. Furthermore, the minister's role makes him a natural for this kind of limited marital and family counseling because of the ease with which he can enter the home. He is enabled thereby to discover what the family members do individually and as a group, and to develop insight into the activities that are disturbing family equilibrium. He can usually,

---

* Harrop A. Freeman, *Legal Interviewing and Counseling*, American Casebook Series, West, 1964, pp. 244–246.

within his ministerial program, give a troubled marriage support and an educational type of help once a week for a limited number of sessions. This arrangement permits ventilation and catharsis so that, depending on his ability, he may eventually be able to open up some communication between husband and wife. He may even help them begin to explore some of their attitudes and behavior.

Some might tend to call what the clinically untrained minister does a patchwork job, and so it is. However, what he does has its place in the help troubled families need, provided that the minister is aware of his clinical limitations, stays within them, and has recourse to referral.

Ministers who enter training programs in pastoral care can be —and should be—suitably trained to cope with marital distress within the second dimension of counseling—the basic dynamics of the wide range of interaction found in marriage. Such training would equip ministers to achieve a somewhat more satisfactory resolution of the marital difficulties that present themselves in their parishes. Once they understand what marital partners can do to each other, they can begin to help them see what they must do if they want to keep their marriages.

Marriage-counseling training within the pastoral care program should do much toward helping ministers make the premarital counseling so many are attempting today a more meaningful and worth while experience. Most ministers do a large percentage of their premarital counseling just prior to the ceremony. At best, the most significant value of this kind of premarital counseling lies in the establishment of a relationship between the minister and the couple so that they will know where to go if they get into trouble in the future.

With training, the parish minister stands in a unique position to do much in the way of family education which is to be distinguished from premarital counseling. Family education is a preparation for marriage that is not limited to a few sessions at a time when young people are not in the mood to listen but, instead, spans their lifetime. If he has a good working relationship with his teachers, workers, and congregants, the minister can make certain that emphasis is placed on the positive values of human life and on how they can be reflected in marriage. The minister who has an involved relationship with his congregation may, through his sermons, personal contacts, and programs, inculcate values so that he is giving the young members of his congregation a form of premarital counseling as they grow. Then, when the need for actual premarital counseling arises, young couples will seek much more from him than a mere official stamp of approval for the ceremony.

Recent years have seen the development of the pastoral counselor, a minister so clinically and psychologically trained as to be able to do intensive counseling, with the primary focus, like that of the psychiatrist, usually on the intrapsychic level. The assumption is that when the client's feelings are clarified and he feels better about himself, he will be able to do better in interpersonal relationships and do the right thing for himself in regard to social institutions, including his marriage. In contrast, as we have seen, the clinical marriage counselor's primary focus is on intervention in marital crisis and on the interpersonal, particularly on marital interaction, even though he is clinically equipped to treat, if necessary, those dimensions of the marriage involving the unconscious relationship between husband and wife and the intrapsychic conflicts of each. When treatment of the latter two dimensions is in order, the marriage counselor, should he decide to continue treatment himself, never lets go of the primary focus —the marriage. The theory is that simultaneous treatment of the marriage and the individual spouses will result in reciprocal growth. Time and again the marriage counselor finds that as the marital relationship is improved, this helps to resolve or diminish the intrapsychic conflicts enough to permit individual growth. This growth process carries the client away from intense self-involvement so that he is able to become more constructively involved in the marital relationship, thereby helping it and his partner, as well as himself, to a better life.

It is certainly a paradoxical turnabout from the moralistic approach adopted by ministers in the past for those who have been trained in pastoral counseling to become exclusively devoted to therapeutic concern for the feelings of the disturbed person. This means that they tend to leave the disturbed person's conflicts of behavior and attitudes involving other people and institutions for resolution at some undetermined future time when that person emerges from the therapeutic process. On the other hand, any clinical marriage counselor who is exclusively concerned with interpersonal conflicts and conflicts with institutions sets himself on the road to becoming a zealot. I have noted that the marriage counselor's goal is to help each partner toward sufficient personal growth and ego strength so as to be able to make a decision either for the marriage or against it and to take responsibility for that decision. (To this point, my own view is that to be really competent a clinical marriage counselor must also be a divorce counselor able to help those who divorce with their many feelings and problems.)

Because of the demand for and need for help presented by marriages today, it becomes imperative that pastoral-counseling training programs include a schedule of instruction in clinical marriage counseling. Even more valuable and less obvious, perhaps, is the fact that such training, since it focuses primarily on the interpersonal, with an underpinning of education and clinical experience involving the intrapsychic, can help pastoral counseling to achieve a balance between psychiatric emphasis on the intrapsychic and emphasis on counseling interpersonal and behavioral conflicts. Some mistakenly consider that these two theories of therapeutic technique with their differences in focus are mutually exclusive, but all this does is create another conflict, with those who seek help becoming the innocent victims. A "marriage" of these two theories, rather than any cleavage, must be achieved in the interest of the realistic needs of those who seek counsel.

Inevitably, questions concerning religion arise in marriage-counseling sessions. Ministers, of course, are particularly trained to give specific help in this direction, provided that there is awareness of the differences in the ways of life that different religions propound. Pastoral counselors doing marriage counseling must be prepared, as are lay marriage counselors, to refer to the appropriate clergyman when necessary.

When we think of religion we think, among other things, of values and morals. Furthermore, anyone who does marriage counseling is proclaiming that he is a moral person, since he must believe in the institution of marriage to want to help those with marital troubles. The minister, more than anyone else, is expected to be a moral person to whom one can turn for help with marriage and family problems. He may, in addition, be well trained clinically for marriage and family counseling but, as with the clinical marriage counselor, this training is meant only to enhance what positive values he has as a person—not to give him a rationalization for his negative attitudes. He cannot simply expect to be a representative of values; he must really believe in them for himself and his children, for this is what will ultimately come through and count with the people he sees. The compassion he displays to those he counsels will reflect the sincerity of his belief in the constructive, positive elements of human personality and growth, of his deep belief in life, of his love, hope, and faith—all this, despite his awareness of all the destructive elements that reality can present. He will hold out a kind but firm hand, and the troubled will take that hand to help themselves out of the morass of their despair onto the road that leads toward life and well-being. His help will be imparted not so much by means of transference and countertransference, of which he may be aware as a trained counselor, as by the development of a human relationship established and maintained on a realistic basis, within which a working rapport is achieved.

The extent and the intensity of the marriage counseling done in actual practice by the minister trained in pastoral counseling depends very much on the professional setting in which he finds himself and his personal interests and abilities. The small parish does not always lend itself to extended counseling because of the parishioners' potential embarrassment, particularly when marriage counseling is sought, whereas the large city congregations are far from personal and even employ ministers to be pastoral counselors primarily. What the minister does will also be tempered by whether he presents himself as a pastoral counselor first and minister second, or the other way around, or as both simultaneously. In any case, whether he wears the pastoral counselor's hat for the most part or not, those who seek his help generally tend to see him as a minister to whom they have gone for counsel.

This is not any different, I would think, from Jewish congregations that have two rabbis, one for the ministerial role and one for the educational role. There is no dichotomy—both men are rabbis. Nor is it different among lawyers who specialize in criminal law, tax law, realty law, matrimonial law, and so on— they are basically lawyers who have more closely defined their roles. The same is true of doctors, of course. Finally, underlying all the specialization and definition of roles is always something that must never be forgotten—what the person himself really is.

The additional skill of pastoral counseling, whether specifically used in the congregation or not, means that the minister has the groundwork for insight into the needs of those seeking his help. Also, he has established, at the very minimum, a referral system on which he can depend. He should, as much as possible, know the professionals to whom he refers personally. He should ensure, too, that his parishioners do not feel rejected by the referrals he may make, but believe that the minister has their welfare in mind when, for example, if they have a troubled marriage, he refers them to a marriage counselor.

## THE SOCIAL WORKER

There are more similarities than differences between the social worker's approach to marriage counseling and that of the clinical marriage counselor. Whatever differences there may be are due to personalities, with the disciplines coloring and enhancing the personalities. Since both disciplines are trained to do the job, there is usually no need for referral between them. However, there may be moments when the clinical marriage counselor finds it necessary to consult with the social worker about certain practical matters—placement for a retarded child, foster home placement, the problem of where to locate an aged parent, adoption.

The social-work profession is completely identified with crisis. People go to social-work agencies and offices exactly as they go to marriage-counseling clinics and offices—in utter distress, feel-ing the long brewing difficulties over the many years that on that day, at that hour, just cannot be borne any longer, and projecting their dilemma on either the situation or the marital partner. This is a far cry from the applicant for mental health services who is prepared to give his contribution to his problem, or the applicant to a psychiatrist's office who is fully prepared to settle down to self-investigation over a long period of time, prepared emotionally, mentally, and financially, even when putting up much resistance.

The social caseworker is trained to have two particular skills. More than anyone else, he is oriented to helping people with environmental adjustments and, in recent years, with internal adjustments. Such professional skills obviously lead toward good marriage counseling. Because the social worker is trained in the family approach, he has a somewhat broader focus than that of some clinical marriage counselors. He is trained to seek the essence of the family's situation. Rather than ask a spouse how he got along with his parents, the social worker asks how is he getting along with his children, deliberately focusing on the here and now and seeking a broader sense than the couple—not just how husband and wife are getting along but how this affects their children; in what kind of environment they live—how many rooms the family lives in, what the sleeping arrangements are (especially if there is a problem with money), who else lives in the family. These facts may not be brought up by the couple and yet may be important for the counselor to know in counseling them in their marital difficulties. In other words, the social worker emphasizes the horizontal approach and then seeks the vertical.

The clinical marriage counselor tends to integrate the whole and goes backward as well as forward—how a wife relates to her children affects her relationship to her husband, but how she feels about men because of her feelings about past relationships also affects their marriage. Perhaps not enough emphasis is placed on the "horizontal" approach by marriage counselors and they should seek the broader picture sought by social workers.

---

Trends for the future indicate that eventually all the helping professions will include in their training programs education to help their students become aware of and understand marriage counseling problems when they meet them in practice and be able to know when to refer. More and more, the clinical marriage counselor will be a much needed specialist. He will have to be a professional person who will be discriminatingly able to encompass and embody the techniques, processes, procedures and orientations of individual, family, and group psychotherapy developed by all the different helping professions. He will have to be able to function not only in a clinic or a private office but also in hospitals or courts, or on campuses, and wherever else he is needed.

There are many different ways therapists can function in therapeutic situations; certainly all have the right to their differences of opinion with the expectation that they will command respect. No one profession, professional person or professional technique is ever clearly so right that there can be only "either/or" in helping people in trouble; rather, there has to be "both/and." Far from being superficial, marriage counseling has a great potential for intensive treatment depending on who is doing it, with whom and in what setting.

# 13

# *Marriage Counseling*
# *in a Clinic or Private Office*

The setting for marriage counseling, whether it be a clinic or family agency, a court * or a private office, influences the counselor's approach, since each has its unique characteristics, although all settings are basically interested in helping keep marriages and families together.

In recent decades marriage counseling in clinics and family agencies seems to have gradually evolved from the more limited casework approach of crisis intervention to concern about how two people behave toward each other consciously (interaction); then to the unconscious reasons why they interact as they do (interpsychic factors); and, in psychiatrically oriented marriage counseling, to the unconscious feelings of each partner (intrapsychic factors). The result is that more and more psychiatrists are being used in marriage counseling for purposes of clinical training and for case consultation and supervision, whereas formerly they generally tended to be involved only by way of referral. In the movement toward consideration of the whole marriage, the process has come to involve a team approach, so that other professionals functioning in or connected with a clinic may be consulted—the clinical psychologist, the physician, the lawyer, the social worker, and the clergyman.

Because of the demands made on the personnel in clinics, process in a clinic is frequently affected by this team approach, so that clients are apt to see several workers before settling down with one. No one person can be all things to those with

---

* See Chapter 16 for a discussion of conciliation proceedings in the courts.

marital difficulties, and there is often need for the help of other professionals, but at the outset it is most important for the troubled spouses to see only one person. They are divided enough already, and what they need at first is exposure to one person who can act as a unifying force and who can eventually direct them to other professionals for help if necessary. Experience indicates that it is often confusing and even divisive for a couple to consult different counselors. Except for special clinical reasons significant to the needs of a particular couple, the philosophy of marriage counseling demands that every effort be made for one counselor to work with both husband and wife from the outset.

In private practice, the marriage counselor faces the constant need to crystallize his philosophy of marriage counseling without the confrontation by his peers that he experiences in a clinic—his clients are his challenge, and his psychiatric supervisor his stay, but above all he must answer to himself for the therapeutic help he administers. He has a freedom to develop his philosophy, theories, and techniques that he may not have in a clinic, and he must take responsibility for this freedom.

Marriage counseling procedures as practiced in clinical and private settings vary, of course, with the particular clinic and the particular marriage counselor. The following discussion is based primarily, although not exclusively, on my experience in a mental-health clinic and in private practice.

INITIAL INTERVIEW

When people seek marriage-counseling help, both partners are given an appointment as quickly as possible for an initial interview of two consecutive sessions. When they appear, the counselor might ask which one would like to be seen first or whether they would prefer to be seen together. Frequently the spouse who wishes to be seen first has some serious grievance and wants to tell his story first to gain an advantage and win the counselor to his side. The marriage counselor, alert to this possibility, is careful to maintain objectivity. If they choose to come in together, the joint session is best kept to a minimum, allowing just enough time for each to voice what he believes to be the problem. After this, one is asked to wait outside while the other is seen alone. The theory here is that distressed husbands and wives struggle to voice their deepest feelings in front of each other in an initial interview and are likely to voice their hostilities instead, which can accomplish nothing but further hurt and destruction, especially since a third party is present.

In the initial individual sessions it is important for the counselor to establish who referred the clients and why. (There can be considerable difference, for example, between the case referred by a lawyer and that referred by a minister.) It is also important for him to learn whether one partner determined to seek marriage counseling and the other acquiesced willingly or with resentment, or whether both made the decision, since this gives some indication of the motivation each has toward doing something about keeping the marriage. The counselor then attempts to establish what the problem is in terms of the marriage and of the individuals. Most problems are so urgent that clients tend to plunge right into them and begin to talk, which allows for catharsis and ventilation of feelings. If a client does this, the wise counselor starts where the client is with his feelings. If, however, the client finds difficulty in getting started in the initial session, the counselor may help him to explore this, but usually the counselor asks questions and supports the client as he stresses how the two of them, together, are going to attempt to resolve the client's problem.

In any case, it is important for the marriage counselor to get a clear statement of what each partner feels is the problem; when he feels it began—that is, when he noted the onset of change in his spouse's behavior—and how each has tried to deal with the problem. It is at this point that the counselor can perceive each spouse's capacity for awareness, insight, imagination, and responsibility. Finally, the question to be answered is where the client sees himself and his spouse in all this. In most cases each spouse comes in pointing his finger at the other; rarely does the client point a finger at himself. It is in this area that the extent of communication, projection versus reality, and understanding of the self and of the relationship is revealed.

The identities of husband and wife as individuals must be explored at least superficially in the initial interview—the marriage counselor must know with whom he is concerned. To accomplish this, he obtains all kinds of information including the personal histories of husband and wife and the history of their marriage. As he does this, he observes how questions are answered about parents, siblings, and other relationships—words may communicate one thing, tone of voice and behavior another.

Having seen husband and wife individually, the marriage counselor calls them both in for a short joint session to clarify his role, the kind of help he can and cannot provide, and the confidential nature of his relationship with each partner. In summary, the counselor advises that he is not a judge or referee; he is only someone who will now represent their marriage and, from as objective a standpoint as possible, will reflect back to husband and wife what they are doing to each other. They are told they will not be permitted to use the counselor to attack each other but only to help each other. Everything that each says in individual sessions will remain confidential unless there is agreement that the counselor can speak of it to the other spouse or the counselor feels it is something that can be used constructively. Neither spouse is permitted to seek information about what went on in the individual sessions, lest disclosure be made out of context and so be misjudged. On the other hand, everything that is said in joint sessions is to be common property and can be discussed by husband and wife when they are by themselves, providing they can do this constructively. The marriage counselor may discuss with husband and wife how they feel about being in a counseling situation, since some clients, particularly men, believe that there is an implication of weakness or lack of capacity to use their intelligence and that the marriage counselor will have the power of a judge and reject them for their weaknesses.

Finally, arrangements are made for future sessions in light of a treatment plan. This is based on an evaluation of the problems the marriage counselor has already shared with the clients in either individual or joint sessions. The counselor may disclose in the initial session, either directly or through suggestion, some of the underlying dynamics that make each spouse function as he does in the marital interaction. Clients can accept this at this first contact if they feel the marriage counselor to be supportive, kindly, and objective. The arrangements depend on the urgency of the case and are shifted according to the needs of the clients as treatment proceeds. Because so many cases tend to have an emergency quality about them, the marriage counselor makes every effort to stop the bleeding at the initial interview, even if it is sometimes at the expense of history-taking or of getting involved in diagnosis. He may become active and, if need be, directive in order to accomplish this.

### INTAKE PROCESS

As can be seen, the marriage counselor hopes to achieve much in the initial interview. If he does not, his safety valve is the intake process, which may last three to six sessions. During this time he continues to work with the presenting problems, but attempts to reach a tentative assessment of the marital inter-action and pathologies. He may make use of psychological testing to enhance his understanding of each spouse and to help each eventually to turn the finger back on himself and see his role in the problem more realistically. In a mental health clinic, or even in private practice, the counselor may have husband and wife evaluated by a psychiatrist. He then makes a tentative prognosis and sets the goals for treatment. In this period, on the other hand, he may determine to refer a spouse showing obvious signs of deep pathology and will seek to motivate him for psychiatric treatment, while continuing with the other spouse in marriage counseling.

The focus in the intake process usually remains on the situational and how it affects the marital relationship. It is the rare client, as we have seen, who seeks help with his marriage and can take anything more at the time. He wants help with what is going on right now with his spouse. He is not ready to accept any suggestion that his whole personality may have to be reworked and his whole life investigated and rehabilitated—and, again, the fact is this is not always necessary or advisable.

In the event that the counselor is seeing only one spouse, he refuses to accept complaints against the absent spouse, nor does he permit himself to be drawn into the position of being a gossip or a one-sided court. At best, treating one partner is treating only half a marriage. I make it a point during the intake process to try to get the other in, either through the one whom I am seeing or through direct contact. My experience has been that about 70 per cent do come in and are frequently anxious to tell their side of the story. The counselor must be aware that it is not unusual for a client to say his spouse will not come in because of fear of what that spouse might reveal about him or because it would mean sharing a relationship that is becoming quite comforting. The theory behind calling in the other spouse early in the marriage-counseling process is that the longer the marriage counselor waits to do this, the harder it will be for him to build a relationship with the second spouse, who is likely to feel that the counselor is only on the side of the spouse being seen. In other forms of therapy, spouses are frequently called in as collaterals at a later date to help the therapist and his client in the therapeutic process; in marriage counseling, on the other hand—and this is an essential point— the other spouse is never a collateral* since both spouses are directly responsible for the marriage.

In the course of the intake process the relationship and working rapport between marriage counselor and client are initiated and established. It is also essential to establish the concept that, as the counseling proceeds and the clients gain insight, understanding, and awareness, they must eventually accept the responsibility to do something about what they have learned— they can no longer plead ignorance or use the defense of anger and develop into armchair philosophers.

PSYCHOLOGICAL TESTING

As we have seen, the marriage counselor, more than any therapist, looks to the healthy aspects of the individual spouses and their marriage as a means of resolving the difficulties presented. He asks many questions to this end: How strong an ego does each spouse have? Is the spouse's difficulty only with the marriage, or is there difficulty in other areas? What are each spouse's expectations? In what is he disappointed? How does each handle disappointment? How much confusion is there as to roles? What is the extent of their devotion to each other?

---

* "Collateral" as used here refers to a person who has an indirect relationship to the client's difficulty.

What are their values? Their goals? Their hopes? Their dreams? How much of their difficulty is due to situational distress? How much is due to the treadmill they have gotten onto and from which they need to be extricated?

A number of marriage-evaluation tests help to supply some of the answers. Many counselors find them useful. However, in a recent interview with me, a doctoral student investigating the matter for his thesis produced findings that indicated that clinically trained marriage counselors able to go into some intra-psychic depth did not use these tests, turning instead to the clinical psychologist for the administration of a battery of tests ranging from I.Q. to the Rorschach.

The clinical psychologist seeks to uncover the pathological aspects of personality, whereas the marriage counselor looks for the healthy and sees the cross section of what is happening to the client at the present time. This being the case, why should a marriage counselor use psychological testing as part of his treatment plan?

My experience has been that psychological testing can be most helpful when the client is properly prepared for it, and if the testing is put into its proper place in the treatment as part of the process. There is something about the test situation that makes the results more readily respected by a great many clients, although not by all. Psychological testing can be a dynamic experience for clients in marital distress, cutting through many feelings and defenses and awakening them to core problems with a clarity that might take many counseling sessions to achieve. Since time is so often of the essence in marriage-counseling cases, this can be most helpful.

The testing often breaks through the miasma of accusations so that the pointed finger each spouse is directing at the other turns inward and husband and wife are enabled at long last to sit down and, with help, take a good, long look at themselves. The depth of pathology is rarely equal in both spouses—usually the pathology is more severe in one than it is in the other— and the tests may indicate that the clinically healthier-looking spouse is the sicker of the two. The objective appraisal of the psychological tests can do an enormous job in aiding the marriage counselor to deal with obstructive, unrealistic, or highly intellectualized self-deceptive types. Lack of communication is frequently involved in marriage-counseling cases, and the test experience frequently has a way of opening up the lines of communication between husband and wife.

For the marriage counselor the tests are not only an X-ray of the pathology of the individual spouses but of their marital interaction. The marriage counselor uses the tests to get at major sources of friction, to help each spouse accept himself and his spouse, and to show them how to handle their relationship more constructively. Some psychologists put together the individual pathologies of husband and wife to depict the resultant inter-psychic pathology in the marriage, which can help marriage counselors understand more fully what is behind the marital interaction. However, the experienced clinical counselor is likely to use only the description of each spouse's intrapsychic problems as the basis for determining for himself what the interpsychic elements are.

People in marital difficulty often feel certain that the differences in their personalities are the cause of their difficulty. They find it hard to see that, paradoxically, their problem is really due to the similarities in their personalities and that only their dynamics are different. They find it hard to comprehend, too, that they both have the same frustrated need for affection, but it is only that each spouse seeks its fulfillment differently. The marriage counselor, using psychological tests constructively to indicate the similarity of need attempts thereby to institute growth in the relationship. Intelligence tends to marry intelligence. Even when the woman is not as educated as her husband, the innate intellectual potential generally proves itself to be more or less equal. Yet, in many such cases, the wife feels intellectually inferior to the husband so that it becomes a basic problem between them. In other cases, she has been sold the idea of how inferior she is to her educated husband. Clients often place more emphasis on problems of their intelligence than they do on those of their emotions. Since the test findings as to intelligence and intellectual ability are likely to show both spouses to be fairly equal, this can prove to be a decisive turning point in marriage-counseling cases. Clients begin to realize that they are worthy of setting educational and work goals that heretofore they did not think they could achieve. Once this begins to happen, they are able gradually to get off their partner's back, stop some of their demands, and achieve some satisfaction independently for themselves.

In some cases, at the time of meeting and decision to marry, the developmental pattern of both spouses was almost equal. They fitted into each other's needs very well at the time, but with the years one progresses and the other regresses and there is an imbalance. Trouble in such marriages frequently crystallizes somewhere between eighteen and twenty-five years of marriage, since this is the beginning of the empty-nest period and is a crucial time for marital problems to come to the fore. Testing that shows temperament, personality structure, defenses, ego strengths and weaknesses, and concepts of masculinity and femininity can be of great aid in helping such marriages.

At no point does the clinical psychologist who gives the test become involved in marriage counseling as such. He stands aside and focuses on the person. The psychologist administers the tests blindly, without discussing the case with the marriage counselor. However, if the clients have had some counseling sessions and have developed some insight and the psychologist finds them attuned, he may make a point on which the marriage counselor has already focused. This tends to reassure the client so that he gains confidence in the therapeutic procedure. Clients are aware of the objectivity of testing and are more likely to accept what the marriage counselor has to say later if the insights already advanced are borne out by tests. The psychologist's role in a marriage-counseling case is to reinforce the marriage counselor and motivate the clients to work things out together. He observes patterns but he never tries overtly to fit them into the marriage.

The success of testing depends on the marriage counselor's timing of the psychologicals, his preparation of the clients, his understanding of the language of the particular psychologist, and the way in which the counselor is able to use the results in counseling sessions.

After the marriage counselor has intervened in the crisis, developed a relationship to the clients, and begun to deal with their problems as presented in the marriage, he can suggest their taking psychologicals. To bombard distressed marital clients with psychologicals before they feel that any help is being given them with their problems might alienate them or frighten them off. When the time is appropriate, the counselor conveys to both spouses the fact that their marital difficulties are a symptom of personality disturbances. He explains the testing and makes the point that the results act as an X ray that will help both clients and counselor to see more clearly the emotional problems with which they have already begun to deal.

He may indicate that no one test is of too much significance and that the results of a battery of tests have validity only when matched with the counselor's clinical observations, giving those observations another dimension. Reserving the diagnostic labels for professional use, the counselor tells the client that he will read the results to him and that he will refer to the report as treatment proceeds. The testing results of each spouse are read to him alone. They are confidential between the client and the counselor unless the client cares to have his spouse know them. If he does, the reasons are explored and then, if the result is expected to be constructive, they are read in a joint session.

For the testing results to have depth of meaning to the counselor, he must already have formulated his clinical findings on the positive and healthy as well as the negative and sick aspects of the clients and their interaction. When the results come through he must be able to understand what the psychologist is saying; for this reason, communication between psychologist and marriage counselor needs to be clear, to accomplish which they must have conferences on the results of many tests over a long period of time. Only then can the marriage counselor feel free to use the tests as he sees fit.

As for myself, having captured the pathology described, assisted by the tests, I then tend to put away the testing results the better to focus dynamically and constructively on the human beings before me and what they do to themselves and to each other.

INDIVIDUAL AND JOINT SESSIONS AS COUNSELING CONTINUES

Individual and joint sessions are used in the ongoing process of marriage counseling. The focus in individual sessions is kept on attitudes, feelings, and behavior that precipitate emotional stress in the client and in his spouse, while hostility is reduced by ventilation. At the same time, the marriage counselor helps each spouse toward an understanding of unresolved early experiences that are causing psychic difficulties in the marriage. Psychological support is given as each spouse develops insight and objectivity and goes through a reorientation process in regard to his problems and life situation. Re-education and help are given husband and wife toward clarification of role concepts and expectations. Each is helped to develop a new perspective on himself and his marriage and to set and implement long-range goals for himself as well as for the marriage. The counselor particularly tries to help husband and wife reopen and strengthen emotional and verbal communication. This last can be most successfully accomplished in joint sessions.

The general experience of marriage counselors indicates that the dynamics of the joint session can do a great deal for the marital relationship. Aside from enhancing communication, each partner gains even further insight into the painful areas of conflict and has the opportunity to hear what the other's needs are. As the interaction becomes manifest, each can better comprehend what he is doing and how the other reacts.

Joint sessions can be most destructive if not used properly. Not only must the marriage counselor be clear in his purposes—to help with communication, to help the partners recognize what they do to each other and to help them solve mutual problems—he must also make quite certain that these effects are likely to take place. To accomplish this he sets limits within the counseling situation and makes sure that both partners have their hostility under some control and that they trust him. Ugly words said between husband and wife in a joint session before the marriage counselor may take on a significance they might not otherwise have.

The joint session must be carefully structured by the counselor, which, in this context, means establishing the format for dealing with problems in terms of the relationship of the spouses to each other and to the marriage counselor, and of the counselor's relationship to them and to their marriage.

The first element in the structured joint session is authority.

Troubled husbands and wives seek a marriage counselor because he is an authority and is paid for being helpful. This does not mean that they should expect him to be an omnipotent judge, an infallible referee, or a mystic soothsayer, but that people who seek help are not, for the moment, in a position to be co-equals with the marriage counselor, whoever they may be. I am reminded of the help I have given ministers who were in marital difficulty. The first thing I say after I have heard their story and we settle down to considering what can be done is: "We shall talk of many things that you have spoken about in a far more beautiful and brilliant way from the pulpit, but your difficulty seems to develop when you leave your pulpit and go home. Apparently it is hard for you to carry out what you can say so well—this is where I have to help you if I can."

The marriage counselor has the responsibility of fulfilling his role with *benign* authority. When husband and wife are going in different directions, the counselor must take over and point out what is happening and how different their behavior is from what prevails in a good marriage. Spouses in trouble are frequently unable to see eye to eye. As they speak of their life together, with each one treating his version as the truth, I usually comment to them that it is difficult to believe that both were there at the same time. The marriage counselor must help them to reconcile their disparate views of the marriage so that they can see what is happening between them in a more realistic light and with understanding and acceptance of each other's perspective.

Once the marriage counselor's authority is established, both spouses are usually able to accept his analysis of their interaction. He is able to point out how they perform in the marriage —how, for example, they do not come to each other's defense, how neither gives what he wants of the other, how they denigrate each other, how they consciously or unconsciously act out old neurotic patterns with each other. Using gentleness and tact, a "perhaps" or a "maybe," the counselor lays the real story of their lives before them, as it were, so that possibly for the first time they can really see themselves.

Usually the counselor's authority is established early in the relationship. Sometimes this becomes difficult if there is much friction in the marriage and one spouse wants out, for then he treats the counselor as he treats the marriage. If matters get out of hand in joint sessions, the counselor may stop them and see each spouse individually. In any case, the counselor remains in control at all times.

The second constructive element in a structured joint session is respect. The marriage counselor listens respectfully, gathers the facts and feelings, and then presents what he sees and hears as calmly and objectively as possible. He acts as a mirror for the turbulent husband and wife and, therefore, is as impartial as a mirror. If he can reflect with accuracy, intelligence, and insight, the counselor will be able to teach his clients how to differ with each other in a respectful way instead of bickering or battling as they do. This may well introduce an entirely new element into their relationship.

The marriage counselor's emphasis here, obviously, is to demonstrate in joint sessions the value of exercising control over feelings, whatever may be going on in individual sessions. This is the antithesis of the free-associational technique used in individual therapy, in which the person is encouraged to say whatever comes to mind. The marriage counselor does not speak spontaneously in a joint session; he thinks before he speaks and then voices differences respectfully and tactfully. If he does not do this he may well foster disruption. A primary tenet is that if a marriage counselor cannot help, he does not hurt.

Respect involves the channeling of feelings and must be worked out in joint sessions. The joint session must not be used by one spouse to belittle the other. If it is so used, the counselor must step right in and show how resolution of the problem is being hampered. When spouses discuss their differences, the discussion must be without mutual derogation. The marriage counselor must keep this aspect under close scrutiny if much is to be accomplished.

The third element in the joint session is the requirement that the marriage counselor accentuate the positive in the marital interaction. He must be aware of any underlying pathology and be able to determine its extent clinically, but he must not emphasize it in joint sessions—instead, he moves on to using the existing positives. If he sees the need to examine pathology, he does so in the individual sessions; to do so in a joint session is, generally, to disrupt the marriage further. However, there may be times, after some insight has been developed, when an observation by the counselor in individual session, together with dynamic portrayal in a joint session, may, for example, help a woman to understand her husband's limitations sufficiently to reduce her expectations, aware at last that his behavior is not necessarily a rejection of her but something he cannot help.

While the marriage counselor is accentuating the positives in the relationship, he tries to eliminate as much concern as possible over the negatives. If this succeeds in bolstering the warmth and the bond between the spouses, their ability to deal with problems may become stronger, too, so that their need for the counselor can gradually be reduced. Often a person's intentions and motivations are good but his execution is bad, and this is what his spouse is complaining about. To circumvent mutual recrimination, the counselor points out to the complaining spouse that the intent was good and to the recalcitrant spouse just how the execution and behavior might have been different.

The content of the joint session may cover a wide range of topics so that the marriage counselor must set limits if anything is to be achieved. This does not mean that clients cannot talk freely and, if they feel the need, speak about what is bothering them most at the moment, providing they do so with some diplomacy.

Joint sessions are particularly useful if a crisis occurs during marriage counseling, for then steps can be taken toward evolving a joint resolution. They are invaluable in defining problems if there is a gap between the views of husband and wife concerning what is going on, so that a picture can be drawn about which husband, wife and marriage counselor agree. Getting insight into how battles develop helps the couple learn how to prevent them.

Problems of interaction are most frequently interwoven with the specific problems of money, sex, children, in-laws, and so on. The marriage counselor is able to see the problems of interaction in joint sessions. He then frequently uses the technique of confrontation—that is, he uses himself as a mirror to reflect what husband and wife do to each other to help them better understand what goes on between them and what their real problems are. He quickly cuts through the details of external problems presented by the clients to their feelings of anger, derogation, inadequacy, disappointment, and hurt. He shows them how mutual provocation can snowball. Once couples are made aware of this, they are expected to take responsibility for what they have learned about their relationship if they want to keep the marriage. The marriage counselor educates all the time, teaching that people cannot always help losing control and being anxious, and that when this occurs it is a signal to hold tight rather than explode in response, for in this way the marriage and the family can reach greater stabilization.

Paranoid trends in marital interaction frequently need to be resolved. Translated into marriage counseling language, they mean a lack of trust. Many men do not trust women and many women do not trust men. In individual sessions the counselor can pick up what the lack of trust really signifies and bring this out in a joint session so that the spouse who is the target can begin to understand it. Once this spouse is aware that his partner is not vicious but actually fears certain things, or has certain problems that really have nothing to do with him, he can accept the other's behavior with just a little more objectivity so that the marriage counselor can help him begin to rebuild the marital relationship.

In the joint sessions, when the communications lines are being rebuilt, husband and wife are taught to listen to each other in a third dimension that goes beyond hearing what each is saying, to tuning in and understanding the feelings behind what is being said. When spouses are able to add loving cooperation and consideration to this kind of communication, their relationship begins to solidify.

Hostility between spouses is often expressed in psychological terms—the verbiage has become popularized and is very often used to accuse, belittle, or castrate the other spouse. The marriage counselor, knowing the pathology, is nevertheless careful not to use these terms freely and deals with specific issues with the awareness that a person can be simply mistaken instead of disturbed or irresponsible, and that a person can be anxious and worried over a particular life situation without being labeled with psychological terminology.

In dealing with specific problems, the counselor is aware that defining the problem may remove some of the pressure but is not likely to resolve the situation. Defining a financial difficulty, for example, does not overcome a lack of money. There is a tendency to overlook or forget in this psychologically oriented age that stress in a family, which augments the natural irritability of its members, may be due to tangible external factors.

There is no better opportunity for the counselor to observe the interaction between husband and wife, whether good or bad, than in the joint interview. In the joint interview clients can find the way to communication, insight, and understanding of themselves, their roles, and their operation as a unit in marriage —a unit that must be dedicated eventually to common goals rather than to a tug of war between selfish, personal goals. The joint interview demands an active marriage counselor who can structure the sessions for the benefit of the clients and their marital union and not permit them to vent their hostility to the further destruction of their marriage.

### TERMINATION

Ideally, and with some frequency in actual practice, the termination of successful counseling is mutually agreed upon by the couple and the marriage counselor. Not too many specific problems remain with which the counselor can be of help, and the partners are satisfied with the methods by which they have learned to deal with their problems and have become more involved with each other. Their sex life is more satisfactory, and there is a feeling of shared loving and hope. They leave counseling knowing that if they run into difficulties again they should not let them drag on as before and can return to the counselor for help whenever they wish.

On the other hand, termination may occur in a less ideal fashion. It may be premature, as when husband and wife have to move away or when one refuses to come any longer for counseling. In the latter case there is termination of treatment of that spouse but not of the other. Termination may be gradual, and the counselor may in that case indicate that termination will take place at a certain time. Sometimes, on the other hand, a couple suddenly develops a feeling that they can go it alone; the marriage counselor may agree, and termination may take place rather quickly. Other couples may reach a plateau in which no further progress seems to be made, and they and the counselor feel counseling should stop.

In any case, the last session, if at all possible, is usually a joint session in which husband and wife evaluate what they have learned, how they have grown, and what they foresee. They take their leave knowing that they can always return if they feel the need.

# 14

## *Premarital Counseling*

Not too many years ago parents having difficulty with their children hid their troubles behind closed doors. Today it is socially acceptable for parents to seek help when they have disturbed relationships with their children. Since World War II, certainly, the efforts of parents to join in the guidance and welfare of their children have been growing tremendously. This drive by parents to obtain help, together with the guidance of professional workers in psychology and education, has produced a vast number of child-study groups and parent-teacher associations all over the United States.

In more recent years a new demand for help has been voiced by young people themselves—a demand for knowledge and guidance in preparation for marriage. Consequently colleges, churches, community agencies, settlement houses, social agencies, and youth groups have been developing programs in education for dating, courtship, and marriage. What is more, government agencies are doing much to encourage the development of these local resources. Some formal educational programs start in the nursery school and continue through college. Such educational programs are to be distinguished from premarital counseling.

The aim of premarital counseling is to help the healthy with their problems and orientate couples toward further professional help if trouble arises in marriage. Premarital counseling is generally designed to provide preventive therapy against sick marriages and divorce and to promote good marriages. There seems to be no scientifically drawn conclusion as to whether couples receiving such help fare better than those without it. Indeed, there is some doubt among marriage counselors about the actual value of premarital counseling. In such counseling the counselor has to assume that the client has knowledge of the nature of marital conflicts whereas at best such knowledge can only be intellectual and of a second-hand nature. In other words, no matter how much one may learn about marriage in one's original family, it is second-hand knowledge and not first-hand experience of the marital relationship. It is like book learning without life experience. As a result, most premarital counseling is likely to have the limitations of an intellectual exercise.

Though what premarital counseling can be expected to achieve remains questionable, premarital counseling does seem to be something of an answer to the needs of young people and, until proved otherwise, should be encouraged. If such counseling accomplishes nothing more than establishing a professional relationship on which couples may draw if they find themselves in trouble, it is worth intensifying and continuing.

By definition premarital counseling focuses on the relationship between a man and a woman, helps them evaluate that relationship in view of their approaching marriage, and acquaints them with some of the ways in which they can build a fulfilling and successful marriage; or, after evaluation of the relationship, premarital counseling may result in the couple's deciding against the marriage.

The areas of concern in premarital counseling are those that are frequent sources of difficulty in marriage: sex, birth control and children, money and work, in-law relationships, religion, and friends. Beyond this, premarital counseling includes an evaluation of the expectations of the individuals of themselves and each other and the marriage, education and reassurance, and an exploration of any psychological, physical, or emotional differences and handicaps.

All this would seem to be the ideal goal of premarital counseling rather than a definition. The kind of premarital counseling that takes place in actual practice and the nature of its goals depend on who is doing the counseling, his training and philosophy, where and when it is being done, and who is asking for this help and why.

## THE THREE KINDS

Three kinds of premarital counseling have developed: education for marriage, personal (clinical) therapy, and counseling that focuses on immediate preparation for a marriage that is already decided upon.

The trend of family-life education as preparation for marriage is generally away from the use of primarily clinical or pathological materials and toward a more positive emphasis on healthy growth of the individual's capacity for personal and social adjustment. By directing themselves to the healthy, positive, conscious aspects of the personality, courses in education for marriage do not upset potential mates with accounts of the dire things that may happen. Instead, such courses give young people positive images of desirable outcomes and help them to acquire the necessary know-how to achieve them.

This education is much more than the giving of information. In many cases, an emotional re-education is required. For such cases, personal counseling or a dynamic group counseling experience may be offered. Courses in education for marriage and family life also prepare the way for awareness of whether clinical help is needed.

At a recent convention in Philadelphia of the American Association of Marriage Counselors, where the focus was on premarital counseling, one of the conclusions reached was that such counseling seems to go particularly well with courtship and marriage courses on the college campus.

The second kind of premarital counseling is done generally by psychiatrists, psychologists, clinical marriage counselors, and social workers. Couples who seek out such professionals are generally concerned with specific problems that are serious enough to make them wonder about themselves and the marriage they are planning. Some may come seeking premarital counseling, but what they may really want and need is personal therapy. They may even be ready to alter their marriage plans because of the threat presented by the marriage. This group is in the minority of those seeking premarital counseling; the majority are going to carry out their marriage plans whether wise or not.

The third kind of premarital counseling is concerned with the immediate preparation of a couple for marriage in the weeks prior to the ceremony. Such counseling as already noted can be done by physicians. More often, it is done by clergymen, is not therapy and, for the most part, is not undertaken by therapists, simply because couples who are on the verge of getting married usually do not seek out a therapist.

Obviously, clergymen do much premarital counseling because it is to them that most couples go when they want to get married. Some do the premarital counseling carefully and sensitively, others are awkward and inadequate. Clergymen who otherwise do very little counseling often do counseling of this kind, and the likelihood is that the majority of clergymen today do some premarital counseling.

Premarital counseling is a relatively new endeavor for the clergy. In recent years, however, increasing numbers of ministers have been not only offering but requiring some interviews with candidates for marriage. Couples know that a particular minister is not likely to marry them unless they have sessions with him. Such premarital counseling necessarily differs from that received by couples who seek it as a result of an awareness of potential problems in their relationship.

The clergyman usually undertakes a brief series of interviews —no more than half a dozen sessions within the few weeks immediately prior to the wedding—in which he evaluates the backgrounds of the individuals, their relationship, their understanding of the meaning of marriage, their expectations of each other, and their plans. Any existing problems or potential difficulties are explored with a view to helping the couple understand them and to minimize the adverse effects. Occasionally, if the problems cannot be worked out to some extent and accepted by both partners, a decision may be made to call off the marriage or to postpone it.

If the minister is a practicing marriage counselor, he is more aware of the problems to be found in marriage and will tend to do more than explore the areas where there are known difficulties; he will also open up some of the main areas in which problems arise in marriage.

METHOD AND CONTENT

The nature of premarital counseling requires the counselor to structure the sessions and to be more active and directive than in most other forms of counseling unless it be marriage counseling. If the sessions are not structured much time is wasted, and since the counselor is usually working against a deadline, there is little time to waste. Couples may come in as late as a month or less before the wedding and, perhaps, long after the preparations have been made. The counselor, who has to learn quickly what is involved, cannot wait until the couple volunteers information. At the same time, he must remain sensitive to the needs of each couple, dealing with them and their concerns rather than following some outline of what should be covered.

Some counselors bring discussions toward main points by using questionnaires, marriage information schedules and sex knowledge inventories. The large number of these in use are a way of getting information quickly to determine the areas of greatest need. Their main value seems to be in relaxing couples who are especially timid about talking as well as counselors who are inexperienced in interviewing. At best they are not of much use unless they lead into discussion and exploration. Experienced marriage counselors who are able to lead easily into discussion and exploration will probably not find the questionnaires, schedules and inventories too useful. Instead, experienced counselors will structure the sessions themselves, using what material and subject matter they consider most valuable for the particular couple.

The areas of concern in premarital counseling have already been indicated. The following discussion attempts to touch briefly on how those areas might be handled in counseling prior to a marriage.

What does each person expect of the other in relation to marriage, sex, money, in-laws, children, friends, religion, and so on? The counselor might explore the fantasy that each has of the other and of what a spouse is, and might help the couple to do some reality testing. The purpose of this is to narrow the gap, albeit not very much, between the real person and the idealized image each has of the other. If this is successful, it can make adjustment to the marriage a little easier.

What are their attitudes toward money, possessions, and work? Is the bridegroom's income going to be adequate to meet expenses? Will the bride work? How do they plan to handle their money? Budget details should not be gone into unless the couple specifically asks for such details or unless they are uninformed.

The time is usually better spent trying to explore why they cannot set up their own budget.

If there is extreme guilt because there has been premarital sex, the cause of this might be explored, though there usually is not enough time to get into it deeply. The door should be left open for further discussion after marriage if need be. If premarital sex has been unsatisfactory, the causes for this might be discussed briefly and some reassurance given to minimize the problem in marriage. The reassurance might follow the line that the circumstances in which premarital sex takes place are usually unfavorable and marked by a conflict with ideals.

Many a bride today is pregnant at the time of marriage. Feelings of guilt, of being trapped, of anger and resentment, are often contained until things go wrong in the marriage, and then the accusations begin. If the premarital counselor knows of the pregnancy, wisdom may dictate holding individual sessions to explore the feelings of both partners regarding the pregnancy.

Attitudes toward sex in marriage, the use of birth control, and pregnancy are, in a psychological sense, far more important than what actually takes place. If the counselor is uncomfortable in discussing these matters, he should refer the couple to someone else. Family planning needs to be discussed with the couple: Do they share the same ideas about families? Do they expect to start a family? How many children would they like? Are they thinking of birth control measures and if so, have they chosen a method that will be safe, secure, and satisfactory to both of them? The marriage counselor should refer them to their family physician or a planned parenthood center for specific information. If the counselor believes that there may be a problem in the area of pregnancy, he can ask how they would feel if the wife became pregnant. This often discloses hitherto unvoiced attitudes and doubts.

In-laws may be a major cause of concern for some couples and can, indeed, be a source of much trouble unless the relationship is explored and prepared for in premarital counseling. I remember the B's, who had met in their early college days. Their parents had permitted the relationship without voicing any feelings or opinions. Neither set of parents felt however, that their child was marrying well enough. When the B's became engaged, they felt the tensions between their parents, but, being young, they hoped to dispel those tensions somehow by the time of the wedding. Things went from bad to worse and the wedding turned into a fiasco. The families did not speak with each other or with the bride and bridegroom, who never were able to overcome the vendetta and eventually sought a divorce. Their marriage had never been given a chance.

Cultural backgrounds are important and need to be faced and accepted, not rationalized. A young American-born woman of English extraction married a man of Italian stock. In his family any decisions, major or minor, were made by the whole family; the purchase of a lamp was not a decision the couple made, it was the family's prerogative. The young woman had not known this. The repetitive exercise of family prerogative was undermining the marriage. Her husband and his family could not understand why she was disturbed since this had always been their way.

Unresolved, immature feelings toward members of one's own family are not helpful in marriage. The triangle of mother, husband and wife just does not bode well. A man's loyalty to his mother must be subjugated to the loyalty he must build to his wife. Later, when husband and wife know and feel they are at one, they can return together as a unit to his family and to hers. The same is true of the wife's loyalty to her parents.

The premarital counselor performs an important service when he tries to dispel the myth that when people marry they are not becoming involved with each other's families. The statement, "I'm not marrying her family, I'm only marrying her," warrants a vigorous reply from the counselor because it bespeaks a misconception. When two people marry, whether they like it or not, they marry each other's families, too—their parents, their siblings, their aunts and uncles, and their grandparents as well. No matter how far they may move away, each carries his family inside himself. While each may be different from his family in many ways, he will also be like it in many ways. Each had better take a good look at the other's family and recognize that he is marrying into that family, with its culture, customs, and traditions, and that he is going to have to come to terms with it.

On the other side of the coin, the counselor may emphasize that these two people are now leaving their families to establish a new family and that they will owe their first loyalty to the new. If they are not going to be able to make this shift in loyalties, they need to seriously consider whether they are mature enough to marry. To make the change both partners have to be independent of their parents. Should there be indications of overdependence on the one hand or open rebellion on the other, it is not likely that the marriage has a sound basis.

Interfaith marriages are on the increase, as we have seen. To raise questions about a particular marriage on the basis of religion may bring a charge of narrow-mindedness or bigotry. Such a charge is based on shallow thinking if not on outright ignorance of facts and reality. To begin a marriage with a fundamental difference in something as basic as religion, if religion has been important and meaningful to either one or both partners, puts a great strain on husband and wife. Inevitable questions arise: Where to be married and by whom? What will the parents think? Should one convert? In what religion should the children be reared? What will be the effect on the children if the family is divided in religion? There are those who say that if two people are mature enough, significant differences in religion can be worked out, but there is some question whether a couple with the requisite degree of maturity would enter into this kind of marriage in the first place. Again there are exceptions, although the general experience seems to be that many interfaith marriages reflect rather serious emotional or personality difficulties. Young people frequently go into interfaith marriages propelled by unconscious reasons such as the need to rebel against parents or to avoid a man too much like father or a woman too much like mother because of unresolved incestuous feelings. The premarital counselor must make every effort to help both partners understand something of what is involved for themselves, their children and their families.

---

Most couples are on Cloud Nine when they appear for premarital counseling, especially if they seek or are given such help by their minister. His role is often to try to calm them down and get one foot back on earth. Few couples are aware of their problems and few are ready to enter into serious discussion. Most are wrapped up with wedding plans and it is hard for anyone to get through to them. The hope, really, is to set the stage for the future. Months or years later when problems arise, they may remember something that the marriage counselor or minister said and return for help before the situation becomes too serious. Perhaps counselors themselves need some reassurance, too. They should not set their goals in premarital counseling too high. In all short-term counseling there are limitations on what can be accomplished, yet there are some worthwhile things that can be done if a counselor is technically able to work within those limits.

# IV

# *Death of a Marriage*

# 15

## *To Be*
## *or Not To Be Divorced*

A forty-year-old woman client sat in my office one day considering whether she should continue in her nineteen-year-old marriage or get a divorce. "Tell me about divorce," she said. "What can I expect?"

I knew I could easily convey some understanding of the many areas in which she would need to make new adjustments. But how could I communicate the bitterness, the frustration, the despair, the unbearable loneliness, and the deep feelings of failure and isolation that are the experience of most divorced persons?

If she made the decision to divorce, the first thing she would have to do would be to obtain a good matrimonial lawyer who would be her champion in the legal arena against the man she had once promised to live with as one until death did them part. The choice of lawyer would be important, for he would have to take care of the division of property, financial support, custody of the children, and visitation rights and help her determine how to go about obtaining her legal divorce. One could say he would assume the role of undertaker for her dead marriage and make arrangements for the coffin to be closed, sealed, and buried in the cemetery called the court.

This done, then what? What would happen to her? How would she manage her feelings? How would she adjust to life after divorce? Inevitably, she would find that having discarded one set of problems, she was faced with another set in a totally new and potentially difficult life situation.

Left to her own devices, she might help herself by trying pseudo-adjustments like talking too much to others about her divorce to achieve what she would need so much—attention and acceptance while she vented her feelings. After a while she would learn that she had to set limits on this, for even the best of her friends would become bored and turn from her. Or she might resort to the past for consolation and continue to see and even have sexual relations with her ex-husband, despite the divorce. She might try to control his life. Lawyers are constantly used to fulfill this need to control, which is detrimental to both spouses and wastes their lawyers' time. Then again, she might seek to move to another neighborhood or another city. Unfortunately, this too would bring little satisfaction, for sooner or later she would have to come to grips with the realization that one takes one's feelings wherever one goes.

On the other hand, she might begin to idealize the past, particularly the early phase of her marriage, and so begin to feel sorry for herself and not accept her present life. Since my client was forty and attractive, she stood a fairly good chance of marrying again. Without therapeutic help, however, she would have little or no awareness of the complications that remarriage presents or of the difficult and confused feelings that might hamper its success.

She would eventually have to realize that pseudo-adjustments bring little compensation or consolation and that to lead any kind of a satisfying existence she would have to make deeper and more meaningful adjustments in many areas of her life. How successfully she would achieve such adjustments would principally depend on two factors: how deeply unhappy and insecure she was as a person, and whether she was positively motivated to get therapeutic help, aware that this was a peculiar time when she needed such help to reconstruct her life. Divorce counseling would add to her self-understanding as well as help her to resolve the problems her new life presented.

DIVORCE AMERICAN STYLE

Divorce in America is viewed as a solution for unbearable marital conflict, although it is not universally approved or accepted. Approved or not, the fact is that divorces continue to occur and the rate of divorce is very high. Although this rate fluctuates from year to year and varies from state to state, it can be generally said that in recent years one divorce has been occurring, on the average, for every three or four marriages made that year (in California, the ratio is almost one to one). Until now, as a society we have not wanted to take too close a look at what has been happening to marriages that break, so that the statistics on divorce are sometimes vague and not too well developed. Death of a marriage, by divorce, separation, or annulment, seems not to have been fully accepted as yet as a social institution.* This is indicated by the fact that there are no prescribed rites and rituals attendant on the marital demise, with the result that people tend to feel uncomfortable and do not know how to help the divorced as, for example, they do the widowed. This adds to the distress of the divorced person, who struggles to help himself, with little enough knowledge and aid at a time when he must make basic decisions important to his well-being and future.

Divorce, like sex, is much talked about and has the aura that everybody's doing it; but, like sex, it is an area where there are discrepancies between attitudes, feelings, and behavior, and there is widespread ignorance. Nowhere is it more evident than in the area of divorce how much we tend to say one thing and then proceed to do another. We say we accept divorce but as a society we are just not ready yet to accept and help those who do divorce.

Myths about divorce abound. For example, we say divorce is accepted by our society. We know this is not entirely so—as we have said, there are no rites and rituals for a dead marriage —and the role of the divorced person is not clearly defined for him.

Then, too, there are those who say that every marriage can be saved. Though many more marriages could be saved than are being saved, not every one can be. Some marriages are too far gone, some should never have been made in the first place, some are too destructive emotionally or physically, or both, to warrant being saved.

---

* William J. Goode, *After Divorce*, Free Press, 1956, p. 10.

Some people still think divorce is evil. Perhaps it would be wiser, instead, to consider divorce as a safety valve for bad marriages, for at the very least, divorce protects people from being trapped and possibly destroyed physically and emotionally in the imperfect institution we call marriage.

There may be those who still think of the divorcée as a gay girl. The truth is that she is frequently depressed and lonely, feels rejected and a failure as a woman, and tends to use sex to prove her femininity and to find some human warmth. Similarly, the divorced man may be envied the happy times that are open to him now that he is free. The truth is that the percentage of gay blades is small. The divorced man has lost not only his wife, but his children and a way of life, and he must carry the financial burden for maintaining them anyhow. Remarriage is frequently a financial impossibility, even if the opportunity presents itself.

Some believe that lawyers welcome divorce cases and matrimonial litigation for the big fees involved. Some lawyers may—most do not. If anything, it is not unusual to find that the man behind the lawyer may find divorce repugnant to his personal value system or a divorce action too complicated and difficult emotionally to handle comfortably. The fact is that some lawyers are unable to set time limits in emotionally charged divorce cases so that divorce cases become too time-consuming to be financially worthwhile. The specialists (matrimonial lawyers) in this field are few, although growing in number. Some of these specialists are usually able to deal with cases involving marital breakup with a fair degree of objectivity and expedition.

Lastly, people say that if there are children, the first duty is to keep the marriage for them, which means that an unhappy marriage is better than a divorce if there are children. Marriages kept for the sake of the children alone are frequently futile because they are emotionally bleak, with the unhappiness of the parents seeping down to and often hurting the children. Good intentions are never enough; if a decision is made to remain in a difficult marriage, then one spouse, and preferably both, should get counseling help to achieve as constructive a relationship as possible. By the same token, divorce is no solution if strife continues with the children as the battleground. At the very least, divorce should give surcease from the wars of yesteryear.

## BASIC REASONS FOR DIVORCE

As we have seen, inevitably there have to be mistakes in judgment in choosing marital partners and wide discrepancies between the expectations and the realities of marriage. These difficulties are compounded by the hypocritical lip service our society pays to the acceptability of divorce as a way out if young people do not find "happiness." Since the emphasis is on "happiness" in marriage, somehow they never hear of the un-happiness of the divorced. Yet, why does one marriage dissolve into divorce and another not? Because of the many psychological and sociological unknowns, we do not have all the answers. However, clinicians observe certain broad psychological under-currents.

Immaturity is most often considered the basic reason for the failure of marriages today. A catchall that includes a variety of intellectual and emotional factors, immaturity usually means a lack of commitment. The inability to become dedicated to anything is a problem of the immature, so that it is not sur-prising to find they lack commitment to the marriages they make. Young people who enter into marriage with the feeling that if their marriage does not go well they can get a divorce do not have the requisite sense of commitment. Those who marry to get out of a bad home situation are frequently not fully committed, and when matters become difficult, they leave their marriages as they did their parents' home. Immaturity means that the autonomy of the individual has not been as yet established, so that there is a romantic or unrealistic search for "happiness" and fulfillment that no marriage or marital partner can be expected to provide, and which can wreak havoc. Ignorance of what marriage really involves can do the same. The inability to define one's own role and that of one's partner causes confusion, as we have seen. Above all, there is the in-ability of the immature to love on a day-to-day basis, to become involved with a spouse, to care about his feelings and well-being, and to give because he is there to be given to. The immature, who really are involved only with themselves, expect to receive rather than to give. People who marry solely for what they can get out of a marriage are doomed to disappointment, and the immature have little tolerance for disappointment.

Neurotic elements may be another reason. The use of the marriage to work out old, unresolved relationships is behind many of the problems that people bring to marriage counselors. Early ties to parents that continue, consciously or unconsciously, into adult life do not permit for healthy marital relationships. Marriage has a way of crystallizing feelings, particularly those toward parents and siblings, and the price is often paid by the spouse. The unresolved feelings about parents too often breed hatred that is vented on the spouse in subtle ways more frequently than people may care to believe. Still another neurotic element is the latent antagonism that many men and women seem to have for each other; their hostility to each other is always there to come into play when things are not going well. There is no room for a power struggle in a loving marital relationship. Where the need for power and the need for love are very strong, one must give way to the other; when divorce occurs, the need for power has often pushed love out.

Needless to add, those who suffer from borderline or actual mental illness are generally not good marriage material. If immature and neurotic spouses find it difficult to give to each other, those who border on psychoses or are psychotic not only find it difficult to give to the marriage but make impossible demands or sadistically create chaos.

LEGAL GROUNDS FOR DIVORCE

Legal grounds for divorce vary from state to state and reflect, in part, the problems people present as reasons for marital distress. They are generally confined throughout the United States to behavioral fault without any dimensions of emotional depth. Lawyers are generally aware that the legal ground pursued is not usually the real reason for a divorce—it is a legal expediency. They usually tend to leave the emotional and psychological factors to others.

Most states do not regard unhappiness, no matter how deep, as a reason for dissolving a marriage. It is notable that three states—New Mexico, Oklahoma and Nevada—and the Virgin

Islands have recently added incompatibility, indicating a more widespread recognition of unhappiness itself as a suitable cause for divorce. Although the basic legal concept is behavioral fault, some states permit divorce without looking for behavioral fault if physical separation has lasted for a stated number of years, usually two to five. Despite the emphasis on behavioral fault, there are indications that courts and lawyers are giving more recognition to marital discord itself as a ground for divorce.

The newly liberalized divorce law in New York is another indication of the direction the legal tide is taking. This law is a progressive step that reflects a transition in judicial thinking from the theory of fault to recognition of the realities of marital breakup. Despite negative features, about which legal arguments may continue, the law furthers the concept of reconciliation and the use of marriage counselors, albeit at what may be the eleventh hour. Perhaps the time is not too distant when state laws will provide for conciliation proceedings within the judicial framework that will mean not only the rehabilitation of marriage but the personal adjustment of those husbands and wives who decide to divorce.*

Because of the timing, a distinction needs to be made between the reconciliation efforts of the lawyer and the marriage counselor prior to and even after the decision to divorce and the conciliation efforts of the court in conciliation proceedings. As people move along the continuum from bad marriage to divorce, counseling techniques, goals, and efforts at keeping the marriage must change and become more intense to fit the needs of the crisis at hand.

## FROM THE LAWYER'S OFFICE TO THE MARRIAGE COUNSELOR

How the decision to divorce is made is of importance to the spouses not only in dealing with the realities of the situation but in the struggle for the eventual adjustment they must make. Who asked for the divorce first and who left whom have tremendous impact on feelings. Decisions to divorce are sometimes made alone in the heat of anger, and sometimes they are made

---

* See Mitchell Salem Fisher, "Matrimonial Turmoil—The Law and the Lawyer," *Journal of Family Law*, University of Louisville, Spring, 1967.

with the aid of interested and concerned relatives. Needless to say, despite their good intentions, relatives are usually too personally involved to give objective advice, and, as a matter of fact, consciously or unconsciously they not infrequently have their own axes to grind.

The role of the legal profession in marital distress tends to be somewhat neglected by those involved in marriage counseling, and yet the ultimate decision to divorce is frequently made in the lawyer's office. Though the ethics of the legal profession are high, there is something not quite right about any decision involving a professional person who has an economic stake in which way the decision goes. There is always the danger that the fees the lawyer would receive in marital litigation might unconsciously cause him to push the marriage precipitately to its termination. Good matrimonial lawyers make a sincere attempt at reconciliation before starting divorce proceedings. Often this attempt will include recommendations for help from a psychiatrist or marriage counselor.

The marriage counselor who cooperates with the matrimonial lawyer and seeks to help clients who have already crossed the threshold of the lawyer's office has some special problems. He is frequently considered by the troubled couple, and possibly by the lawyer, as a combination of an inflexible marriage advocate and a miracle worker.

The first thing that clients (and the lawyer) must learn is that the marriage counselor is not for or against the marriage but rather for helping the couple come to grips with their problems. The decision to divorce or not will be theirs. The only time the marriage counselor makes a decision for divorce is when physical or emotional destruction of a deep-rooted nature continues despite efforts to the contrary. Otherwise, whatever decision is made should come after exploration of both spouses' attitudes and feelings and when they have gained enough strength to take responsibility for their decision.

When there is close cooperation with lawyers, the marriage counselor becomes acutely aware that time is of the essence. There is urgency about most marriage-counseling cases—there can be unusual urgency in cases referred by lawyers. In these cases, the marriage counselor cannot await the slow tide of personal growth and emotional development. Rather, if he can, he must seek to accomplish a quick stabilization, a quick order out of chaos, if he is to achieve any counseling momentum within the scope of his professional dimensions. He must be quite reality-oriented and ready to take responsibility, where necessary, for a technique that is, at the outset, more directive and dynamic than is usually considered appropriate in counseling. The counselor cannot wait—the hour is late—and he must be willing to take more than usual responsibility. Tempered by clinical knowledge, education, and experience, this approach can often produce good results.

When clients are sent to a marriage counselor by a lawyer, the counselor knows they have been considering divorce and that their suffering is intense. There is an urgent need for release, for one understanding and empathic relationship in which a qualified person can hear out one or preferably both spouses without the clamor for revenge and expressions of hostility that the lawyer's office so often symbolizes and encourages. Both spouses need quiet, kindly, intelligent, nonadversary objective guidance and help without ugly recriminations or legal technicalities.

Answering these needs for emotional release, together with kindly, directive guidance, tends to ease the tensions. The marital coin begins to turn just a bit from the side of hostility, hatred, and aggression to the side of friendship, love, and pliability. Control and reason become activated and make possible a mutually calmer and more objective consideration of the marriage.

Assuming that the diagnosis indicates hope (most marriages can be saved and many of them should be saved), the couple must be influenced at this point to do the right thing for the marriage. How far and how speedily a husband and wife will accept this emergency directive advice will give some indication of their motivation to keep the marriage and their emotional strengths. This directive guidance is to be distinguished from pressure—no pressure should be put upon them by the marriage counselor. On the other hand, I have found with surprising frequency that a distressed couple will welcome directive guidance dispensed in a kindly manner. Of course, the counselor is aware of the significance of too ready acceptance on the client's part and the psychological problems it presents. Nevertheless, the fact is that during this period both spouses are usually at loose ends, emotionally and behaviorally, and feel the need for direction by a kindly authority.

Such directive technique aimed toward rehabilitation is obviously not a "cure" by any clinical standard; attempts at treatment will come later. The objectives then will be for the clients individually and together to achieve insight into and understanding of their attitudes, their feelings, their behavior, and their marriage. They may then be able to forgive themselves and each other and bring themselves to do the "right" thing—either to divorce or to keep the marriage—but certainly their decision would be based on different insights and feelings than before.

If the clients are separated, the counselor may state the need for them to begin to live together. Marriages are made not by living apart but by living under one roof, and preferably in the same bedroom. Sexual intercourse may or may not follow, but there must be opportunity for it and for the psychological closeness essential to marriage.

Lawyers may rightfully be concerned over such a procedure should the marriage counseling fail. A single occurrence of sexual intercourse consequent to adultery or cruelty raises stiff questions of legal condonation, and may make a good lawsuit shaky. Stipulations might be devised to preserve the lawsuit aspects and grounds in the event that counseling fails. In any case, counseling, even if it fails to keep the marriage, is likely to induce a mood facilitating settlement. Finally, the major concern should be for human beings, not lawsuits.

Marriage counselors are aware that clients can use or abuse them in making decisions to divorce. Not infrequently the decision is in fact made by one spouse prior to entering the counselor's office, and he may try to use the counselor to achieve what he wants. The marital partner clamoring most loudly for a marriage counselor is in some cases the one seeking to break the marriage. The client who professes to come in confused about whether to save or break the marriage may have similar intent. Under the guise of seeking help, he sometimes wants a counselor to do no more than announce how bad the marriage is and prepare the road to divorce. One man, after several sessions, confessed that his real objective was to get me to help his wife gain some emotional strength so she could survive the divorce he was planning.

Some people come to the marriage counselor seeking to assuage their guilt about breaking up their marriages. There was the case of a man who struggled with the need to keep his mistress as well as his wife. He was driven to play one off against the other. Divorce proceedings were started, but he lived in a dilemma. He wanted the marriage counselor to induce both women to accede to and accept the situation or for one of them to make a decision for him so that he could refer the losing woman to the counselor and relieve himself of responsibility.

The marriage counselor must be able to spot clients using these deceptive maneuvers and eventually confront them. The counselor is never in collusion with anyone—husband, wife, or. lawyer. His purpose is the honest objective of helping all three entities—the husband, the wife, and the marriage—if possible.

There is a special problem that arises for the marriage counselor when a client has been referred by a lawyer and his spouse does not know about this. To most people the term "lawyer" in a marital situation means divorce, and to consult him is considered an act of war and a breach of the marital relationship. If the marriage counselor informs the other spouse, this may only widen the breach. Many a marriage has been saved with only the marriage counselor and one spouse knowing that a lawyer was once consulted.

The shadow of the courtroom must not be permitted to darken the office of the marriage counselor. When necessary, the marriage counselor may ask that a written stipulation be signed by both spouses ensuring that the acts or events during the reconciliation period will not be used in any later lawsuit. The confidentiality of marriage-counseling interviews is sacrosanct, and the marriage counselor must make clear that he is not to be hauled into court by either spouse. If the marriage counselor is a physician or minister, he may have some protection under those statutes prohibiting forced disclosure of confidential communications. If not, some protection can be afforded by having the counseling done under the authority of a physician or minister, and having a letter so stating. Nevertheless, a wise marriage counselor carries professional liability insurance and knows a good lawyer. Society professes deep interest in saving the American home from the blight of divorce. Legislation is required to shield the marriage counselor and the marriage-counseling function from intrusion of the cold hand of the law in what should be a warm, spontaneous salvage attempt free from litigative considerations.

Marriage counseling may not succeed in saving the marriage. The marital discord may be too extensive and the couple may have waited too long before seeking help. Perhaps there has been improper counseling that cannot be undone. There are times when individual psychiatric or psychoanalytic help has been obtained and the operation on the spouse or spouses has been successful but the patient, the marriage, has died. Some marriages were mistakes initially; others are too destructive emotionally and physically; still others have been undermined by one partner's persistent adultery or determination to leave the marriage. In such cases, clients should be prepared by the marriage counselor for the alternative of divorce.

The decision to seek the lawyer's office and the courts belongs to the client. The marriage counselor has no vested interest in which way the decision will go. Some clients prefer to bear the responsibilities of a difficult marriage. Others prepare for the difficulties and responsibilities attendant upon divorce. Still others find they have no choice but to adjust to the divorce situation. Clients have the right to decide that divorce is, for them, the lesser of two evils. In my experience it is rare that the divorcing person is against marriage and for divorce. Rather he accepts the fact that his has been a bad marriage and that divorce is a necessary way out. The client's decision should be respected; the marriage counselor's role is to help, not to judge.

PREDIVORCE COUNSELING

Let us take up the case of Mrs. E, which was discussed in Chapter 8 (p. 101). She was dependent, felt inadequate, and sought love, but had been seduced by the intellectualism of her detached, rigid husband, who thought in black and white terms. He had originally sought the help of a matrimonial lawyer,

who recognized Mr. E's need to explore his decision to divorce
and had recommended that he visit me for marriage counseling.
After interviewing Mr. E, I called his wife in with his agreement.
I told Mr. E that his wife would not be told by either of us
that he had already gone to a lawyer, for to tell her would
only mean further weakening of their marriage.

Despite Mr. E's protestations to the contrary, I found his wife
most anxious for help, but depressed. Both continued in counseling for almost a year, with Mrs. E making every effort and
Mr. E assuming the passive, uncooperative, "show me" role
that devastated her. She came to recognize the hopelessness
of the marriage.

When her husband finally decided that divorce was the only
answer and left the counselor's office for that of the lawyer,
Mrs. E became even more depressed. She spent many a session
crying over something she could do nothing about and over
what her future might be. Interspersed with her tears were
explosions of hatred and anger at the man who had made her
life so miserable.

The predivorce counseling that continued helped her to find
a good matrimonial lawyer who would show understanding
and kindness. It helped her to accept the limitations of her life
situation more readily. Whatever excess monetary demands she
made on her husband through her lawyer were small compared
with what she would have made had she not been getting the
counseling. She eventually agreed to a legal and financial
settlement.

There followed a year of postdivorce counseling in which she
also reached an emotional settlement with herself as a woman,
wife, and mother. She selected the kind of work she felt she liked
and for which she was best suited educationally and emotionally
and went into training for it. She recognized and accepted the
fact that her marriage could not have continued without destroy-
ing her emotionally, and she felt relief with little accompanying
guilt. She saw the desirability of seeking her own independent
goals as a person, with the hope that some day she might marry,
but with acceptance of life and herself if she did not. She also
accepted her ex-husband's continuing role as father to their children and did not belittle him to them; she gave them freedom

to maintain contact with him and see him whenever he and
they wished.

The marriage counselor's function need not and, indeed,
should not end with the decision to divorce. He may continue
to help both husband and wife during and after the proceedings.
In actual fact, few cases of actively litigated divorces are so
amicable that both parties can be seen or wish to continue to
be seen by the same marriage counselor. Nevertheless, much can
be done to help the family that remains. Husbands and wives
who are concerned over the feelings of the children or visitation
rights, or over support, work, sex, a way of life, and disturbed
feelings, can use the predivorce period to try to achieve with
help an understanding of what is needed to deal with their
life situations.

Ironically enough, what predivorce counseling does is to help
two people, who were unable to agree in marriage, to agree
to disagree and to have a minimum of trust and faith in each
other where they did not have it before. This is seen most
frequently in legal settlements about money and children.
Almost inevitably, wives feel that they are getting too little
money and husbands that they are giving too much. Very often,
with little or no justification, wives feel that their husbands are
making excessive demands for visitation and will somehow hurt
the children, and husbands feel that the wives are too incompe-
tent to have custody of the children. Predivorce counseling can do
much to help those who are divorcing to understand the process
and what they have to expect of themselves and each other
in the roles of ex-husband and ex-wife. The counseling, as a result, can help lighten the emotional burden that divorcing couples
present to lawyers and courts, thereby expediting the legal
proceedings.

Society spills much of its tears (sometimes hypocritically)
over the divorced woman. Most divorcing and divorced women
do need understanding and help; as for myself, I have been
repeatedly shocked by the loneliness and distress of the divorcing or divorced man. Husbands suffer death of the marriage,
death of their entire family as they have known it, death of a
way of life, and the loss of that continuum of relationship to

children which is one of the joys of parenthood; and, to top it all, they must continue to pay financially for something that no longer exists. Predivorce counseling should help these men to come to terms with divorce and its consequences.

# 16

## Divorce: Lawyers, Courts, and Marriage Counselors

The process of most marital battles that terminate in the death of the marriage entails emotional divorce, physical divorce, and finally legal divorce. Husband and wife may have been emotionally divorced for a number of years before anything further occurs. The real pain over the dying marriage comes most frequently when physical divorce takes place and the couple's friends and family know they are no longer living under one roof. Emotional separation or emotional divorce is difficult enough but may be bearable if husband and wife continue to live together. It is when physical separation or physical divorce takes place and becomes public knowledge that the suffering over feelings of guilt and failure becomes the greatest. This is particularly true for the person who, at least overtly, has not asked for divorce. Legal divorce comes as an afterlude that may or may not involve deep emotional reactions, particularly when the physical separation is of long standing. Therefore, when physical separation and legal divorce coincide, suffering can be very intense.

The professions, exclusive of the law, to whom the divorcing and divorced turn for help (the disciplines concerned with marriage and the family—psychiatry, psychology, social work, education, the ministry, medicine, and marriage counseling) are generally oriented toward preserving and promoting stable marriage. In the effort to find a cure for marital breakup, much time and effort have been spent by these various professions in seeking the causes for marital unhappiness and dissolution. One gets the uneasy feeling as one reads the literature that each discipline experiences self-righteous justification for its own particular labors as a new cause for marital breakup is brought to light.

If one accepts the fact that those in the helping professions generally tend to concentrate on marital happiness as a goal in dealing with marriage and family life, then their behavior and attitude are understandable. Divorce is official recognition and acceptance of unhappiness, a final commitment to the fact that the relationship of two people is finished. To those professionals whose goal is to "help" the marriage and enhance the partners' happiness, divorce spells failure. We live in a society bent on success that does not believe in accepting failure but in giving individuals opportunities for achieving success. Since divorce is an unbearable finality spelling unbearable failure, divorce becomes something to be punished. It is not surprising, therefore, that the helping professions generally pay only a limited amount of attention to divorce and tend to view the postdivorce period as a destructive time with which few want to become involved.

## MARRIAGE COUNSELORS AND DIVORCE

My observation has been that marriage counselors, as a group, tend to limit their help and their thinking to keeping marriages intact. They focus on individuals who are faced with divorce problems and yet generally do not speak of helping those who have gone through the divorce process and need guidance in readjusting. If marriage counselors do help the divorced, they generally tend to put their therapeutic aid within the framework of individual counseling, and they separate (divorce, if you will) what they are doing therapeutically from marriage counseling *per se.*

It is as if there were general acceptance of a more sickly quality in those who are divorced or as if an indefinable change for the worse were expected to occur in the divorced person. Some marriage counselors tend to ignore or forget the fact that many people do not go for help when they are in the "want to divorce" period. These people are not stopped in their tracks; their marriages are not saved. Why should the divorced, as a group, be so regarded and neglected? What makes them so different as a group from what they were just before getting the divorce?

A common misconception is that marriage counseling aims to help people stay married and nothing more. The marriage counselor's job, as we have seen, goes far beyond helping the marital relationship. The ultimate goal is to help clients learn how to handle their individual as well as marital problems so they can satisfy their own integrity. The decision whether to continue their marriage is their own. The stumbling block to the wider concept of the marriage counselor's role is the premium that society puts on the married state and the extent to which this is part of the individual marriage counselor's value system.

Whether the marriage counselor believes in divorce or not is not the issue. We assume he stands for marriage; why else be a marriage counselor? Divorce is the other side of the coin of marriage. If there were no bad marriages, there would be no divorces. Therefore, the marriage counselor must know, understand, and accept the reality of the experience of divorce as part of the continuum of life, for, statistics tell us, at least a fifth of the men and women in this country who will live out an average life span will experience divorce. If we add to the divorced population those whose lives are intertwined with theirs, we find a substantial percentage of the population involved in divorce.

Marriage counselors presumably approach marriage and its attendant problems from a broad over-all perspective. Their educational and professional preparation gives them an awareness of the kaleidoscopic impact of social change upon the marital relationship. They are aware that the social, legal, and religious controls on marriage have lost their effectiveness in large measure, and they are looking more and more to the psychological controls that are necessary if the relationship of husband and wife is to be maintained. I would suggest that as a group they need to go further and free themselves from the feeling that there is still a stigma attached to those who divorce. Despite what is said, there are those counselors who continue to act as though all who divorce are unstable or immoral. The implied attitude is that divorce as such is not the concern of the marriage counselor, committed as he is to the stable marriage.

Marriage counselors who do not wear intellectual and emotional blinders, who have a perspective on the continuum of life, and who have personal stability and integrity have much to offer the distressed client. There is a point even in traditional marriage counseling at which it may well become necessary for the counselor to be able to say: "This marriage is too destructive physically or emotionally or both; perhaps a divorce should be considered." The only value—and the only way—does not always lie in the married family unit and the warding off of its potential breakup. The divorced family unit and its needs for the better life are realities too and must receive much more professional recognition and acceptance. This approach does not imply that marriage counselors would be *for* divorce as such; rather, it means that they are not thinking of what *should* be but of what *needs to* be done when certain conditions prevail.

The philosophy of marriage counseling, its aims and objectives, are in flux. Marriage counseling in this country has traveled far from the view that the purpose is, evangelistically, to save every marriage. The marriage counselor whose aim is not to save every marriage but to help husband and wife move toward personal growth, away from aggressive destruction of others and self and ultimately toward love and life, is aware that this at times may mean only partial success, the price being the death of the marriage. The intelligent marriage counselor will be ready at such times to accept the cooperative role a competent matrimonial lawyer can have in the healing process.

If the success of marriage counseling is doubtful and if circumstances warrant, as when one spouse has gone to a lawyer, the marriage counselor who becomes aware of this has the duty to suggest to the other spouse the advisability of obtaining legal counsel. The counselor cannot be part of a conspiracy in which only one side is guided by a lawyer. Likewise when divorce has been decided irretrievably by the client, the marriage counselor should not be timid in suggesting that a matrimonial lawyer be consulted or retained.

Marriage counselors, in my experience, are sometimes naïve or timid about using and cooperating with lawyers. Perhaps underlying this, as I have suggested, is some sense of failure or hopelessness concerning clients who are already or are about to become involved with lawyers. Counselors also suffer a general lack of knowledge about the law and lawyers. The marriage counselor must not play the role of lawyer or of half a lawyer. He should not deter clients from obtaining legal advice. In predivorce counseling as well as in marriage counseling generally, the counselor must not invade the lawyer's province; he must be careful not to employ legal concepts or to give what may be advice on conduct in the light of what he may think are legal considerations.

There is increasing specialization in the field of matrimonial law, as indicated by the establishment of the Family Law Sections of the American Bar Association and of local bar associations, and by the establishment of the American Academy of Matrimonial Lawyers, the *Journal of Family Law* and the *Family Law Quarterly*. The bar is slowly developing a nonadversary approach to the family problem; much needs to be done, and much is being done. To this end there is a need for opening communication lines between matrimonial lawyers and clinical marriage counselors.

LAWYERS AND DIVORCE

The matrimonial client who seeks the aid of a lawyer has three sets of problems—personal, legal, and economic. In addition to handling the legal aspects, the lawyer can give some suggestions and direction on the economic aspects. However, short of some low-key advice in the area of personal problems, he generally cannot and should not do anything else.

The lawyer tends, by reason of his profession and art, to be somewhat autocratic and directive. He does not interview the client with psychological problems in mind; rather, he is trying to get an over-all view of the situation. His function is to get his client what he wants within the bounds of ethics and practicality. To this extent, he is a partisan, an advocate. Lawyers are generally aware that they literally hold the life of the marriage and the family in their hands, the future of both frequently entirely dependent on the lawyer's wisdom and insight. The problem is one of knowing limits.

In the realm of the psychological, the good matrimonial lawyer makes certain that decisions made are those of the client. The client must make the decision to divorce. The lawyer cannot and should not make such a decision, for it is not his function, nor is it within the scope of his training. The multiplicity of his observational experiences with couples in marital distress is no substitute for formal psychological education and guided clinical experience. The decision to divorce is best made by the client outside the lawyer's office in a completely objective atmosphere, even away from friends and family. No matter how empathic and good-intentioned the lawyer may be, the atmosphere of his office is too often colored, perhaps unwittingly, by the adversary approach of the law.

Even though the client states emphatically that he has reached the limits of endurance, has thought the matter over carefully, and wants the lawyer to move promptly, the lawyer is not free to accept the decision and begin to act on it. Consciously or unconsciously, many people go to the lawyer to use him as a whip to shock their spouses into realization of the depth of their misery and dissatisfaction. They hope to move their spouses to repent, change, and mend their ways. These clients do not really want a divorce. Some want to use the lawyer and judicial techniques in a power struggle with their spouses and without having a genuine desire for marital separation. Some think they *must* divorce, especially when they have learned of adultery. Self-respect, society, and family seem to demand it, and adultery supplies legal ground for divorce.

If the lawyer is not aware of such possibilities, he will go ahead and serve the summons and complaint, and the client who wanted only to frighten or punish his spouse ends by losing him. People frequently go to a lawyer's office with no regard for their own destinies, only with bitterness and hostility. They repress any sense of having done any wrong themselves, and focus on the enormity of what their spouses have done. The experienced matrimonial lawyer is aware that husbands and wives too often seek to work out their psychological difficulties in his office.

The average lawyer engages in some suggestions toward reconciliation, especially when there are children. Too often this appears to be lip service to a duty he feels he must perform. Some lawyers who have goodwill, good intentions, and vast professional and life experience go to the other extreme and become involved in reconciliation without too much sense of their own professional dimensions. The matrimonial lawyer should not attempt, in his efforts at reconciliation, to engage in intensive marriage counseling unless he is among the few who have had psychological education and clinical experience. Without such training, lawyers tend to think in terms of situational changes and verbalisms. The lawyer's office is not a clinic for emotionally disturbed persons, nor is he equipped to serve as a clinician, no matter how much he has read or experienced.

Yet the lawyer cannot simply reject the causes people present to him and he does have a role to play in the critical period in which an unhappy spouse first enters his office. He has the duty to explain matrimonial and divorce law and to survey the client's experience and cause in relation to that law, pointing out the strengths and weaknesses and explaining the rights involved. He engages in legal diagnosis and gives a tentative legal prognosis, advising the client of the timetable of legal procedure, carrying on his interview objectively, and never assuming the role of the avenger. A successful technique that the experienced matrimonial lawyer can use in this first interview, after the facts have been reviewed and the diagnosis and prognosis have been made, is to sit back and ask the client, "What do you want?" Lawyers have often been amazed at the answers to this simple question. A woman, who throughout the interview has been burning with indignation and demanding that the lawyer hit her husband for everything he has, begins to cry. She answers that she wants happiness, love, peace, quiet, a home, and family. She says that she wants her husband but that her husband does not want her and insists on divorce.

At this point the matrimonial lawyer interested in exploring the possibilities of reconciliation will begin to cooperate with the helping professions, referring the client to a marriage counselor or psychiatrist. He suggests to the client that as long as she has not really reached a decision, perhaps she should consider going to a marriage counselor. If there has been a history of treatment by a psychiatrist, the lawyer may suggest that the client return and talk the matter over. Lawyers tell me that they frequently find clients resistant because they feel that the psychiatrist will not tell them what to do. Some lawyers reply that a marriage counselor will also not say anything directly, but will be more direct in assisting the client, and they refer the client to one. The client may still resist by saying she will go only if her spouse goes. These lawyers, nevertheless, persist in the referral since they know that marriage counselors have their own techniques of inducing the recalcitrant spouse to come in. In any case, granted the other spouse does not cooperate, the marital illness requires a nonlegal as well as a legal specialist.

Most lawyers are agreed that an attempt at reconciliation should be made, and the highly specialized matrimonial lawyer has accepted the value of referral. Except for a rare seminar, law schools offer little or no preparation for counseling, and, at best, the practice of the law does not lend itself to extended hours of marriage counseling, so that proper referral and cooperation between the lawyer and the marriage counselor are essential.

The lawyer and the marriage counselor have to communicate and genuinely cooperate. The fact that difficult cases end in divorce anyway is beside the point. If anything, once such a decision is made each spouse can be prepared for divorce by the marriage counselor with a resulting diminution of hostility. Every lawyer and judge bewails the bitterness attendant upon marital litigation, in which all reason disappears and children suffer. Assuming that divorce is to be had and without encroaching upon the lawyer's prerogative and duty to do his utmost for his client, marital litigation must cease to be so adversary in character. The time must come when a case of marital distress will be labeled and treated as "In the Matter of the Family X" and not as it generally is today—"Mrs. X *versus* Mr. X." As things are the marriage counselor skilled in divorce counseling can do much toward reducing this hostile condition by paving the way to more amicable settlements of marital disputes.

CONCILIATION AND THE COURTS

In recent years the courts of some states have developed conciliation proceedings in connection with matrimonial actions. Since the philosophy and process of conciliation counseling are still in the making, there is much confusion and debate as to what courts can hope to achieve by the use of such proceedings, what the goals and focus should be, how much judges should be involved with them, who the counselors should be, whom they should help, with what that help should be concerned and, finally, how the whole effort should be administered.

Conciliation is a court-sponsored form of marriage counseling that seems to be regarded by some of the judiciary as a means of reconciliation and by others as a process by which communication is facilitated between spouses so that they are able to make mutually satisfactory decisions in their marital disputes whether they go on to divorce or not.

Although all these courts basically hope for reconciliation, experience has generally tempered their goal. As a result, the goal ranges from reconciliation, to having the contending parties carry out their mutual and reciprocal roles as parents, to more sophisticated suggestions like that made by the California Governor's Commission on the Family.* These suggestions advance the view that the parties should be helped to reduce the areas of controversy if divorce is inevitable, and then should be helped to respond to the divorce experience so that there is the least possible damage to all concerned.

The focus of the counseling that has been done in various courts, and as seen by them for the future, is on communication, in an attempt to make each spouse aware of his own and his partner's perceptions, interpretations, and feelings, as the spouses relate to each other as husband and wife and as parents.

Although the increase in divorce throughout the country has given impetus to conciliation efforts, the courts that have seriously attempted to mend and stabilize breaking marriages are in fact few and far between, although they are on the increase. Counseling is viewed by those courts as a means by which spouses arrive at the ability to reconcile their differences not by quarreling and domination of one by the other but by communication, cooperation, and consideration for each other's uniqueness. Whatever is achieved is not brought about by any direct attempt at changing the personalities of those involved.

To understand court-sponsored counseling and the problems it presents, one must keep in mind the adversary procedure that exists in our courts. Intrinsic to marriage counseling is objective,

---

* *Report,* December, 1966.

nonpartisan, time-consuming consideration of emotional problems, with primary emphasis not on the rights and wrongs but on the realities of the marital interaction. The adversary system is inherently ill-suited to the solution of emotional problems because of the uncompromising nature of its assumptions about innocent and injured spouses. This conflict between the philosophies of counseling and the law's adversary system becomes even more sharply defined in view of the fact that the vast majority of divorce cases are uncontested. Particular judges have too often become rubber stamps, without making much effort to examine the allegations, the assumption being that divorce is what both recriminating parties actually want. This puts the court in a quasi-punitive role in contrast to the helping or healing one that is assumed by marriage counselors and other therapists.

For some time the suggestion has been made that matrimonial disputes be kept apart from the adversary system and, along with other problems concerning the family, be placed within the framework of improved family courts, where an attempt would be made to understand and resolve the problems that marriages in conflict present without anyone being the winner or the loser. Family crises of all kinds are presented to the family court, which, if it had jurisdiction, would be able to capture the marital problem and recommend marriage counseling before the problems reach the court in the full-blown state of a divorce suit. The idea has yet to take wide hold in our courts, although there are hopeful indications.

Thinking, humanitarian judges are often unwittingly trapped by the adversary system within which they perform their duties. In talks from time to time with some non-family court judges in New York City, I have found that they generally have little respect for members of the helping professions. An obvious reason for this is the frustration judges so frequently feel when they cannot obtain the unequivocal answer they expect from a professional witness. A more disconcerting reason is their feeling that the helping professionals, usually psychiatrists, are not to be trusted. It would appear that in response to the requests of lawyers who hire them, some psychiatrists give professional opinions to meet the needs of the side that has employed them, with the result that they too frequently seemingly become not the objective professional who is testifying in a given case but a quasi-advocate. This seems to me to be an unfortunate outcome of the combination of the law's adversary system and a therapeutic system whose primary concern is the pathology of the individual. As a result the combination of these systems sets up both the judge and the psychiatrist for partisan participation in a matrimonial dispute, despite any personal feelings or opinions they may have to the contrary.

Judge and psychiatrist also experience disharmony because of the difference in their professional focus, which must inevitably create a gap in communication. Judges are primarily concerned with overt behavior and the truth as to the external events, while most therapists are primarily concerned with feelings and dynamic truth based on feelings and perception.

Recently there has been an effort to establish marriage counseling as part of the court's system for dealing with marriages on the brink of breakup. Although the marriage-counseling process functions better in a less adversary environment, to some extent, perhaps, the clinical marriage counselor could prove to be a compromise between the judge and the traditional therapist, since the marriage counselor is concerned with the behavior of both partners in marriage as well as the pathology behind that behavior. So as to come closer to the truth, he is accustomed to fitting together what a husband and wife say, and his techniques include the directive, guiding, educational techniques necessary for crisis intervention and problem solving that the court understands. Nevertheless, mutual trust and understanding have to be established between judge and marriage counselor if they are to be a successful team. Each must allow the other his professional uniqueness and must make an effort to become informed in the other's field, not to wear the other's professional hat, but simply to facilitate communication.

Before deciding the problem of who should be offered conciliation counseling, every court will have to determine the limits of the counseling it intends to offer. This will depend on who the judge is, the character of his court—whether it is a family court or not— and what he believes the practical goals should be. There is little evidence to indicate the value of counseling for reconciliation purposes alone, although the Los Angeles Conciliation Court seems to have achieved something in this direction. Since most divorces are granted by default, implying that neither party is interested in continuing the marriage, some courts may feel that the advantage of any counseling would lie not in reconciliation but in assuaging divorce-related conflicts over custody, visitation, support, alimony, and property settlements. Few courts are ready to go beyond this point.

At this writing, the practical issue for interested courts is both the inadequacy of public funds for counseling purposes and the lack of qualified marriage counselors or professionals with clinical marriage-counseling training to do the job. Suggestions to overcome this have been made: having an experienced marriage counselor see the couple for one interview upon their filing suit and classify them as to their potential for counseling (New York courts are now directed by law to appoint a conciliation officer for this purpose); or having them see the judge first and then see the principal marriage counselor, who would either refer them to an outside agency or arrange a limited number of sessions with another staff counselor who, in turn, might refer them.

The ideal, it seems to me, would be a nonadversary court in which specialized judges who have been clinically trained or oriented would sit primarily as judges and would be able to act at the same time as clinical intake workers, determining the direction matrimonial cases should take. This would reduce the number of professional people involved with the case, which would be excellent emotionally for the disturbed spouses and practically for the court. If the judge felt that he could not wear two hats well, he could do the next best thing and have an experienced marriage counselor sit with him to help him determine the direction the cases should take.

There is some question whether counseling can be foisted upon clients by making it mandatory and, if this is done, whether such counseling will be of any value. The experience of the marriage counselor in private practice indicates that this might well have merit. The marriage counselor frequently finds one spouse pulling the other in for counseling or sees only one spouse initially and then calls the other in himself. Limited mandatory counseling can have merit if the counselor can give enough time and effort and has enough flexibility to abandon the effort with those who do not want or need it. Timing is always important, and counseling in conciliation proceedings is coming very late. Yet much can be done for those already in court, since people in the midst of crisis are likely to be amenable to the suggestion of counseling. However, they need to save face, and the authority of the court can help them do so, while providing the opportunity not only for reconciliation but for rehabilitation.

The experiences of various courts in conciliation proceedings indicate that the framework has to be short-contact marriage counseling in which the court acts like an emergency receiving hospital for sick marriages.* Clients in extreme marital crisis are not usually able to think in terms of a long-range counseling or psychotherapeutic program to save the marriage. They are often willing to accept short-term marriage counseling.† Those who do this kind of counseling find that the client can be helped to function more effectively even if he does not always know the origins of his problems. If one or both partners are really too ill to function effectively in the marriage or in other areas of their lives, then they must be referred for more intensive help. Although the goal cannot be to save all marriages, many divorces can be prevented—the question is frequently one of saving face once the proceedings have started.

Since the court is a powerful authority figure in the client's eyes, the court is able to play a strong supportive role when the marital situation is in turmoil. Male clients in particular find the court setting easier to take since they perceive it as more masculine. In general, the framework of the court permits people under stress to accept the sort of help that otherwise is widely regarded in our culture as a sign of weakness rather than strength. That framework also enables the counselor to surround a collapsing marriage with some external structure that, like a splint on a broken arm, permits healing to take place. This external structure helps clients to cast immobilizing feelings aside

---

* The simile is that of Meyer Elkin, speaking of the Conciliation Court, Los Angeles.

† Even in private practice I frequently indicate to clients that marriage counseling is not an arrangement for all time, and that how long it takes depends largely on them—my job is to help them move out on their own as quickly as they can.

and permits husband, wife, and counselor to search more deeply into the disruptive factors in the relationship and to try to determine whether a workable solution is possible.

Process in the Los Angeles Concilation Court includes one to three counseling appointments of two hours each. Husband and wife are first seen together briefly to enable the marriage counselor to define his role as an impartial one and to emphasize confidentiality and the court's function. Husband and wife are then seen separately, after which another joint session is held. In the first session the counselor strives to achieve some understanding of the dynamics of each personality and of the marital interaction. He then provides intensive short-term treatment focusing largely on immediate problems. If he feels that there are sufficient internal injuries in the marriage, referral is made to community and private nonprofit counseling agencies. Various techniques can be used in this kind of short-term marriage counseling—the directive technique, the confrontation technique, and the joint-session technique.

Clearly, marriage counseling in a court setting cannot be the same as that done in a family service agency, clinic, or private setting. Yet all are interested in keeping marriages and families together. Helping professionals from all disciplines might take some lessons from the Los Angeles court and others to heart. The down-to-earth philosophy and process they are evolving are to be highly commended. Over and beyond this, they are demonstrating how the unification of different disciplines can offer the much-needed services of marriage counseling in a court setting.

---

More often than not, unfortunately, counseling may stop for both husband and wife when the formal legal procedures begin. If there has been a good relationship with the marriage counselor, that relationship may continue for one or both spouses after the divorce decree. Payment of the lawyer's bill may or may not be the last act in the legal drama, since custody and support proceedings can be endless. Such payment is certainly not the final curtain in the marital divorce drama.

Although divorce may appear to be an accepted phenomenon, the divorced person struggles in his aloneness, and few helping hands are extended to him. Just as premarital counseling has been frequently found to have value in the relationship achieved between marriage counselor and couple should marital difficulty occur later, so predivorce counseling may have similar value for the peculiarly difficult period that follows divorce.

Marriage counselors must be prepared educationally and clinically to give predivorce and divorce counseling whenever necessary. Such counseling tends to be complex and difficult, but can also be very rewarding. In *The New York Times Magazine,* on January 1, 1967, Morton M. Hunt wrote an article, "Help Wanted: Divorce Counselor." The title is indicative of a need, and the need becomes increasingly greater although there are marriage counselors who are already doing divorce counseling. For such professionals, the title "marriage counselor" is limited and misleading. There have been a number of clients in my experience whose spouses have refused to come to see me because they were uncertain whether to keep their marriages and felt they wanted no help from someone who stood unequivocally for preserving marriages. They were obviously wrong, and perhaps this was their way out of taking responsibility; nevertheless, they make the problem clearer. When marriage counselors are in fact doing divorce counseling, they should be known and accepted as "marriage and divorce counselors."

# 17

# *Life After Divorce*

The divorcing or divorced person is caught up not only in the morass of his own personal disorganization and emotional upheaval, but also in the morass of our changing society and of his potentially ambiguous relationship with church and state—both institutions usually permit divorce and at the same time generally treat it as something only to be tolerated. Moreover, the divorced person's difficulties increase when he comes to the realization that the divorce to which he had looked for surcease is perhaps not the cure-all, the magic for that new life of "happiness" that he believed he had every right to achieve. For most persons there comes a moment somewhere in the divorce process when they feel that they may have been shortchanged, that this new, shining existence to which they had looked forward is perhaps not quite so shining after all.

The last person officially concerned with those who divorce is usually the lawyer. Once the decree is obtained, he assumes that his task is ended. The client may receive from the lawyer a parting shot of advice not to rush into remarriage, with an indication (depending on the client's wealth) that there may be a need, if he does remarry some day, to consider the possibility of an antenuptial agreement. After that directive, there is nothing—only oppressive silence, perhaps a feeling of relief if the marital turbulence has been great, loneliness, depression, and feelings of failure and concern over practical problems that vary in kind and magnitude, but most of all, there is nothing to assuage the peculiar pain and silence that follow.

An analogy can be drawn between the feelings of the divorced and those in mourning. The Jewish people show deep psychologi-

cal insight in their approach to the emotional problems that beset
the living when a dear one has died. Part of this approach is in
the use of time. They reckon that a year usually must pass for
the survivor to get over intense mourning. After this period,
he is expected to take his accustomed place among his fellows.
It takes at least as long for the divorced to recover as it does
the widowed, though both may remarry before the healing
process is finished. During this period of "mourning," the
divorced need a large amount of emotional support and understanding. Generally, the divorced are highly motivated to seek
help with their life situations and their emotional problems; the
difficulty is where to get that help. A small number of divorced
persons, more fortunate than the rest, rely on members of the
helping professions; the vast majority get little or no help.

DIVORCE COUNSELING

Divorce offers a closer look at the pathology of marital conflict. The problems the divorced person presents are as wide
and deep as life, so that the substantive part of divorce counseling is vast. There are problems that concern his feelings and
emotional well-being, those that concern others with whom he
is involved, and those that involve practical matters of his everyday living. Maturity, mental health, and divorce adjustment
that is based on personal growth; being able to cut the psychological umbilical cord in the struggle to be; the significance
and meaning of freedom; the need for evolving inner strength,
becoming a person in one's own right and able to cope with isolation and loneliness although alone; the meaning of love and
God, faith and hope—all this needs to be explored with the
divorced in their anxiety.

The divorced person stands in a peculiar position in society.
He is not married and yet he is not really single. He may be a
parent but he is neither a married nor an unmarried one. The
law does not help any because it labels the divorced persons
as ex-husband and ex-wife, as though they were negative
counterparts of what once was. The divorced woman, who usually continues to be known by her ex-husband's name, is ob-

viously not a virgin, but some people may expect her to act more or less like one.

Unlike other social roles, the role of the divorced, especially in relation to others, has not been clearly defined. As a result, many divorced people flounder at a traumatic period in their lives when there is a tremendous need for something to grasp and hold onto. They are expected to use their judgment at a moment when, realistically or not, they have every right to question their judgmental abilities. Already confused by events not yet seen in perspective, they must make decisions about their lives with little to go on beyond kindly advice from the well-meaning, unless they seek professional help.

The general goal of the marriage and divorce counselor in helping the divorced is to reduce the influence of any negative, passive cultural traditions and internalized values and to enable the divorced person to become his own judge of what is good and bad, wise and unwise, and to develop a rational role for himself. If society can give him but few answers to his problems, the divorced person must learn to seek them within himself.

The divorce counselor must be careful not to foist his own values on the client. This is easier to do with the divorced than others because they are confused and bewildered, and many of them live, for the moment at least, in a moral vacuum. The aim should be to help them build their own structure within the framework of social standards in regard to behavior, beliefs, and values, with a recognition of the differences in subcultures and among individuals.

Awareness of this need for the divorced client to build his personal structure does not permit the divorce counselor the luxury of a value-free approach. The competent counselor's value system, like that of other therapists, is based on his background, clinical research, and experience, and the ideals peculiar to each of us. The counselor's values will never be more challenged than by the divorced client. The counselor has the responsibility of helping the client to clarify the client's values and to understand their application in reality. To do this, there will be times when the counselor's responsibility will be to state his own values. The counselor's avoidance of ethical issues by adhering to a value-free approach does not help most clients in marriage counseling; for the divorced it may well be destructive, since their need for a definition of standards and the structuring of their lives is urgent.

The problem for the divorce counselor lies not in the mere stating of his value system but rather in the manner in which he presents that system to the client. The divorced are frequently confused about values as well as about their goals and their attitudes toward life. Where regressions to childhood occur in counseling, I believe, the counselor should speak with conviction and authority rather than to support values and goals that he honestly feels to be destructive, but he must do this in an atmosphere of compassion, understanding, and acceptance.

The focus of divorce counseling is on helping the divorced to achieve an adjustment through personal growth. Personal growth may be defined as a maturation process by which the individual moves away from egocentricity toward altruism and a desire to contribute to society. Inner conflict is a characteristic of personal growth. The desire to remain self-centered, gratify selfish aims, and assuage inner conflicts battles the desire to gain social acceptance through sharing and belonging; the result can be frustration, hostility, anxiety, and guilt.

Sometimes a person believes he meets the requirements of adjustment and maturity and then circumstances such as illness, death, or divorce throw him into emotional imbalance. Counselors must be on guard for this and not categorically treat those who are suffering emotional stress and strain as a result of some catastrophe on the assumption that they are emotionally ill in any fundamental sense. Personality is dynamic, and the individual responds to life with constant readjustments to maintain his emotional and social equilibrium.

The disturbed divorced person who is basically a fairly well-adjusted adult may be helped to aim for more intellectual and spiritual growth and more effectiveness in his various roles. The disturbed divorced person who can be said to be basically maladjusted may strive for personal growth, but he must first be helped to rid himself of unhealthy attitudes, feelings, and habits that hinder his personal growth.

I do not believe that there is justification for considering all divorced persons as hopeless neurotics who must inevitably repeat their failures should they marry again. The divorce-prone (the third or fourth decree begins to raise doubts) and those whose deep-rooted problems make them poor marital risks are good newspaper copy and establish the divorced person's prototype. They are comparatively few in number. Neurotics may choose for divorce or marital unhappiness, but then so do so-called normal people. Marital unhappiness may be due to what we can call a team factor, so that conceivably a distressed person married to someone else might do fairly well. Perhaps a more reasonable and realistic view is to say that the majority of the divorced population may be considered normal in the sense that they have the potential for achieving average success in a second marriage, especially if they have obtained interim therapeutic help.

Postdivorce adjustment is widely viewed as the process by which a person comes to perceive himself as no longer an "ex-spouse" but as a single individual who is eligible for and interested in remarriage. Ours is distinctly a marrying society; the question remains whether everyone must marry in order to be accepted as well adjusted. If one defines postdivorce adjustment as personal growth, such adjustment need not always involve remarriage in fact, in intention, in desire, or in eligibility. Post-divorce adjustment might include a variety of other goals for the divorced person: a return to social activity, a reduction in feelings of bitterness and hostility, more understanding and acceptance of self, of children and ex-spouse, and of society generally, better management of his affairs so that he is able to handle the new problems that follow divorce—in general, changes in attitudes, feelings, and behavior with regard to sex, marriage, divorce, work, hobbies, and life as a whole.

The divorced do not stand alone in their feelings of emptiness, although their feelings may be more poignant. One grows to the adult state best who discovers for himself the profound truth that the purpose of life is to live and who, having determined to live, is committed to accepting the responsibilities inherent in his decision. If the divorced person could not carry on a love affair with marriage, he may, with help, have the potential for carrying on a love affair with life.

The situation of the divorced makes it imperative for them to review and determine where they are going—what their long-range goals are as well as their more immediate goals concerning work and remarriage. When someone has lost out in life, a deeper significance is attached to understanding of self and others, democratic values and goals, self-discipline, feelings in regard to freedom and responsibility, faith and hope, and attitudes toward life and its purposes.

Should the divorced person be told to be loving and accepting? Can he be? If he can, whom should he love and accept? His children, perhaps? But should he love and accept his failure? His ex-spouse's failure? There is tremendous emotional disturbance in the early periods of the divorce situation, with anger and hatred playing leading roles. The divorced person should, at best, strive to express love and affection only when he can do so spontaneously, for otherwise such an expression becomes self-defeating. The divorced person is in the position of having stated openly that he has loved and lost; one cannot expect him to love because he is told to do so.

To help the divorced person gain some outer security is not enough—he must be helped to develop inner security. To do this means helping him come face to face with the facts of his life and his emotional and behavioral errors and inadequacies. To help the divorced client define his role, increase his problem-solving abilities, become in part his own judge of good and bad, achieve self-awareness and self-acceptance and awareness and acceptance of others, arrive at competence in establishing and achieving personal goals—this is the task the divorce counselor must assume in trying to meet the divorced client's needs.

HALF A FAMILY

Personal growth can be seen most clearly in the stages the divorced person goes through in his feelings toward his former spouse. They range from violent hostility and even hatred in the beginning, to guilt, to being sorry for the ex-spouse and, finally, to indifference. How soon the final stage is achieved, if at all, depends on the maturity and life situation of the divorced person. Much depends also on who left whom. The divorced person tends to focus superficially on the mere fact of the physical departure—who forced whom out or who left of his own volition absorbs their attention and feelings. Frequently, ongoing problems of support, visitation, and custody are symptoms of an unresolved relationship with the ex-spouse. Only with courage and honesty and, perhaps, with help can they go more deeply into the destroyed relationship to determine when and how the emotional leave-taking took place. Few have the insight or courage to admit the role they played in the emotional departure.

To attain better insight and behavior, the divorced person must evaluate objectively the sort of person his former spouse is; why he married that person in the first place; the expectations in and disappointments of the marriage; how well each knew the other before marriage; who really left whom and when; and what part each played in it—and he must develop an awareness of remaining feelings toward the ex-spouse and acceptance of the fact that a relationship continues between them as ex-spouses, which means he must explore his feelings about remarriage for himself and for his ex-spouse. The anomalous relationship between ex-spouses can be difficult if there are children, for there remains the relationship of natural parents to the children of a marriage that no longer exists—inevitably, they must be able to close the book on what once was, only to open it from time to time as special life events occur affecting their children.

Buddy was a rotund nine-year-old who was failing at school. His father and mother had finally separated after many arguments and were seeking a divorce. His younger sister had died two years before and Buddy had taken her death badly and was ridden with guilt about it. Now his parents' decision to divorce had precipitated many strange feelings. He wanted them together and yet he did not. The feeling of relief at finding his home quiet was colored by a feeling of guilt that perhaps this too was his fault. He was angry at his father for leaving and yet he did not blame him since his mother yelled so much. He liked having his mother to himself but he felt uncomfortable when she came near him. Most of all, he felt rejected and abandoned—his parents could not love him very much if they were getting a divorce. He bet that if his sister were alive they would not be doing this—he always knew that they loved her more than him.

Several hours of counseling with Buddy made us great friends. Gradually he determined for himself that whatever was wrong with him, there was much more wrong with his parents. The guilt began to drain away and he began to take up his own life and interests.

Every once in a while, for some two years, he would appear at my door to show me something he had received, to sell me a magazine, or just to see what I was doing. His parents divorced but Buddy gradually extricated himself from their morass so that he was able to say, "I'm okay. I just was unlucky in the way I picked my parents."

Children are often anxious and uncertain over changes taking place in the family, and the knowledge that their parents are considering divorce may bring on many feelings with which they cannot cope. They must be helped to accept the reality of divorce, for their fantasy and hope are that Mom and Dad will resume the marriage and the family will be whole again. Deep feelings of rejection and abandonment that leave their mark for life are experienced by children of divorce. The idea that "my parents did not love me enough to keep the marriage" may well pervade their spirits. Added to this is a sense of guilt, for when unresolved oedipal fantasies and wishes are realized, the fright and guilt may be overwhelming. A boy may wish his father out of the way; to have him really leave is much too threatening.

Divorcing parents need to understand the effect on the children. Although there are cases where the marital relationship is so bad that divorce can only bring relief to children, by and large the experience is a destructive one for them. If older children have been made aware that divorce is under serious consideration, a session with the marriage counselor may be warranted so that they can gain reassurance that the divorce of their parents is not the end of their world and, if necessary, so that they can be motivated for referral to a child psychologist or a child psychiatrist.

Divorcing parents should convey to their children the idea that, despite their disappointment in each other, they will always be loving and concerned parents. Each parent must also refrain from tearing down the other in the eyes of the child. It cannot be emphasized too strongly that, whatever the impact may be, the shock of divorce can be assuaged with the resolution of the parents' feelings about themselves as persons. If they could not agree about their children in marriage, they must find a way—with help that is objective and not judgmental—to agree now that they are divorcing. Custody and visitation conflicts are an all too common and destructive tug-of-war for the child, who becomes the prize and the loser. Since neither spouse can genuinely be called the innocent victim or the guilty party, both must search for what is best for their children's growth and development and arrive at a mutual decision.*

This can be more easily reached when both partners are still involved with the same marriage counselor who, respecting the decision to divorce, sees each partner individually to help reduce hostility. Then he might hold a joint session to help the couple to communicate enough to be able to arrive at agreement. In some cases, communication may improve after the decision is made to divorce, since it frees husband and wife of the demands and expectations of marriage.

Parenthood is a difficult enough role for those who maintain their marriages—with divorce it can become overwhelming. Failure in the marital relationship need not mean failure or potential failure in the parent-child relationship. Marital failure does, however, give cause for review in this most crucial change of circumstances for parents and children. The peculiar and unnatural parent-child relationships that frequently follow upon divorce are further disturbed by a lack of knowledge and experience and by confusion about parental roles and goals. Both the father and the mother suffer, each unable or unwilling to comprehend the suffering and difficulties of the other in relation to the children.

---

* The use of the children as an emotional football between divorced parents is very common. This is only too well known to lawyers engaged in custody and visitation contests. In fact, my awareness of what happens to children in the legal field was one of the major factors that initiated my own interest in marriage and divorce counseling.

There has been much complaint about juvenile delinquency in relation to the broken home. Not enough can be done or is being done with respect to children in the period when the home is breaking. The marriage counselor's involvement with a marriage is also an involvement with the family. The counselor who does predivorce and divorce counseling helps establish the mood for divorce negotiation in the interest of both children and parents, without championing either side and in the hope that the disturbance to the parent-child relationship will be reduced and the broken home atmosphere will be kept to a minimum. A clinical marriage counselor does not presume to take the place of the lawyer or the judge; his role simply places him in a position to reduce the partisan adversary character of the legal process.

I find that comparatively few in the divorced population have experienced a good family life and know what it implies. Since custody of the children is generally granted, for better or worse, to the mother, she must be made aware of her responsibilities. If she failed as a wife, she need not fail as a mother. The father who has only rights of visitation must become keenly aware of the impact of his relationship upon his children. He, too, may have failed in his marriage but he need not fail as a father. Bitterness, hatred, and despair do not help make loving parents. Both parents require help along the way back to living normal lives. The family left by divorce is half a family—a sundered family—and it becomes necessary to define the whole so that the divorced can understand what remains. Strong family life shapes the individual, and half a family is better than no family at all.

To make for strong family life, basic material needs must be met; values must be agreed upon on the basis of rooted moral and ethical concepts and they must be imparted to the children; reasonable long-term goals must be arrived at, and they must be related realistically to current needs and circumstances. The family, and therefore the half-family, helps the individual members to build realistic goals and provides the opportunities for their realization.

We say that parents should be in general agreement in regard to the rearing of children. The divorced parent has only the conflict within himself with which to deal, but he has to be doubly careful not to exploit a child for his own unconscious purposes—as when a divorced woman, consciously or unconsciously, uses her son as a kind of substitute husband. To this end, the divorce counselor may ask such simple questions as where the members of the half-family sit at the dinner table and what the sleeping arrangements are—a son who consistently sits in his divorced father's chair may be inadvertently taking over his father's role; a daughter sharing her mother's bedroom by sleeping in her divorced father's bed may be struggling with many troublesome feelings about herself.

A discussion with the divorced client about the relationships that prevail in a good marriage clarifies the ideal and gives him a better perspective on the failure of his marriage and his future prospects. The divorced have much to learn in distinguishing between dependence, independence, and interdependence in a marriage. They must learn to recognize that each spouse is a major source of security, satisfaction, and love for the other, but that neither can meet every need of the other, and also to accept the fact that members of a family can appreciate one another's satisfactions without necessarily sharing the same interests. In a constructive family life, positive feelings of warmth, mutual respect, and love gain ascendance over negative feelings, so that anger may be expressed without fear that the family will break up. The divorced, who have experienced great hostility and the dissolution of a relationship, must come to understand that anger can be expressed without dire consequences. They need to know that communication, consideration, cooperation, and self-discipline are foundations of a good family life.

Perhaps divorced people should know that in a good family the relationships between husband and wife, parent and child, child and child criss-cross and fuse to create an ongoing maturing experience. There is a sense of the exciting adventure and challenge of life and the joy of achievement, plus a feeling of belonging and the pleasures and ills of one member reach all and resentment is kept at a minimum. Understanding and awareness of each other's needs and differences and caring about each other's welfare, together with mutual recognition, respect, and acceptance, form a framework for everyday living. In such family life, anger can be expressed without fear of abandonment, and forgiveness is the order of the day. Each member is a separate growing person, yet all are united by ties of blood, love, faith in life and trust in each other, work, shared laughter, sorrow and tears, hopes and dreams, memories, triumphs and defeats.

RELATIVES AND FRIENDS

Once a break is made, most of the divorced seem to have little or no contact with their former in-laws. Some feel resentment because they are forced to end the relationship; others project their hostility for their ex-spouses onto the in-laws; still others are indifferent. The relationship between the divorced person, particularly the woman, and his or her *own* family is not so simple. A divorcée may move in with her family and rely on her mother to help with the children so that she can work. On the other hand, she may have limited contact or none at all. These relationships are often pervaded by ambivalent feelings— wanting and not wanting help, appreciation and lack of appreciation, dependence and independence. It is not too surprising that among the divorced there should be extensive unresolved relationships with the members of their own families since original unresolved relationships in the parental home are often reflected in marital breakdown.

The divorced tend to leave their old friends behind and make new friends, primarily among the divorced population. Since they want to remarry, they have to circulate socially as they did before they married, but they find it more difficult. There is a constant search among the divorced for social contacts. Some seem to have little difficulty in meeting new people and making friends. Others try through all kinds of artificial means to achieve the warmth of a relationship that will assuage their loneliness.

DATING AND SEX

Desperate for companionship and still bemused by the American dream of romance, despite what has happened to them, some divorcés think they have to whoop it up as though they were sixteen in order to be successful; many others tend to date persons of whom they do not approve and whom they would not consider marrying. The majority have many questions to ask the counselor about their behavior on dates—especially divorced women in regard to their children. There is important need for discretion around children—a fast social pace involving a sequence of men hardly helps them.

If a dearth of sexual activity is a barometer of unhappiness in marriage, an excess of sexual activity is a barometer of unhappiness after divorce. Feelings of inadequacy and of a need to establish a relationship with someone—anyone—at all costs lead the divorced on to sexual activity that becomes its own goal. Instead of being part of a relationship between a man and woman, sex is abused to meet the needs of the individual, to bring him out of the chaos of his confusion, and to help him bridge the gap between himself and others. Sex among the divorced, more than in any other group, tends to become sex for one rather than sex for two. Nevertheless, it should be noted that sexual activity among the divorced ranges from promiscuity to continence.

The attitudes and feelings of the divorced were dramatically displayed in a series of meetings I conducted for groups in Education for the Divorced.* The participants ranged in age from twenty-seven to forty-two. There was, particularly in the beginning, much pressure to talk about sex. Yet at the final individual interviews sixteen of the twenty-one participants said that they felt the most important topic discussed was "the Role of a Woman" and "the Role of a Man," while only one person felt that "Sex" was most important.

If the divorced abuse sex, they do so in their profound unhappiness and because of their misconception that sexual activity will prove their femininity or masculinity. Seemingly, the less they know what it means to be a woman or a man, the more they need sexual activity. If their expressed failure in marriage proclaims them inadequate in their roles as men and women, they are determined that their sexual success outside of marriage will proclaim them adequate. So they search endlessly, unsparingly.

---

* Esther Oshiver Fisher, *Education for the Divorced,* unpublished doctoral thesis, Teachers College, Columbia University, 1962.

WORK

The divorced man's concern over work can be a strange mix-
ture of hope and hopelessness. He is concerned because he is
aware as never before that divorce is an expensive proposition.
Having lost the home he knew, he must help maintain it,
and he has the added burden of setting up a new home for
himself. Many men end up in furnished rooms or hotel rooms.
If they hope to eventually remarry, they must increase their
income in some way so that they can maintain two families.
Unfortunately, just when the need is greatest to put forth
effort and achieve in work for pure monetary return as well
as to keep their grip on life, divorced men are frequently
hampered by deep feelings of depression, loneliness, anxiety,
and despair.

Most divorced women have to work. Work for the younger
woman who has young children and who must work in order
to support herself and them takes on peculiar significance.
While she may have worked during her marriage, work has other
connotations now that she is divorced. During her marriage she
may have worked for various reasons, not the least of which
may have been to escape her role as housewife and mother.
With the advent of divorce, work is something she usually has
to do to live. Ironically enough, she is compelled now to play
an impressive segment of the man's role at a time in her life
when her feelings of inadequacy as a woman are being tested.
Her feelings about work can therefore become quite ambivalent.
This is not so for the older woman. Although she may be placed in
the same position in regard to work, depending on her life experience and situation, she generally feels a greater need for work as
a satisfactory way of expressing herself as a person. As a result,
work does not seem to become so deeply involved with her
feelings of adequacy as a woman.

EDUCATION FOR THE DIVORCED

Adult education has become established as part of social and
intellectual life. The impact of such education becomes dramatic
if one observes that the parent who is troubled and perhaps
failing in his role can, if he wishes, attend PTA meetings. There,

ideally, he can hear how others are handling their parental problems. Less than fifty years ago such activity would have been unacceptable. Within the range of possibility, therefore, a program of adult education that focuses on the problems of the troubled divorced person might become acceptable.

The need for such a program is starkly seen in the way in which the divorced population, in its desperation, has tried to help itself. Parent education is respectable, so the divorced have created an organization called Parents Without Partners (which includes the socially acceptable widowed) for the ostensible purpose of helping their children. Friendship, dating, and sex are subtly placed in the background, but in fact the activity is intensive. Here, at least, is a façade of respectability that can be widely accepted by the confused and conflict-ridden among the divorced. Why not? Has it not become socially acceptable to admit frankly that there is difficulty and even failure in the parent-child relationship? Parent education has achieved this in the last three decades.

It follows that programs of education for the divorced, established to help groups of divorced persons, when such programs become professionally and socially acceptable, should eventually produce a more honest environment that will prove therapeutic for those who divorce. Here, at least, those troubled by their failure in life's most intimate relationship can acknowledge such failure and yet feel that they are socially acceptable as individuals and not part of some subterranean, unrecognized culture. Divorce counseling and groups set up within the framework of education for the divorced have much to offer the troubled divorced population. Such groups are limited as to time of participation and their goal is to help the divorced move toward and become a part of the general population.

Because of this philosophy, I became interested in exploring what could be done for the person who, no matter what the reasons may be, finds himself divorced. To this end I developed and carried through the idea for my doctoral thesis of groups of divorced persons within the same age range meeting for ten to twelve sessions in what I termed Education for the Divorced. I concluded, among other things, that such groups not only would be a way of reaching many of the divorced population, they could be highly beneficial and effective in helping the divorced person rehabilitate himself and reconstruct his life.

The divorced person may feel that a part of himself has died but, particularly with help, a heightened awareness of the possibilities of life and of self may follow. When one consciously chooses to rejoin the living, his responsibility for himself takes on new meaning, for then he truly wants life so that discipline from the outside is converted into self-discipline.

# 18

## *The Widowed*
## *Also Have Problems*

Not long ago I stood waiting to speak to a mixed audience about
remarriage. A woman in her mid-thirties approached me and
whispered, "Talk about the widowed and their troubles—we are
always hearing about the problems of the divorced, but we have
problems too, only nobody ever seems to consider them." That
young widow spoke with some justification and probably reflected what the widowed population at large feels—that too
much attention is being given today to the divorced and not
enough to the widowed.

There is some reason, if not excuse, for this neglect. Society
has a vested interest in the family because of its concern for
children and is more likely, therefore, to turn its attention to that
which most  threatens family stability. In the beginning of this
century, death at an early age was the primary factor disrupting
marriage. The number of divorces was small and little attention
was paid to them; at that time the many orphans under eighteen
far outnumbered the children of divorce. Now not only has the
rate of divorce become one of the highest in the world but,
increasingly, divorces tend to occur early in marriage, involving
far more children than those who experience the death of a
parent. Almost 90 per cent of the children available to be stepchildren in 1900 were orphans, whereas today 30 per cent are
orphans and 70 per cent are children of divorce.* Slowly  and
surely society is having to do a turnabout and become concerned

---

* Ann Simon, *Stepchild in the Family,* Odyssey Press, 1964, p. 60.

251

primarily with the problem of what happens to the children of divorce.

Put another way, the percentage of young married adults affected by divorce is increasing, whereas the percentage for the same segment of the population that is affected by death continues to decrease, in large part as a result of modern medicine. Short of an increase in widowhood caused by war casualties, the likelihood is that the major number of marriages ended by death will involve older people. There is general recognition of the problems of young adults when they divorce and of the effect on young children. On the other hand, the problems of the young widowed tend to be thrown into the catchall basket with those of the older population, whose problems have begun to be recognized, explored, and dealt with comparatively recently. The result is that many problems peculiar to the minority group of the young widowed are likely to be overlooked or thrown together with those that are presented by the divorced. This is unfair to both the widowed and the divorced.

Experience with the widowed indicates that though they may be resentful of the emphasis placed on the problems of the divorced, they generally consider themselves separate and apart and look upon the divorced as a somewhat lesser breed of humanity. This attitude would seem to stem from differences in the area of feelings and not from similarities in external problems that present themselves to both groups. Particularly in dealing with the widowed, the individual must be extracted from the group and observed in his own right, taking age, sex, and his life situation into account. The fact is that women tend to live longer than men, but little preparation is made or pattern of life suggested for a widow.

If we consider that divorce is the death of a marriage, it would appear, at least superficially, that divorce and bereavement are somewhat the same in the extent of suffering and trauma. Yet there are sharp and important differences that affect the feelings of the widowed. The divorced notably fare badly because of the lack of social support and a well-defined role to play at a time of disruption and disorganization. In contrast, we like to think that the widowed have social support and that their role is defined. The facts are that although many friends and relatives are around before and at the time of death, they gradually withdraw into concern for their own lives, leaving the widowed in a position similar to that of the divorced, in which they must face alone the task of taking up life again.

There was a time when rituals concerning death set standards of behavior upon which the widowed and their friends could depend. Today, except for a few subcultures that retain them, those rituals are being eliminated, so that the widowed come closer to experiencing the void that the divorced encounter. The difference lies in the fact that although the divorced suffer a social finality that we can compare to death, the widowed suffer both the biological finality and the social finality. As in the case of the divorced, much depends on the personal capacity of the widowed for rehabilitation and the reestablishment of social relationships.

## LONELINESS, ISOLATION, AND BEING ALONE

Divorce is inevitably preceded by a long period of conflict in which the emotional attachment between the spouses is deteriorating, so that the finality of legal divorce tends to be less upsetting than the finality caused by the death of a spouse with whom there may have been conflict, but not to the point of divorce.

Loneliness besets both the divorced and the widowed. If the widowed person had a good, meaningful marital relationship, it implies that there existed an interdependence between two independent persons, each of whom had the capacity to go it alone. Left alone because of death, such a person is likely to be temporarily paralyzed. He will nevertheless eventually move away from loneliness and isolation toward an independent life in which he might live alone and still be able to go out beyond himself toward others. Independence, to which we attach so much value, has its price of isolation unless a person is willing to move toward life and human relationships, for we are not really meant to live alone in isolated independence but rather in involved interdependence. Some of the widowed may be mature, independent people, but they depended on their spouses for this basic human relationship, and it is to be expected that the depth of their feelings of loss and deprivation will be in direct relation to the years spent in the marriage and that those feelings will not be easily overcome. Once the feelings are worked through, the ability of the widowed to establish new ties will increase.

This is in contrast to the divorced, who rarely, if ever, have experienced interdependence in marriage and knew only dependence and the need to make constant demands on the other partner. The divorced are likely, therefore, to struggle differently with their feelings of loneliness. They tend to compensate by being overactive sexually and socially, but they remain lonely and isolated unless they come to grips with the meaning of adult independence. The quality of the feelings of deprivation and loss tend to take a more neurotic turn based on the extent of their former demands and dependency needs. The divorced may turn more quickly to others. They turn not to give as much as to gain satisfaction for their insatiable demands.

### GRIEF, ANGER, AND GUILT

In the personal growth process of the divorced, which runs the gamut from deep emotional disturbance to postdivorce adjustment and rehabilitation, the person goes from anger to hatred to pity for the ex-spouse and, it is to be hoped, he ultimately arrives at a stage of indifference. The widowed tend to run the gamut from fear and feelings of deprivation, frustration, rejection, and impotence to anger and resentment. Ultimately they too must close the book of their past marriage and place it high up on the shelf of life, as do the divorced. Yet there is an important difference with the widowed. The widowed do not have the target of a living spouse that the divorced have upon whom to blame the breakup of the marriage. The widowed, as it were, cannot talk back to death and a dead spouse. We tend not to think or speak badly of the dead but, rather, to recall the good.* The conflicts and difficulties that beset the marriage are pushed aside, and the dead spouse is made over in memory to conform to what the widowed spouse had wished him to be. This may arouse feelings of guilt over irritations expressed in the past and may even prolong the period of grief. To compound this, the widowed may internalize their increasing anger—anger that is born of fright

---

* Shakespeare's Mark Antony to the contrary notwithstanding.

at suddenly having to handle so many new situations, not the least of which may be the raising of children alone.

Children, depending on age, can understand a widowed parent's grief to a point; they cannot be expected to comprehend his total feelings. Even adult married children who may be sincerely concerned for a parent's welfare are likely to be impatient because of their need to return to their own lives. Younger children have many feelings when the death of a parent occurs that they must repress from sheer fright. The fact that they may look as though they have little or no feeling does not mean that this is so. The widowed parent who has a need to overextend the period of grieving has little love to offer his children—he is too embittered and involved with his feelings of guilt—any more than the endlessly embittered, hostile, divorced parent has to offer his.

The problems that children present to the widowed depend in large part, of course, on their ages and that of the parent. The widowed do not have to deal with the complications of visitation and custody that plague the divorced, nor do they have the problem of an ongoing relationship with a former spouse because of children. They do have the total burden of raising and supporting the children. As with the divorced, establishing authority and defining the role of the widowed parent can prove to be quite difficult, though not insurmountable, tasks.

INADEQUACY AND INSECURITY

Whatever feelings of inadequacy and insecurity the widowed may have, they are not proclaimed to the world at large as are those of the divorced, who by the intrinsic nature of divorce make a public declaration of their failure. Feelings of inadequacy and insecurity are frequently expressed in sexual behavior. The need for sex may be the same among the widowed, but as a group they are not propelled into sexual activity. Since a distinct social pattern for the widowed no longer exists, their social as well as their sexual lives become a matter for individual determination.

The decisions are not easy ones for many widowed women to make. They may have been aware in marriage of the changing mores in regard to women. Then they felt safe. Now they are placed in the position of wanting the company of men but of being uncertain of what to expect. When they were single their peers were single; now they find themselves single again when most of their peers are married. The widowed woman, like the divorced woman, must make the shift from living as a married woman to living as a single woman—a single woman who was once married. Among other things, this means resolving the problem of her relationship to men.

VALUES AND GOALS

The divorced, as a group, tend to be confused as to values and goals; the widowed may or may not be. If there was integrity, feelings of self-worth and adequacy as a person as well as a man or a woman, a commitment to life and acceptance of responsibility for it, dealing with others with loving kindness—if these patterns and other sound ones existed before, they will return to stand their owner in good stead. If there was confusion before, confusion will undoubtedly compound itself. Like the divorced, the widowed often need help to clarify and reassess their values so that they can set appropriate goals for themselves in their new way of life.

---

In a previous chapter the suggestion was made that the marriage counselor be known as a marriage and divorce counselor. The title is not adequate, for it seems to exclude counseling the widowed. No other title comes to mind that will inform the public that the widowed, like the divorced, can seek and find appropriate counseling help. Perhaps the lack of nomenclature is symbolic of the times, which place so much emphasis on the divorced to the exclusion of the widowed.

The widowed need the widowed as the divorced need the divorced to help them return to a place in society. Groups organized under competent leadership for education for the widowed similar to those already suggested for the divorced could do much toward easing the pain, redefining values, setting standards for behavior, determining goals, and helping the widowed to move away from the excessive self-involvement that death can bring, toward involvement with life and other human beings.

# 19

## *Is Remarriage*
## *the Answer?*

Since 1900 the remarriage rate has more than doubled; whereas one marriage in ten was a second marriage then, the figure now is one in four. The situation is still in flux. As might be expected in view of the rising divorce rate, most remarriages involve the divorced rather than the widowed. This means that those who remarry are younger and have younger children. Yet remarriage remains a phenomenon of middle age despite the fact that young formerly married people tend to remarry more quickly.

The remarriage rate among the divorced is higher than that of the widowed at any given age, and both the divorced and the widowed tend to marry those who have been married before more than they do single people. At twenty-five, for example, the divorced person stands a 99 per cent chance of remarrying, the widowed a 93 per cent chance, whereas the single person has an 88 per cent chance. By forty-five, men are more likely to marry than women, especially widows. The strong trend toward remarriage among the divorced may indicate that there is more acceptance of the divorced woman as a respectable and integrated person than in the past. Virginity seems to have little, if any, significance these days. Moreover, more single men are marrying divorced women, suggesting that more men are finding it psychologically difficult to initiate the establishment of a home and family. These marriages seem to meet with some amount of success because of the women's experience. This cannot be said so readily for single women who marry formerly married men. Theirs is potentially a most difficult situa-

257

tion, for their lack of experience prevents them from meeting the unexpected demands that are placed upon them by their more experienced, and often impatient, husbands.

There is a dearth of research data on remarriage. The general impression has been created that more remarriages end in divorce than first marriages. This may be due to the hyperactivity among the divorce-prone. Although Roman Catholics and some Protestants still forbid remarriage after divorce until a spouse dies, most Protestants and Jews are more liberal. As for the law, about a third of the states impose a waiting period on the "guilty" party to divorce before he can remarry, or some other technicality, such as the requirement for court permission. These restrictions are not usually effective, since the remarriage may then take place in another state. In contrast, no state restricts the widowed; Puerto Rico prohibits remarriage until three hundred days after the death of a spouse.

The growing rates of divorce and remarriage make it imperative for those involved with marriage and the family to achieve a perspective and to accept them as part of adult life. Even if remarriage be considered the only satisfactory answer to divorce —the only adjustment to divorce—the ceremony is not enough on which to base any conclusion that an adjustment has been made; it is what goes on in the new marriage that is significant, for the achievement of unity in the new family is the ultimate adjustment to divorce. Any person who consciously or unconsciously prevents this unity cannot be said to be adjusted.

Marriage is complex and difficult enough, and remarriage by its nature creates even more complexity; yet the divorced, who have suffered and know the difficulties of marriage so well, seem propelled to remarry. Why do they really want to marry again?

There is much talk about love, and love is certainly expected to play a role among young people, but love is not fully understood or expected to exist among the middle-aged. Despite the extent of sexual activity among middle-aged divorced people, sex as such is not usually a compelling reason for marrying again; rather, there is a need for reassurance and love that offer the opportunity to express feelings. Those who have been emotionally deprived in a first marriage cherish the opportunity for a loving relationship. This intense need for someone with whom to share one's feelings is added to several other needs expressed by the divorced: the desire for a partner to share one's social life, the desire for stability, the difficulty in living alone after being married, the need to regain the status that marriage confers, and the problems in being a lone parent.

Everyone has the need for support, emotional or financial or both. This need is not to be confused with the need some people have to exploit others. Among those who remarry there may be some who are motivated to exploit those they marry—the older man who marries primarily to get a housekeeper and a mother for his children, or the woman who marries primarily for financial support or to get a father for her children. These people, however, do not reflect the more general motivations for remarriage.

Family and friends frequently pressure the divorced and the widowed to remarry. Young children, seeking to be like everyone else and have a complete family, urge it; friends who may feel the divorced person to be a competitive threat to the well-being of their own marriages exert their influence. Above all, our marrying society expects it.

Beyond these reasons and pressures, neurotic needs and compulsions may play a role: the need to assuage deep personal conflicts and hurts, to prove that one is a man or a woman and can therefore be a good husband or wife, to punish the ex-spouse, and above all to prove that one is lovable. Such neurotic factors tend to color our ideas about the divorced who remarry, but the fact is that they are encountered in only a part of the divorced population who do so. The divorce-remarriage prototype, like many prototypes, is only a limited expression of reality.

Unfortunately, all this motivation for remarriage does little to overcome the complexity of the problems that remarriage inevitably presents since remarriage involves many more people, feelings, attitudes, and beliefs than a first marriage. Although the areas of adjustment in remarriage that are sensitive and call for serious attention are more or less the same as those in first marriage, children by previous marriages and former spouses com-

plicate the remarital picture, so that far more emotional strength
may be demanded of the husband and wife than in a first
marriage.

REMNANTS OF THE PAST

From the start, remarriage begins with a harsh liability in
terms of residual emotional attachments. The previous spouse
plays an inevitable role in remarriage, and the new partners must
be able to adjust to this peculiar negative relationship if their
marriage is to flourish.

Mr. A was divorced by his wife after seventeen years of marriage and when their son was fifteen years old and their daughter
twelve. He had not wanted a divorce because of the children,
although he recognized that he no longer loved his frigid wife,
toward whom he felt intense hostility. A year later he became
engaged to a divorced woman with two children of her own.
They sought help because they were disturbed over Mr. A's son's
threats of suicide at hearing of the prospective marriage. Mr. A
felt insecure, inadequate, and confused. He blew hot and cold
about his children and had deep feelings of guilt concerning
them. His fiancée had good insight into his problems, but there
was some question whether she would have the strength to
sustain the relationship because of them. Nevertheless, the
marriage took place and the couple continued counseling.

Mr. A still felt deeply lonesome for his first family and said
that if he had the choice, he would choose the children and
unhappiness rather than his new marriage. He felt financially
burdened and said that his new wife, who had appeared to be
warm and accepting before marriage, was cold and hostile. The
thought of his old home now seemed inviting and warm. He was
self-involved and could not imagine his new wife's need for him,
feeling such a need to be unbelievable to the point of being unbearable—after all, it was he who needed her help! Most of all,
the weekends—when he was caught between being with his children and with his new wife—were intolerable. His son was a
problem because of the son's insatiable demands, and Mr. A was
overinvolved with his daughter, putting her ahead of his wife
when she visited his new home, so that the child had little respect for her stepmother.

Mr. A projected his feelings onto his children and was constantly concerned lest they feel that their stepmother stood between them and him. He spent far more money on his children than had been agreed upon and gave so little to his wife as to deprive her; when she objected, he told her to stop acting like a stepmother. Mr. A's relationship with his stepchildren, who were living with him, also left much to be desired. He ignored them as much as possible and refused to accept them on any terms.

Mrs. A used everything she had learned in analysis in the attempt to keep the marriage, but she could not hurdle the deep rejection she constantly experienced. Furthermore, she would have spurts of jealousy when she realized that her husband gave little thought to her and was preoccupied with thoughts of his first wife and their children. She saw that she would never be able to wipe out the seventeen years of the prior marriage— at best, it would always be Mr. A and his children and herself and her children. The remarriage ended in divorce.

When a divorced person remarries and his former spouse does not, this is likely to be an obstacle to the success of the second marriage, especially if the woman is the one who remains single. A man's feeling of guilt may well intrude upon his second relationship. Compensatory devices are frequently developed and used—the husband indicates too great solicitude for his former spouse, whom he now sees as difficult but weak and alone, or he has too great hostility against her, which is at least much better than directing that hostility on himself, or he may assuage his guilt by having too much or too little solicitude for the children of his first marriage. Guilt feelings over having deserted the children are difficult to handle. If the children are permitted to become overinvolved in the new marriage, they can precipitate its breakup.

It was the second marriage for both Mr. and Mrs. B and the marriage was not going well. There were many reasons for this; one obviously destructive factor emerged after several sessions. Although Mr. B gave the impression that he was finished and done with his first marriage, he was far from having relegated what had happened in the first marriage to the past. He refused to see his part in the failure and felt that he had been the injured, abused party. One thing was certain—he was going to control his new wife's every move and thereby avoid repeating the disaster he had experienced in his first marriage. Mr. B refused to see her as she really was and treated everything she did as an indication that she was going to turn out like his first wife. His first wife had been a chain smoker, and he would become distraught when he saw his second wife smoke several cigarettes; he was certain that his second wife was an alcoholic when she took several drinks socially because his first wife had been an inveterate drinker; his first wife had had a series of affairs and Mr. B needed to control his second wife, who was young and pretty, because he was afraid she would leave him for someone more interesting. So it went—nothing Mrs. B did was good enough, and it took very little for Mr. B to point out to *her* that her first husband had probably been right to divorce her since she really did not make a good wife.

A dependent woman, she had married Mr. B thinking he was a kind, fatherly man who would answer her needs. After marriage she realized that he was an omnipotent, controlling man who had little awareness of her feelings. Mr. B left counseling because he felt there was nothing wrong with him. As Mrs. B continued to get help, she became aware of how frightened her husband was that she would leave him, as his first wife had done, and she saw that this was the reason why he was compelled to control her. Her fear of him diminished and she determined to start pleasing herself instead of seeking constant recognition and approval from her husband and so setting him up to reject her. She began to assert herself more and was less affected by her husband's demands. This decreased her feeling of pressure, and she began to set her own standards for behavior, recognizing that no matter what she did, he would have the need to pick at something. Her growth made Mr. B very anxious, but he needed her too much to leave the marriage; instead, he withdrew, becoming somewhat less oppressive.

Divorce is an ego-wounding experience, and when a former spouse remarries, the hurt is intensified. The divorced person's role requires that he appear indifferent. It is difficult to accept a situation in which not only has he lost but someone else has won. This can result in jealousy, paranoid trends, and a strong desire for revenge that can precipitate actual intrusion into the second marriage. Jealousy may lead to checking up on the remarried spouse's activities through children or friends. Paranoid trends are manifested in the unmarried rejected spouse's feeling that everyone has ganged up against him, particularly the spouse who has remarried, the children who continue to see that spouse, and that spouse's family and new spouse. The desire for revenge may be acted out by the unmarried spouse in vicious gossip, by outrageous financial demands, by preventing the children from seeing the remarried parent, or by assuming a martyr's role.

On the other hand, an ex-spouse may not be active at all and may still exert influence on the new marriage. For example, in the new marriage a man may use his wife's former husband to remind her of her capacity for failure in marriage, or he may use his own ex-wife to enlarge upon defects he may find in his second wife, or he may consider the former husband as a rival.

Mr. C, sixty-four, became a lonely, frightened man when his wife died after thirty-five years of marriage. Shortly after her death he met an attractive but discontented married woman whose relationship to her husband had been close to breaking for many years. They began to have an affair, and Mr. C felt that he was a man again. His mistress gathered enough courage to divorce her husband and marry him. She soon realized that she had married a rigid, ungiving man who wanted everything as it had been when his first wife was alive. The first wife had been a plain woman who had attended to his every comfort, was frugal and saved money, demanded little for herself, and permitted her husband to come and go as he pleased. The new Mrs. C felt that she could not measure up to such a standard. She had married Mr. C in the expectation that he would answer her needs and be concerned for her feelings.

Mr. C felt restrained by Mrs. C's demands, did not trust her with his money, and believed that since she was attractive, she would not continue to be interested in him and would find someone else. His guilt about his first marriage became apparent when he confessed privately that actually the first marriage had been very unhappy for the first twelve years and only tolerable the rest of the time. He had always traveled for business purposes and had had several affairs, one of which his wife had broken up. He had had little sexual activity in his first marriage—only out of it. What really made him uncomfortable was having intercourse with his second wife. He agreed that perhaps she had shown some real insight when she had said that all he really had wanted was a mistress and not a wife.

Mrs. C's dependency motivated her to accept the limited marital relationship she had made, and she settled down to living under her husband's thumb.

If a widowed person remarries, there is always the danger that the ghost of the departed spouse will intrude on the marriage. Because we cannot fight the dead and vent our anger upon them, the feelings are insidious. The problem of idealization of the dead spouse may haunt the second marriage, to its detriment. Then there is always the queasy feeling on the part of the second spouse that the first marriage did not end voluntarily. Friends and relatives do not always help, especially when they feel that the new marriage is an act of disloyalty and that the new spouse is an intruder. The widowed partner may be harassed by an underlying sense of guilt that the first marriage was in fact not a success. In older marriages, children may further complicate the second marriage, particularly when property is involved.

Emotional disturbances over a prior marriage have impact on the second marriage. A remarried person may become consumed with guilt, especially if the second marriage is a success. He will then have to explore why he has so much need to keep the past marriage alive. Frequently the past is made into a fantasy with which to be preoccupied to avoid dealing with present reality and becoming committed to the new relationship.

Much depends on the second spouse. If the second wife feels secure as a person, then the former wife becomes a common enemy and this feeling can contribute to the solidarity of the second marriage. Of course, this depends on the extent of the husband's resolution of his feelings about his prior marriage and his ability not to be defensive about his first wife, intellectualizing with statements to the effect that divorce does not prevent them from continuing to be friends. If, on the other hand, the second wife feels insecure or full of resentment toward her predecessor, she places an added burden on her new husband, who is torn between his troublesome first wife and his insecure, angry second one.

When a divorced person and his second spouse concur in their attitudes toward the former spouse, and the attitudes take on a flavor of indifference, an adjustment has been made in the second marriage that is about as ideal as can be expected. When the partners to a second marriage have negative attitudes toward a former spouse, then the adjustment is not too good. They may say they are indifferent, but their remarks are filled with hostility.

## ADJUSTING TO THE USUAL PROBLEMS OF MARRIAGE

The initial difficulties that mark sexual adjustment in a first marriage are generally limited in remarriage. Sophistication and knowledge take their place. If anything, experience prior to remarriage may have been so great that an ineffectual sexual partner has been avoided. In any case, the excitement is qualified by past experience. If it is the second time around for the wife and the first for the man, they start out more or less equal, unless he happens to be inexperienced, in which case he has the advantage of a more sophisticated partner. When the marital situation is the reverse, the wife (whether a virgin or not) may well profit from her husband's experience. Of course, if both have been married before, the situation becomes even easier.

However, previous sexual experience is not always an advantage when, for example, a formerly married person seeks someone to solve his conflicts, is hiding from his own personal defects, or is promiscuous outside of marriage but impotent or frigid in it; or, being troubled by feelings of inadequacy, is tortured by the thought of the sexual adequacy of the other's previous partner, or is inhibited out of fear of indicating the extent of his knowledge (this is particularly true of some women).

Age must be considered in sexual adjustment. The young bride is usually below her peak of activity and drive while that of the bridegroom may be high; couples in their late twenties and early thirties tend to be more evenly matched. The older woman is frequently an attractive partner because of her accumulated experience, her fewer anxieties, and her better understanding of men.

Omitting the neurotic exceptions already noted, there is, generally speaking, a better likelihood of achieving a good sexual adjustment in remarriage than in first marriage. The effect of a new partner is usually favorable and even rejuvenating. Also, sex can be especially exhilarating if there was sexual maladjustment in the first marriage. After the rigors of a broken marriage and the uncertain sexual activity of the courtship period during divorce, sex in remarriage can become a new source of reassurance and surcease.

Practical considerations are likely to be more prominent in remarriage. Love and kisses are usually enough for the young but not for the middle-aged. The partners in a remarriage have to be even more realistic than those in a first marriage. Too often they are not. Second marriages are frequently handicapped in regard to income. The less hesitation there is to discuss finances honestly prior to the second marriage the better. Many divorced persons, perhaps afraid of rejection, tend to be over-delicate in discussions regarding money—to the point of being foolish. If the prospective partners are mutually aware of and accept their financial potential and limitations, they can reduce their conflicts over aspirations and avoid unnecessary emotional upset.

Mrs. D, a pretty, vivacious, talkative woman in her thirties who had a son by a prior marriage, had married a man who had four children whom he was supporting on a minimal level. His first wife had not remarried and was working for additional income. Mrs. D, a professional woman of some ability, had continued to work throughout her first marriage and was doing so in her second. She was highly disturbed that her second marriage was not working as she had expected. She talked about many things that troubled her but never about money. When I asked her about it, her eyes opened wide and she said she did not want to talk about it. After some time, she disclosed that her unhappiness was really caused by the fact that her husband was not supporting her but expected that she turn all her earnings over for the upkeep of their marriage. After much discussion in joint sessions with Mr. D, it was agreed that Mrs. D retain from the money she earned a sum equal to what her husband gave his first family that was to be considered her own to do with as she pleased. This arrangement satisfied Mrs. D enough so that she did not have the feeling that she was working to support her husband's first family.

The financial obligations to a first wife can harrass a second marriage to destruction. If too much money goes to the first wife, the second may become embittered. If the first wife thinks that too much is going to the second wife as a result of new affluence or otherwise, the first may become resentful and seek legal help. If the first wife never gives up alimony and will not work or remarry, the second wife may well become embittered, especially if she is living on very little. Many remarried women work, whether they have preschool children or not. Second wives may be understanding to a point, but when the budget is slim and the alimony continues to be paid, it is easy to foresee what they will eventually feel. The minor children of the wife's first marriage may complicate the finances in the second. The father's legal and moral responsibility for support may exist, but he may leave it to the stepfather to pick up the tab.

Generally, in-laws do not constitute too great a problem for the remarried since the spouses are older and the original parent-child relationships are usually not as intense. Nevertheless, there can be severe problems if the family of either mate takes sides or if both the parents and the former in-laws take sides against the new spouse.

Adjustment to friends and community is a lesser problem. When only one partner has been married previously, he tends to determine the social set. There may be some embarrassment if references are made to the prior marriage. Yet, if the remarriage is satisfying and both partners are mature, there is little damage. When both spouses have been married before, the friends of each are usually determined by their relative congeniality. Those who were primarily friends of former spouses tend to drop out or be dropped.

The social life of the remarried couple may be difficult if they remain in the same circles with a former spouse. Former friends are afraid to take sides, and there can be awkward situations when old and new spouses meet. Despite the modernization of attitudes, biases are inevitable, and the remarried must take this into consideration in planning their way of life.

THE PACKAGE DEAL

Children by a prior marriage involved in a remarriage add another dimension to the marital relationship. In the ordinary family, the union of its members takes place slowly, without deliberate cultivation. In the remarried family such unity has to be built and achieved with much time and effort because the stepparent and the children have different histories, expectations, and emotional patterns.

The establishment of a new family with children from a prior marriage takes knowledge, insight, patience, faith, and hope. The first problem to be hurdled is the introduction of the new parent, who must develop his own relationships in the family. Not too much can be expected too fast, and yet it often is. The sudden acquisition of a new parent can throw children off balance as much as the death of a parent. If children are given the chance to meet and know the prospective parent, the chances for acceptance are improved. If the marriage is discussed with them in advance and they are given the illusion of having some say in the matter, acceptance of the new parent becomes easier.

What should be said and done depends on the age, sex, and attitudes of the children. Many people have the feeling that if a couple are going to divorce, they had better do so when they are very young because their children are infants and can even be adopted if there is a second marriage; there will be no conflicting loyalties and the children can accept the new parent without qualification. In reality, not many children are very young, let alone infants, at the time of remarriage, so that their personalities have already been shaped by the biological parents, by the divorce trauma, and perhaps by the fact that they have lived for a time with only one parent. More often than not, this is the mother, so that the children may have lived for a number of years with no adult male in the house at all.

The very young and the quite grown-up tend to accept a new parent more easily than those in between, particularly adolescents. Age differences are complicated by sex differences. Young boys do not like the feeling of being different, so that they welcome a second marriage, particularly of their mothers. However, adolescent boys, because of unresolved relationships they may have with their mothers, may resist acceptance of a new father. Older girls do not find it easy to accept the new father, since he is the symbol of their mother's sexuality, and they may resent the remarriage as a betrayal of their natural father.

What to call the new parent becomes a problem for many children, and how they feel about him is reflected in their choice. Calling the new parent by his first name usually means minimum recognition of the relationship. The child may take a long time to work through his relationship with the new parent, and he should be allowed the time within reasonable limits. Eventually, recognition that the relationship is more than a friendship must be made. There are many names for parents. If a child called his original parent by a particular one, this should be respected, but he should eventually come around to calling his new parent by another name that recognizes the relationship.

Mementos of the first parent may pose a problem for the newly remarried woman. She does not wish to interfere with the original relationship, and yet she wants to protect the child and integrate two families. Much will depend on the amount of insight and tact that is used.

Adoption by the new parent gives symbolic security and helps to solidify the new family emotionally. Adoption does not of itself improve the parent-child relationship. In fact, some children resent adoption, especially if the relationship to their natural father is a close one.

One would think that the acceptance of the package deal of remarriage—the new partner and his children—with all it entails would be an obvious and decisive factor in the decision to re-marry; yet there are many who consider this a secondary matter, only to find it an overwhelming one later.

What does it mean to be a stepmother or a stepfather? There are many myths about these relationships. Being a stepchild has long meant mistreatment or neglect in the pattern of Cinderella. As for stepmother, folklore and literature are abundant with tales about how horrible she is. The myth persists as a symbol of what everyone experiences in childhood—the loving mother who says "no," who gives but also takes away.

A woman may possibly marry a man for prestige or support, despite a lack of affection for his children. In reality, however, women are not rejecting, malevolent witches; it is simply that a mother—or stepmother—is the central force in a family, so that she inevitably bears the brunt of conflict with the children. The woman who becomes a stepmother starts out with two strikes against her and is bound to find difficulty playing the mothering role in the hostile atmosphere in which she frequently finds herself.

However, the problem of being a stepmother has changed somewhat, since she usually operates at a distance nowadays. The typical family created by remarriage today finds the wife bringing her natural (biological) children with her. Her new husband's children, if any, usually live with their natural mother and are visitors or short-term guests, so that their new step-mother's relationship to them is less time-consuming and in-volves less responsibility. Everything has its price, however, and the new stepmother is likely to find that she must be extremely careful not to indicate disapproval of the children's mother or in any way conflict with her. This makes for new tensions and dif-ficulties in the relationship, particularly with regard to problems of acceptance and authority—if their father and she are not at one, his children can wreak havoc.

The competition for love between the natural mother and the stepmother can be exceedingly intense, but this competitive experience is comparatively rare today because custody is usu-ally given to the natural mother. When a father wins custody, he usually has been able to prove the mother unfit. Not only is the blow to her enormous, but the child may find it hard to accept that his mother is unfit to take care of him and feel torn from her and may act out his protestations by rebelling against his stepmother.

Even if the stepmother is successful in her relationships to her new husband's children, she is not likely to win, since one or even both natural parents may become jealous, or she herself may feel guilty over her success if her competition is with a natural mother who is dead while her husband may also feel he has betrayed his dead wife.

Competition may occur between the stepmother and her husband's children, who may feel she is a usurper and compete against her for status, control of the family, and their father's love. A woman in this position needs to feel certain of her own place in the family to sidestep such rivalry. If she does not, she will force her husband to take sides and the likelihood is he will choose for his children. Children by a prior marriage are a constant reminder of a past relationship—they have a history together and if their father is forced to choose between them and a new wife, he will usually pick his children.

In remarriage, the anxiety over abandonment is intensified, and it is not too unusual for the two sets of children by prior marriages to feel competitive. If the new wife makes a special effort toward her stepchildren, her own children may feel rejected, and if she shows any favoritism for her own children, then the stepchildren are jealous. Altogether, the woman who remarries stands in a precarious position that demands far more effort, maturity, and emotional strength than any position she might have had in her first marriage.

The stepfather generally fares better and is more likely to have an affectionate relationship with his new family. Nevertheless, he too may run into difficulties. Since custody is usually given to women, the new stepfather may find himself living with a whole new set of children and in competition with their natural father for them.

The stepfather is in a position to develop a good relationship to his stepchildren if he is kindly and is not under pressure by their mother to become a father to them all at once. He stands a much better chance if he starts as a warm, accepting friend and develops the deeper relationship slowly and at the children's pace. If the stepfather gives most of the support, he is in the position of being able to buy the children's affections from their father. If he decides to adopt his new wife's children, he must get the natural father's consent, which means that he literally asks the natural father to hand his children over to him. If the children take their stepfather's name, their natural father is almost erased from their lives.

In any case, the natural father is the likely loser as against the stepfather, for there is just too much against the natural father. If the stepfather has money, the natural father may feel that the stepfather should take over support. When the natural father continues financial support, he may feel the child owes him more love and gratitude than the child is able to give him.

We have already seen that a divorced man may experience terrible suffering with the loss not only of his wife but of his way of life and his day-to-day relationship with his children. When his ex-wife remarries, he finds himself set back even further in regard to them. He cannot spend as much time with them as their stepfather; it is embarrassing for him to visit them in their new family, so that his visits frequently have to take place in artificial surroundings. The zoo is a fine place for an afternoon but not as a permanent place in which to build a relationship with your child. Frequently his ex-wife harasses him further by not permitting him the legal amount of visiting time he has been awarded. If, to boot, he is tired, busy in his job, and limited as to money, he may indeed find that he is unable to achieve much of a relationship with his children. The only way he can assuage his feelings is to remarry and set up his life within the framework of a new family. It may be possible then for his children to visit him in his new home and thereby reduce the artificial conditions under which they have been meeting. The alternative to remarriage is for him to eventually stop caring, if he can, about his relationship with his children. The irony is that his ex-wife and society are inevitably the first to condemn him for this—despite the insurmountable difficulties, he is expected to continue his fatherly concern and support.

In some remarriages the stepfather may be able to have an understanding and accepting relationship with the natural father, especially if the stepfather also has natural children. This is to the good and perhaps ideal, except that the basis of this assumption is that too many persons—the stepfather, the natural father, and the natural mother—will be mature in a difficult life situation for it to be achieved in many remarriages.

Competition between the natural father and the stepfather may become a real threat to the child. He needs to think well of his natural parents, and he expects his father to continue to show interest in him. If the child sees his natural father only under artificial circumstances, he may feel uncomfortable. If the child is not permitted to talk about his natural father in the new family, he cannot integrate him into his life and may become emotionally disturbed. If his mother disparages his natural father, the damage to the child can be great, for the child who does not believe in and respect his own father is less likely to believe in and respect himself.

The absence of family history and experience in remarried families prevents feelings of loyalty from developing easily, and breaks that occur between members are not so easily mended. Remarried families, as first families, need to get beyond the level where conflict sets off a form of blackmail, namely, the threat of divorce or, beyond this, divorce itself. For a remarriage to be stabilized there must be recognition of the difference between temporary conflict and anger and long-standing conflict and hostility of a deep-rooted nature. There has to be an understanding of the woman's strategic position, and a perspective has to be achieved about the problems of remarried families so that they are seen as more complicated and intense perhaps, but basically the same as those faced by all families.

SUCCESSFUL REMARRIAGE

Since remarriage presents profound difficulties and conflicts, one wonders what is required for remarriage to be successful. The first requirement is unity. An affirmative reaction from society and the support of families and friends play an important role in making newly married couples feel as one. This support is offered to first marriages. Such support is not so forthcoming to second marriages as it might be—the very occasion when there is a greater need. The new couple may achieve unification also by virtue of the enemy—the ex-spouse. Although community isolation is rare today, some who remarry still have to face such isolation together. This requires inner strength. Guilt feelings on the part of one or both partners have a way of making for unity. Where both have divorced, they can offer each other emotional support since they are both out to show the world they were right to obtain their divorces. The feeling that one failure is enough may give impetus to making an all-out effort toward the success of the new marriage lest the onus of unbearable failure arise from a record of two divorces.

The adaptability of the human being is many-faceted and amazing. Personality growth may be achieved by experience as well as through therapy. An unhappy marriage may prove to be a valuable educational experience for a successful second marriage—the pitfalls inherent in the marital relationship have been encountered and preparation is made to avoid them by acquiring skills in relating to a spouse, and in practical matters and by restraining abrasive personality traits. Frequently, too, the motivation to succeed makes for more flexible standards, so that less is expected and asked for. I have heard the twice-married say time and again that had they devoted as much effort to their first marriage, there would have been no divorce. Then again, if the first marriage was unsatisfactory, the second can seem successful by comparison.

Since personality growth comes with maturity, a remarriage made later in life has, in general, better prospects for success. A person has to have courage to break and start again, be it in work or in marriage. A divorce is not always sought out of weakness; there are times when seeking a divorce is a sign of strength. Many successful marriages are made in the later middle years. Age has removed many of youth's difficulties and life is understood better; there is a tendency to be more tolerant and less demanding; interests have been developed, so that there is not as much absolute dependence on the other spouse's attention; love and faithfulness, with mutual affection, companionship, and interdependence persist.

PRE-REMARITAL AND REMARITAL COUNSELING

The high divorce and remarriage rates make it imperative for the marriage counselor, concerned as he is with the psychosexual relationship of husband and wife, to accept this phenomenon as part of the continuum of adult life. The marriage and divorce counselor who achieves a perspective of life will expand his role to include help for those preparing to remarry and the troubled remarried.

Remarriage among the divorced or the widowed can be a complex process. Once remarriage occurs, there is some question whether the motivation to seek help can be expected. It is when the divorced come for therapeutic help that there is opportunity to include counseling in preparation for eventual remarriage. My experience has indicated that premarital and marriage counseling are frequently sought after exposure to education for marriage and family-life courses. In the same vein, pre-remarital and remarital counseling will be sought when the divorced are exposed to education for remarriage. The divorced in counseling and in education for the divorced groups are anxious about remarriage and they need and seek education and guidance in preparation for remarriage. This is right, for they should explore the complicated state of remarriage and its problems prior to meeting a potential second spouse, rather than wait until the last minute. Remarriage demands that they think first and act second.

Marriage is difficult enough, but in the severity of the demands in remarriage we can learn much about the meaning and significance of the marital relationship and family solidarity. A marriage, divorce, and remarriage counselor has to be sensitive to and have the perspective of the years of living in a marriage and a family, believe in the significance of marriage and family life, and be able to convey their meaning with compassion and understanding to his clients. To create and develop a meaningful husband-and-wife relationship which results in a family is a wondrous and exciting adventure. However, this can only be so where both husband and wife are in love with and committed to life and to marriage, have a sense of excitement and wonder, and have a feeling of security and belonging, and a pride and trust in themselves and each other, together with a sense of awe, humility, love, hope, and faith.

# Bibliography

Much has been written on the topics touched upon in this book. The following list of published works is far from complete, especially since no attempt is made to list the many articles and reports that have influenced me through the course of the years. The authors listed who have particularly helped develop and further my thinking are presented here to assist those readers who may wish to further pursue what has been discussed in this book.

Ackerman, Nathan W., *Psychodynamics of Family Life*, Basic Books, 1958.

Bailey, Sherwin, *Sexual Ethics: A Christian View*, Macmillan, 1963.

Bassett, Marion, *A New Sex Ethics and Marriage Structure*, Philosophical Library, 1961.

Bassett, William T., *Counseling the Childless Couple*, Prentice-Hall, 1963.

Beigel, Hugo G., ed., *Advances in Sex Research*, Harper & Row, 1963.

Bell, Norman W., and E. F. Vogel, *The Family*, Free Press, 1960.

Bergler, Edmund, M.D., *Money and Emotional Conflicts*, Pageant Books, 1959.

———, *Divorce Won't Help*, Harper & Brothers, 1948.

Bernard, Jessie, *Remarriage*, Dryden Press, 1956.

Bier, William C., ed., *Marriage, a Psychological and Moral Approach*, Fordham University Press, 1965.

Blanton, Smiley, M.D., *Love or Perish*, Simon & Schuster, 1955.

———, *Now or Never*, Prentice-Hall, 1959.

Blood, Robert O., Jr., *Marriage*, Free Press, 1962.

Bossard, James H. S., *One Marriage, Two Faiths*, Ronald Press, 1957.

Boszormenyi-Nagy, Ivan, M.D., ed., *Intensive Family Therapy*, Harper & Row, 1965.

Brenton, Myron, *The American Male*, Coward-McCann, 1966.

Brim, Orville G., Jr., *Education for Child Rearing*, Russell Sage Foundation, 1959.

Burgess, Ernest W., Harvey J. Locke, and Mary Margaret Thomas, *The Family from Institution to Companionship*, 3rd edition, American Book, 1963.

Cady, Ernest, and Frances Cady, *How to Adopt a Child*, William Morrow, 1956.

Cahnman, Werner J., *Intermarriage and Jewish Life in America, A Symposium*, Herzl Press & Jewish Reconstructionist Press, 1963.

Caprio, Frank S., M.D., *Marital Infidelity*, Citadel Press, 1953.

———, *The Sexually Adequate Female*, Citadel Press, 1953.

Chesser, Eustace, *Unmarried Love*, McKay, 1965.

Christensen, Harold T., ed., *Handbook of Marriage and the Family*, Rand McNally, 1964.

Clark, Vincent, *Unmarried Mothers*, Free Press, 1961.

Clinebell, Howard, Jr., *Understanding and Counseling the Alcoholic*, Abingdon Press, 1956.

———, *Basic Types of Pastoral Counseling*, Abingdon Press, 1967.

Cuber, John F., *The Significant Americans, A Study of Sexual Behavior Among the Affluent*, Appleton Century, 1965.

Denton, Wallace, *The Role of the Minister's Wife*, Westminster Press, 1960.

Despert, J. Louise, M.D., *Children of Divorce*, Doubleday, 1953.

Deutsch, Helen, *The Psychology of Woman* (2 vols.), Grune & Stratton, 1944.

Dicks, Russell, L., *Premarital Guidance*, Prentice-Hall, 1960.

Duvall, Sylvanus M., *Before You Marry*, Association Press, 1959.

Duvall, Evelyn, *In-Laws: Pro & Con, An Original Study of Interpersonal Relations*, Association Press, 1954.

Eisenstein, Victor W., M.D., *Neurotic Interaction in Marriage*, Basic Books, 1956.

Emerson, James G., Jr., *Divorce, the Church and Remarriage*, Westminster Press, 1961.

Farber and Wilson, *The Challenge to Women*, Basic Books, 1966.

Feldman, Frances L., *The Family in a Money World*, Family Service Association of America, 1957.

Fisher, Mitchell S., "Matrimonial Turmoil," *Journal of Family Law*, University of Louisville, Spring, 1967.

Fox, R. and P. Lyon, *Alcoholism—Its Scope, Cause and Treatment*, Random House, 1955.

Freeman, Harrop A., *Legal Interviewing and Counseling*, West, 1964.

Fromm, Eric, *The Art of Loving*, Harper & Brothers, 1956.

Genne, William H., *Husbands and Pregnancy*, Association Press, 1961.

Gibran, Kahlil, *The Prophet*, Knopf, 1964.

Glasser, William, M.D., *Reality Therapy: A New Approach to Psychiatry*, Harper & Row, 1965.

Goode, William J., *After Divorce*, Free Press, 1956.

Gordon, Albert J., *Intermarriage*, Beacon Press, 1964.

Gottlieb, Bernhardt S., M.D., *Understanding Your Adolescent*, Rinehart, 1957.

Gottlieb, Sophie and Bernhardt S., *What You Should Know About Marriage*, Bobbs-Merrill, 1962.

Grotjahn, Martin, M.D., *Psychoanalysis and the Family Neurosis*, Norton, 1960.

Greene, Bernard L., M.D., ed., *The Psychotherapies of Marital Disharmony*, Free Press, 1965.

Gruenberg, Sidonie M., and Hilda S. Krech, *The Many Lives of Modern Woman*, Doubleday, 1952.

Hamilton, Eleanor, *Partners in Love*, A. S. Barnes, 1961.

Harris, Thomas A., *Counseling the Service Man and His Family*, Prentice-Hall 1964.

Hastings, Donald W., *Impotence and Frigidity*, Little, Brown, 1963.

Hudson, R. Lofton, *Marital Counseling*, Prentice-Hall, 1963.

Hulme, William, *Building a Christian Marriage*, Prentice-Hall, 1965.

Hunt, Morton M., *Her Infinite Variety*, Harper & Row, 1962.

———, *The World of the Formerly Married*, McGraw-Hill, 1966.

Johnson, Dean, *Marriage Counseling: Theory and Practice*, Prentice-Hall, 1961.

Kirkendall, Lester A., *Premarital Intercourse and Personal Relationships,* Julian Press, 1961.

Kling, Samuel G., *The Complete Guide to Divorce,* Bernard Geis, 1963.

Kronhausen, Drs. Phyllis and Eberhard, *The Sexually Responsive Woman,* Grove Press, 1964.

Kuchler, Frances W. H., *The Law of Marriage and Divorce Simplified,* Oceana Publications, 1961.

Lader, Lawrence, *Abortion,* Bobbs-Merrill, 1966.

Langer, Marion, M.D., *Learning to Live as a Widow,* Julian Messner, 1957.

Lenski, Gerhard, *The Religious Factor,* Doubleday, 1961.

Levine, Lena, M.D., *The Frigid Wife,* Julian Messner, 1962.

London, Louis S., M.D., *Sexual Deviations in the Female,* Julian Press, 1957.

Masters, William H., Virginia E. Johnson, and A. Churchill, *Human Sexual Response,* Little, Brown, 1966.

Masters, R. E. L., and E. Lea, *The Anti-Sex,* Julian Press, 1964.

May, Rollo, *Man's Search for Himself,* Norton, 1953.

Mead, Margaret, *Male and Female,* William Morrow, 1955.

Meares, Ainslie, *Marriage and Personality,* Charles C. Thomas, 1957.

Mehl, R., *Society and Love,* Westminster Press, 1961.

Menninger, Karl, M.D., *The Vital Balance: The Life Process in Mental Health and Illness,* Viking Press, 1963.

Morris, J. K., *Premarital Counseling: A Manual for Ministers,* Prentice-Hall, 1960.

———, *Marriage Counseling, A Manual for Ministers,* Prentice-Hall, 1965.

Mudd, Emily H., *The Practice of Marriage Counseling,* Association Press, 1951.

Mudd, E., H. Mitchell, and S. Taubin, *Success in Family Living,* Association Press, 1965.

Mudd, Emily H., and Aron Krich, *Man and Wife,* Norton, 1957.

Nash, Ethel M., Lucie Jessner, and D. Wilfred Abse, *Marriage Counseling in Medical Practice,* University of North Carolina Press, 1964.

Ogburn, William F., and Meyer F. Nimkoff, *Technology and the Changing Family,* Houghton Mifflin, 1955.

Parad, H. J., ed., *Crisis Intervention*, Family Service Association of America, 1965.

Peterson, James A., *Education for Marriage*, Scribner, 1964.

Pike, James A., *If You Marry Outside Your Faith*, Harper & Brothers, 1954.

Polatin, Philip, and Ellen C. Philtine, *Marriage in the Modern World*, Lippincott, 1956.

Reik, Theodore, M.D., *The Need to be Loved*, Farrar, Straus, 1963.

———, *Listening with the Third Ear*, Farrar, Straus, 1948.

Rheingold, Joseph C., M.D., *The Fear of Being a Woman*, Grune & Stratton, 1964.

Rubin, Isadore, *Sexual Life After Sixty*, Basic Books, 1965.

Rutledge, Aaron, *Premarital Counseling*, Schenkman, 1966.

Schur, Edwin M., ed., *The Family and the Sexual Revolution*, Indiana University Press, 1964.

Shipp, Thomas J., *Helping the Alcoholic and His Family*, Prentice-Hall, 1965.

Simon, A. W., *Stepchild in the Family*, Odyssey Press, 1964.

Stein, M., A. Vedich, and D. White, eds., *Identity and Anxiety: Survival of the Person in Mass Society*, Free Press, 1960.

Steinberg, Milton, *Anatomy of Faith*, Harcourt, Brace, 1960.

Stewart, Charles W., *The Minister as Marriage Counselor*, Abingdon, 1960.

Tashman, Harry F., M.D., *Today's Neurotic Family*, University Publishers, 1957.

Taylor, Donald L., *Marriage Counseling*, Thomas, 1965.

Terkelson, Helen E., *Counseling the Unwed Mother*, Prentice-Hall, 1964.

Thomson, Helen, *The Successful Stepparent*, Harper & Row, 1966.

Trainer, Joseph B., M.D., *Physiologic Foundations for Marriage Counseling*, C. F. Mosby, 1966.

Vincent, Clark E., *Readings in Marriage Counseling*, Thomas Y. Crowell, 1957.

Wallis, J. H., *Sexual Harmony in Marriage*, Roy Publishers, 1965.

Winch, Robert F., *The Modern Family*, Henry Holt, 1952.

Wynn, John C., *Sex, Family and Society*, Association Press, 1966.

# Index